Routledge Questions & Answers

# Family Law
## 2013–2014

Routledge Questions & Answers Series

# Family Law

2013–2014

Rachael Stretch

Routledge
Taylor & Francis Group

LONDON AND NEW YORK

Seventh edition published 2013
by Routledge
2 Park Square, Milton Park, Abingdon, Oxon OX14 4RN

Simultaneously published in the USA and Canada
by Routledge
711 Third Avenue, New York, NY 10017

*Routledge is an imprint of the Taylor & Francis Group, an informa business*

First edition published by Cavendish Publishing 1994
Sixth edition published by Routledge 2011

*British Library Cataloguing in Publication Data*
A catalogue record for this book is available from the British Library

*Library of Congress Cataloging in Publication Data*
Stretch, Rachael.
  Family law / Rachael Stretch.—Seventh edition.
    pages cm.—(Q&A, Routledge questions & answers series)
  Includes bibliographical references and index.
  ISBN 978–0–415–69591–6 (pbk)
  1. Domestic relations—England—Examinations, questions, etc.  2. Domestic relations—Wales—Examinations, questions, etc.  I. Title.
  KD750.S77 2013
  346.4201'5076—dc23

                                                                                2012017477

ISBN: 978–0–415–69591–6 (pbk)
ISBN: 978–0–203–08383–3 (ebk)

Typeset in TheSans
by RefineCatch Limited, Bungay, Suffolk

Printed and bound in Great Britain by the MPG Books Group

# Contents

# Preface

Family law can be a fascinating topic; it is so infinitely varied in the different issues that may be encountered, whether in the examination room or in practice.

Each family is different and it is a challenge to try to use the law to achieve a practical solution to the problems encountered.

As a student of family law you must ensure that you master the basic legal concepts that are to be your tools for study, for examinations and, hopefully, for your future practice.

Statute law features strongly in family law, and you must be familiar with the statutory provisions that govern the various areas of the syllabus. Students frequently complain about the wealth of case law that they are exposed to; it may be comforting to remember that cases in the main part merely illustrate how the statutory principles have operated in relation to a particular family. Since each family is different, cases should be regarded as providing guidance, rather than absolute rules, and help to put issues into perspective.

Family law can be an enjoyable and rewarding topic to study and I hope this book will be of use, not only in your revision and question-answering technique, but also in providing you with an enthusiasm for the subject.

Finally, I would like to thank my husband Paul and my sons Elijah, Josiah and Samuel.

**Rachael Stretch**
July 2012

# Table of Cases

# Table of Legislation

## STATUTES

# Guide to the Companion Website

http://cw.routledge.com/textbooks/revision

Visit the Routledge Q&A website to discover even more study tips and advice on getting those top marks.

On the Routledge revision website you will find the following resources designed to enhance your revision on all areas of undergraduate law.

### The Good, The Fair, & The Ugly

Good essays are the gateway to top marks. This interactive tutorial provides sample essays together with voice-over commentary and tips for successful exam essays, written by our Q&A authors themselves.

### Multiple Choice Questions

Knowledge is the foundation of every good essay. Focusing on key examination themes, these MCQs have been written to test your knowledge and understanding of each subject in the book.

### Bonus Q&As

Having studied our exam advice, put your revision into practice and test your essay writing skills with our additional online questions and answers.

**Don't forget to check out even more revision guides
and exam tools from Routledge!**

### Lawcards

*Lawcards* are your complete, pocket-sized guides to key examinable areas of the undergraduate law.

### Routledge Student Statutes

Comprehensive selections; clear, easy-to-use layout; alphabetical, chronological, and thematic indexes; and a competitive price make *Routledge Student Statutes* the statute book of choice for the serious law student.

# Introduction

Welcome to Family Law Questions & Answers. The aim of this book is to help you increase your knowledge and understanding of family law as well as help you prepare for assessments in family law. Family law is an interesting and enjoyable subject and it is hoped that this book encourages you in your study of Family Law.

Most Family Law courses are split between adult relationships and the care of children. The former looks at the formation of relationships, the effects of marriage and cohabitation and what happens when things go wrong – divorce, nullity and domestic violence. The latter looks at who has parental responsibility and how to gain it through adoption, and at both the private and public law relating to children. Financial issues and what rights to maintenance adult partners or children have are also explored. This book follows this plan. The earlier chapters relate to adults, whilst the later look at children. The final chapter contains questions that contain issues relating to both adults and children.

Family law questions can be both essay and problem and this book contains a mixture of both. As always, a good essay question will be focused and will evaluate as well as describe. A good problem question must apply the law to the facts given as well as describe the law. Family law is a largely statute based subject. Students who wish to do well in it must make sure that they understand and can apply key statutes such as the Matrimonial Causes Act 1973, the Children Act 1989 and the Adoption and Children Act 2002.

To finish, one final bit of advice. The best way to use this book is actively, i.e. try and answer the questions yourself before reading the suggested answer. I hope that you enjoy this book, and that you find it helpful.

*Rachael Stretch*
*May 2012*

## Common Pitfalls

The most common mistake made when using Questions & Answers books for revision is to memorise the model answers provided and try to reproduce them in exams. This approach is a sure-fire pitfall, likely to result in a poor overall mark because your answer will not be specific enough to the particular question on your exam paper, and there is also a danger that reproducing an answer in this way would be treated as plagiarism. You must instead be sure to read the question carefully, to identify the issues and problems it is asking you to address and to answer it directly in your exam. If you take our examiners' advice and use your Q&A to focus on your question-answering skills and understanding of the law applied, you will be ready for whatever your exam paper has to offer!

# Nullity of Marriage

## INTRODUCTION

Many family law syllabuses begin by looking at the rules on who can marry and how that marriage should be conducted. Even though very few marriages are dissolved because of nullity, it remains important as the grounds for nullity tell us about the nature of marriage. Furthermore, unlike divorce, nullity enables a marriage to be ended within the first year, and for individuals who are opposed to divorce, nullity may be the preferred way of ending an unhappy marriage.

Some courses will focus on the conflict of laws element to nullity, and the following questions are a mixture of those containing entirely English nullity issues and those containing a foreign element. Cases which involve a foreign element require you to be familiar with the concept of domicile since it affects a person's capacity to marry. Other courses may concentrate on the grounds for nullity and the limitations on who can marry. In this respect the development of the law on transsexuals and marriage from *Corbett v Corbett* (1970) to the **Gender Recognition Act 2004** will be important as will be the law's rejection of homosexual marriage (*Wilkinson v Kitzinger and others* (2006)) and the introduction of civil registration of homosexual partnerships in the **Civil Partnership Act 2004**.

Nullity proceedings may be brought under the **Matrimonial Causes Act 1973 s 11** in respect of void marriages and the **Matrimonial Causes Act 1973 s 12** in respect of voidable marriages. You should ensure that you are familiar with all the grounds for presenting a petition under these sections, and whether there are any bars to the granting of the decree. The different consequences of void and voidable marriages must also be mastered.

## VOID MARRIAGES

Void marriages under the **Matrimonial Causes Act 1973 s 11** are fundamentally flawed from the outset. Students must be able to identify the appropriate part of s 11:

❖ s 11(a) deals with marriages that are invalid under the **Marriage Acts 1949** and **1970**. This is because the parties are within the prohibited degrees of relationship, or either is under 16, or certain formalities are not complied with;

- ❖ s 11(b) deals with marriages that are void because either party is already validly married;
- ❖ s 11(c) deals with marriages that are void because the parties are not respectively male and female;
- ❖ s 11(d) renders polygamous marriages with an English domiciliary void.

## VOID MARRIAGE AND NON-MARRIAGE

There is an important distinction between a marriage which is void for lack of formalities and a supposed marriage which is so flawed it is a non-marriage (*El Gamal v Al Maktoum* (2011)). The latter does not lead to any financial relief (*Hudson v Leigh* (2008)).

## VOIDABLE MARRIAGES

Section 12 deals with marriages that are merely voidable. This means that the marriage is valid unless and until a nullity decree is obtained. Unlike void marriages only the spouses can petition for nullity.

- ❖ s 12(a) deals with the incapacity of either party to consummate the marriage;
- ❖ s 12(b) covers the respondent's wilful refusal to consummate the marriage;
- ❖ s 12(c) renders a marriage voidable on the basis of lack of consent due to mistake, duress, unsoundness of mind, or otherwise;
- ❖ s 12(d) enables a marriage to be ended if either party was suffering from a mental disorder such as to make them unfit for marriage;
- ❖ s 12(e) deals with marriages where the respondent is affected by venereal disease in a communicable form;
- ❖ s 12(f) renders a marriage voidable if the respondent is pregnant by another person;
- ❖ s 12(g) makes a marriage voidable once one of the spouses has obtained an interim Gender Recognition Certificate;
- ❖ s 12(h) makes a marriage voidable on the grounds that the petitioner did not know that the respondent had changed their gender under the **Gender Recognition Act 2004**.

There are no bars or defences to a petition based on s 11 (void marriage). However, in relation to petitions under s 12 (voidable marriages), there are three bars in s 13:

- ❖ s 13(1) contains the bar of statutory approbation;
- ❖ s 13(2) provides a bar once three years have passed for petitions based on s 12(c), (d), (e) (f) or (h);
- ❖ s 13(3) provides a bar of knowledge to petitions based on s 12(e) or (f).

## VOID AND VOIDABLE CIVIL PARTNERSHIPS

The **Civil Partnership Act 2004 s 49** sets out the grounds when a civil partnership will be void and **section 50** sets out when a civil partnership will be voidable. Although there is a great deal of similarity between the two Acts, the main difference is that non-consummation will not make a civil partnership voidable. This is unsurprising given the definition of consummation in English Law which requires penetration of the vagina by the penis and therefore a heterosexual relationship.

## THE EFFECTS OF A VOID OR VOIDABLE MARRIAGE

Despite not being valid, both void and voidable marriages will have consequences.

A voidable marriage is in fact valid until either spouse petitions for its nullity.

A void marriage can still lead to ancillary relief and children who result from a void marriage will nonetheless be legitimate.

## EXAM QUESTIONS

Exam questions on nullity are likely to either take the form of a problem question asking the student to identify whether a marriage can be ended because of nullity and if so under which ground, or an essay question exploring the role of nullity in today's society. Nullity can also be combined with divorce or with financial relief in problem questions.

## QUESTION 1

Jane, an Englishwoman, went to Ruritania to work, and there she met and married Fred, a Ruritanian man with whom she had fallen in love. He told her that although the law of his country allowed him to take more than one wife, he felt that she was so special he would never do so. After a few months Jane tired of his adoring, but boring, company and decided to return home. She soon forgot about Fred and began to form a relationship with Tarzan, who had been briefly married to Jane's mother. Jane's mother had died two years previously and shortly after meeting, Jane and Tarzan married. However, after the ceremony Jane could not bring herself to have sexual intercourse with Tarzan, as she is tormented by the thought of his relationship with her mother.

▶ Advise Jane on the validity of her marriages.

### How to Answer this Question

Begin by examining the validity of the marriage to Fred:

- ❖ consider if both parties had capacity;
- ❖ this depends on where they were domiciled at the time of marriage;
- ❖ the effect of the polygamous, or potentially polygamous, nature of the marriage.

Then consider the validity of the marriage to Tarzan:

- ❖ consider capacity;
- ❖ problem of prohibited degrees;
- ❖ problem if Jane is already validly married to Fred.

Consider also the possibility that the marriage is voidable:

❖    non-consummation (incapacity or wilful refusal?)

## Applying the Law

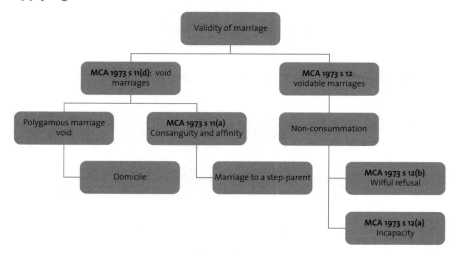

*How the relevant sections of the MCA (ss 11 and 12) affect understanding of the validity of Fred and Jane's marriage is illustrated here.*

# ANSWER

In advising Jane on the validity of her marriages, it will be necessary to first examine the marriage to Fred, which took place in Ruritania. For this marriage to be valid, both parties must have had capacity to marry and the relevant formalities must have been complied with.

Capacity in English law is determined by the prospective spouses' ante-nuptial domicile – *Sottomayer v de Barros (No 1)* (1877). Fred was domiciled in Ruritania. Ruritania was clearly his permanent home: *Whicker v Hume* (1858). Thus Fred would seem to have capacity to marry Jane, although it is arguable whether Jane had capacity to marry Fred. She begins with an English domicile, however, when she goes to Ruritania to work, she may have obtained a Ruritanian domicile of choice. To establish this, it would be necessary for her to have made Ruritania her permanent home, that is, established a physical presence of a lasting nature, with an intention to make it her permanent home. This intention must be positive and demonstrate a fixed and settled intention to remain; mere indifference on Jane's part would not suffice (*Winans v AG* (1910)). In going to Ruritania to work, Jane's intentions are not clear. If she intended this as a temporary or transient measure, then there is insufficient determination to acquire a domicile of choice, however, if on meeting Fred, Jane decides that she should settle in Ruritania then she may have acquired a Ruritanian domicile of choice.

If Jane is domiciled in Ruritania at the time of her marriage to Fred then she will also have capacity to marry, notwithstanding the potentially polygamous nature of the marriage, as Ruritanian law allows polygamy. It is assumed that the requisite formalities of Ruritanian law, which is the *lex loci*, have been complied with, and so the marriage will be valid: *Herbert v Herbert* (1819).

There is, however, a strong possibility that Jane was still domiciled in England at the time of her marriage to Fred, in which case her capacity must be judged according to English law. Lord Penzance in *Hyde v Hyde* (1866) defined marriage as 'the voluntary union of a man and a woman for life to the exclusion of all others' and this definition has formed the basis of the English law rules on capacity. To be able to contract a valid marriage, an English domiciliary must be over 16 (which it is assumed Jane and Fred are); not within the prohibited degrees of relationship (which again appears to cause no difficulty here); not already married; and the marriage must not be polygamous. This is the aspect of the marriage that requires greater examination.

The **Matrimonial Causes Act 1973 s 11(d)** provides that a marriage that is polygamous is void. This means that the marriage is treated as a complete nullity, and there is no need to obtain a nullity decree unless financial provision is to be sought under s 23 or 24 of the Act. In this case the marriage is not actually polygamous, but it has the potential, given Fred's domicile, to become polygamous. In *Hussain v Hussain* (1982) a marriage between a man and a woman in Pakistan which permitted polygamy was nevertheless held to be valid, as the woman had the Pakistani domicile and could not take a second husband, and the man had an English domicile and could not take a second wife, thereby rendering the marriage monogamous. This would not apply to the marriage between Jane and Fred, as the roles are reversed and Fred could still, in theory, take another spouse. Thus the marriage between Jane and Fred, whilst not actually polygamous, is potentially so. Until the provisions of the **Private International Law (Miscellaneous Provisions) Act 1995 (PIL(MP)A)** came into force in 1996, the MCA 1973 s 11(d) had the effect of making a potentially polygamous marriage by an English domiciliary void. This somewhat discriminatory rule was the subject of criticism by the Law Commission in their report on polygamous marriages, which thought that the rule as relating to potentially polygamous marriages was harsh. Accordingly the **PIL(MP)A 1995 s 5** amended s 11(d) to make marriages that were only potentially polygamous valid. The Act has retrospective effect, s 6(1), but it does not retrospectively validate a potentially polygamous marriage if a party to that marriage has gone on to celebrate a later valid marriage, s 6(2).[1]

---

1  Good answers will not merely state that a marriage cannot be polygamous under English Law but will apply this rule to the facts and explain what this means. In particular, it is important that the student is aware of the potentially discriminatory effect of **s 11(d)** and therefore can understand and explain the reason for the **PIL(MP)A 1995**.

Jane's marriage to Fred is however unhappy and she begins a relationship with Tarzan whom she later marries. The next issue therefore is what legal status, if any, this marriage to Tarzan has. Is it a valid marriage? And if not, why? Tarzan and Jane are male and female and above the age of 16. There is, however, a potential problem given that for a short while Tarzan was married to Jane's mother. There would be an absolute prohibition on Jane marrying Tarzan if he were her natural or adoptive father; likewise if she had at any stage been a child of the family whilst Tarzan was married to her mother: **Marriage Act 1949 Sched 1**. However, if Jane had never been treated by Tarzan as a child of the family and Tarzan's relationship with Jane's mother had occurred when Jane was no longer living at home, then provided that Tarzan and Jane are both over 21 they will be able to marry: **Marriage (Prohibited Degrees) Act 1996**.[2]

However, an additional problem may be encountered if the first marriage to Fred was valid. English law requires both parties to be single, and if one or more of them is already married then the subsequent marriage is a nullity: **MCA 1973 s 11(b)**. If the marriage to Fred was valid then the marriage to Tarzan will be void. However, if the marriages to Fred and Tarzan took place before the provisions of the **PIL(MP)A 1995** came into force then the marriage to Fred is void as potentially polygamous, and the marriage to Tarzan will be valid. This is because the retrospective nature of the provisions does not operate if there has been a second valid marriage according to the law at the time it was celebrated.

There are possible grounds for arguing that the marriage between Jane and Tarzan is voidable for one of the reasons in the **MCA s 12**. It does not seem that the marriage has been consummated. Jane's attitude has ensured that there has been no complete and regular intercourse (*D v A* (1845)) once the marriage has taken place. Premarital intercourse does not suffice for consummation. It is then necessary to consider whether this is due to incapacity to consummate or wilful refusal.

Either party can petition on the basis that there is some physical or psychological reason preventing consummation (*D v D* (1982)). Here it would seem that Jane has psychological problems that are preventing intercourse. In order for the decree to be granted these reasons must exist at the date of the petition and the date of the hearing (*Napier v Napier* (1915)), but there must also be no practical possibility of intercourse (*S v S* (1962)). In this case it is not clear what, if anything at all, can be done to help Jane; neither is it apparent whether she wishes to be helped to overcome the problem. If it is felt that there is a possibility of intercourse should Jane accept help which would not expose her to too great a risk, then Jane's refusal to seek such assistance may amount to a wilful refusal to consummate. This would be a settled and definite decision without

2   The concern with step-parent/step-child relationships is that the step-parent might have groomed the step-child and the relationship might be abusive. This explains why the ban on step-parent/step-child relationships only applies if the step-parent has been in a parental position to the step-child.

just cause (*Horton v Horton* (1947)), and would give Tarzan the opportunity to petition for nullity.[3]

A voidable marriage is valid unless and until it is dissolved by way of nullity decree (*De Renville v De Renville* (1948)), unlike the void marriage. Therefore, Jane should seek a nullity decree in respect of her marriage to Tarzan.

# QUESTION 2

Kate was a journalist covering a civil war in the depths of Africa. There she met a fellow English journalist, Leo, with whom she fell instantly and madly in love. They wanted to marry but were in the midst of heavy fighting and were unable to make the journey to the nearest city. They exchanged marriage vows in front of Mike, a missionary who was hoping to become a priest. Both Kate and Leo were captured by rival factions in the civil war, and Kate assumed Leo had been killed when she did not hear from him again. Kate met another journalist, Nick, in the prisoner of war camp she was held in and, finding she was pregnant by Leo, agreed to marry Nick so that her child would have a father. The marriage was intended by both as a companionship only relationship, as neither wished to have intercourse with the other. After Kate's baby was born, Nick found he looked on Kate with increasing affection, and wanted her to be more than his housekeeper. However, Kate refused to have intercourse with him, and Nick has now met Olive, with whom he hopes to have a proper marriage.

▶ **Advise Nick.**

## How to Answer this Question

First consider the validity of the marriage between Kate and Leo as this affects the validity of Kate and Nick's marriage and consequently his ability to marry Olive:

- ❖ examine capacity to marry and the provisions of **s 11**;
- ❖ consider whether the appropriate formalities have been complied with;
- ❖ marriage could be void, or else obtain decree of presumption of death.

Then consider the validity of Kate and Nick's marriage:

- ❖ it appears valid if the marriage to Leo had been void or ended;
- ❖ could be void – **s 11(b)** if marriage to Leo still subsists;
- ❖ if Kate and Nick's marriage is valid – consider **s 12** regarding voidable marriages:
  - ❖ non-consummation and marriage of convenience;
  - ❖ pregnancy *per alium* and bar of knowledge.

Conclude with examination of Nick's ability to marry Olive.

---

3    A spouse can petition for non-consummation on the basis of their own incapacity to consummate, but not on the basis of their own refusal to consummate.

## Applying the Law

*The status of Nick's marriage under the **MCA 1973** is illustrated here.*

# ANSWER

In advising Nick on his ability to marry Olive it will be necessary to examine the validity of his marriage to Kate, which in turn is affected by the validity of the marriage between Kate and Leo. It is proposed that the first marriage to be discussed will be that of Kate and Leo.

The capacity of Kate and Leo to contract a valid marriage is to be judged by the law of their ante-nuptial domicile: *Sottomayer v de Barros (No 1)* (1877). Both Kate and Leo have English domicile and do not appear to have acquired a domicile of choice in Africa. They are present there as part of their job to report on the civil war. It would seem that neither of them has the intention to make this their permanent home: *Winans v AG* (1910).

The English law rules on capacity are based on Lord Penzance's definition of marriage as 'the voluntary union for life of a man and a woman to the exclusion of all others': *Hyde v Hyde* (1866). Thus the **MCA 1973 s 11** requires the parties to be over 16, of opposite sex, not within the prohibited degrees, and not already married. It would therefore seem that Kate and Leo have capacity to marry.

It is also necessary that a valid marriage complies with the formal requirements of the *lex loci*, the location where the marriage is taking place: *Herbert v Herbert* (1819). However, in the instant case, Kate and Leo do not appear to have complied with any formalities prescribed by local law. Indeed, in a civil war situation, it may be virtually impossible for them to do so. The English law will nevertheless recognise such marriages if it is not possible to comply with local law because of insurmountable difficulties, provided that the English common law formalities have been complied with: *Taczanowski v Taczanowski* (1957). This requires the parties to declare that they take each other as man and wife to the exclusion of all others and these vows must usually be exchanged before an ordained minister. This concept has been criticised as artificial, especially where the parties have no connection with England, but it might operate to make the ceremony between Kate and Leo a valid marriage. However, Mike is not an ordained minister, and this may mean that the marriage is invalid unless it can be argued that, in the circumstances, this missionary was the best person available to lend an air of formality as in *Wolfenden v Wolfenden* (1945).

If the marriage is void through lack of compliance with the formalities, then there is no need to seek a nullity decree unless financial provision is sought under the **Matrimonial Causes Act s 25**. If, however, the marriage is valid, then it may have been possible for Kate to seek dissolution of her marriage by seeking to rely on the presumption of death. This would enable her to apply if she could show that no one who should have heard from Leo has done so in the past seven years and if the period exceeds seven years then the presumption that Leo is dead will operate, thereby entitling Kate to a dissolution of her marriage: **MCA 1973 s 19**.

If the marriage between Kate and Leo was void or had been dissolved before the marriage to Nick, then it would appear that both Kate and Nick would have capacity to marry according to the law of their domiciles. English law would be applied, since their capture and detention in prisoner of war camps could not result in them acquiring a domicile of choice. The **MCA 1973 s 11** would require them to both be over the age of 16, of opposite sex, not within the prohibited degrees, and not already validly married. Even if they had capacity to marry, they must comply with the formalities required by the place where the marriage took place, the *lex loci*. It is not clear where the marriage took place and it is therefore assumed that either the necessary formalities were complied with or it was a situation where the doctrine of the English common law marriage would provide validity.

If, however, Kate's marriage to Leo was still valid then the subsequent marriage to Nick is void since **s 11(b)** requires neither party to be lawfully married. Likewise **s 11(d)** prevents an English domiciliary from entering into a polygamous union anywhere in the world, even if the local law permits polygamy.[4]

If the marriage to Nick is valid then it may still be voidable by reference to the provisions of the **MCA 1973 s 12**. It would seem that the marriage has not been consummated; there has been no complete and regular sexual intercourse (*D v A* (1845)). However, there does not appear to be any incapacity; just an initial decision that the relationship would be platonic, followed by Kate refusing to alter the status quo. This may be evidence of a

---

4   This paragraph explains the link between the validity of the marriage between Kate and Leo and the validity of the marriage between Kate and Nick. It is impossible for them both to validly exist at the same time.

wilful refusal to consummate the marriage, thereby rendering the marriage voidable under the **MCA 1973 s 12(b)**. In *Horton v Horton* (1948) it was held that there needed to be a settled and definite decision by the respondent reached without just cause. Initially there was a mutual understanding, and the status quo cannot be regarded as a refusal by either party: *Potter v Potter* (1982). However, when Nick tries to alter the situation and Kate refuses, this may give the necessary definite decision on Kate's part, although it would still be necessary to examine whether her refusal was without just cause. They had agreed at the outset that theirs was to be a platonic relationship: would it be unreasonable for her to refuse to alter the nature of the relationship? Much might depend on how old the couple were; with a young couple, the courts are more likely to hold a refusal unreasonable, whereas *obiter* comments suggest that in the case of elderly couples a companionship arrangement might not be voidable: *Morgan v Morgan* (1959). Since Kate has had a child she cannot be too old and it is likely that her refusal is unreasonable.[5]

Kate was also pregnant by another man at the time of her marriage to Nick, and this can be the basis for a petition under **s 12(f)** – pregnancy *per alium*. However, **s 13(3)** provides a bar to petitioning if Nick was aware of this fact at the time of the marriage. This seems likely given that he did not want intercourse with Kate initially, and so the petition would only succeed on the basis of non-consummation.

In conclusion, if Nick's marriage to Kate is void, then he is free to marry Olive. A void marriage is treated as if it never existed and no nullity decree is required. If, however, the marriage to Kate is merely voidable, then Nick must ensure that he obtains a nullity decree before marrying Olive.

# QUESTION 3

Matthew is 22. He has always had a poor relationship with his parents and two years ago things got so bad that he was told to move out. Matthew moved to London and he began leading a very expensive lifestyle filled with designer clothes, fast cars and foreign holidays. Sadly, Matthew could only get poorly paid work and he soon fell into debt. Having used up his credit cards and after being refused a loan by his bank, Matthew borrowed £15,000 pounds from a backstreet lender. Nine months ago, Matthew realised that he would not be able to pay this loan back and he became very worried.

One of Matthew's friends, Luke, is gay. He suggested to Matthew that they became civil partners. Luke has a well paid job and would be able to help Matthew financially. Luke knew that Matthew was not gay and accepted that they would not have a sexual

---

5    A marriage can be voidable for non-consummation either because of wilful refusal, or because of incapacity. Nick is potentially able to rely on Kate's refusal to consummate depending on whether that refusal was wilful and that means that whether she had a just excuse needs to be discussed.

relationship but he had fallen in love with Matthew and wanted to help him. Five months ago, Luke and Matthew went though a civil partnership ceremony. Sadly, the partnership has not been happy. Matthew now says that he finds Luke repulsive. He brings women back to their home which Luke finds very upsetting. Luke has now met Keith and would like to be free to begin a relationship with Keith.

▶ **Advise Luke on ending his civil partnership with Matthew.**

## How to Answer this Question

❖ There are two methods of ending the civil partnership – through nullity or through dissolution (see Chapter 3).

❖ As dissolution is not possible during the first year, nullity is the preferred option for Luke.

❖ Unlike marriage, a civil partnership cannot be ended because of non-consummation.

❖ Can the civil partnership be ended because of duress – was Matthew's consent genuine?

❖ Can the civil partnership be ended through dissolution because of irretrievable breakdown and, if so, which is the appropriate fact?

❖ What are the financial consequences of ending the relationship?

## Applying the Law

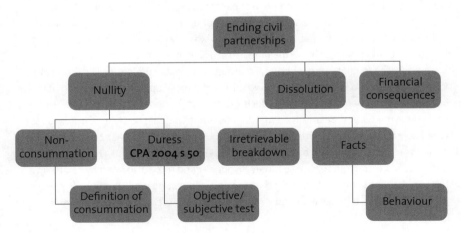

*The key factors to consider in ending a civil partnership are shown here.*

# ANSWER

Matthew and Luke went through a seemingly valid civil partnership ceremony five months ago. Sadly, the partnership has not proved happy and Luke now seeks to end it. The two ways of doing this would be through nullity or through dissolution. As the partnership is not yet a year old, dissolution is not immediately available and therefore nullity will first be considered. From the facts it seems that this is not a void civil partnership. Matthew and Luke are eligible to become civil partners – they are both men, seemingly both over 16, not related and not already married or in a civil partnership (**Civil Partnership Act 2004 s 3**) and the formalities for a valid civil partnership have been complied with (**Civil Partnership Act 2004 s 49**); instead, the question is whether this civil partnership is voidable.[6]

The relationship between Matthew and Luke has never been sexual. Marriage is closely linked to sexual intercourse, and non-consummation, either because of wilful refusal or because of incapacity, is a ground for a voidable marriage (**Matrimonial Causes Act 1973 s 12(1)**). The same does not apply to civil partnerships. The fact that civil partners have never had a sexual relationship does not make their partnership voidable. This is because the legal definition of consummation requires penetration of the vagina by the penis, which means that all civil partnerships by their very nature cannot be consummated.

Another argument that Luke could use is that Matthew did not validly consent to the civil partnership – his financial problems meant that he was forced to agree to the partnership and therefore it is voidable because of duress (**Civil Partnership Act 2004 s 50(1)(a)**). Although it was not Luke himself who was the victim of the duress, the Act is clear that either party can use the duress. The issue of what constitutes duress has been discussed in relation to whether a marriage is voidable under the **Matrimonial Causes Act 1973** and there have been two different judicial approaches. The first, hard-line approach is characterised by the decision in *Singh v Singh* (1971). In this case, the court determined that an arranged marriage was not voidable because of duress as the wife had not feared for her life, limb or liberty. In *Hirani v Hirani* (1982), the court took a more sympathetic approach and recognised that in a close-knit family, it would be very difficult for a young girl to choose family dishonour and to be disowned by disobeying her parents. The court in *Hirani* said that the crucial question was whether the spouse in reality was free to make a decision. More recent cases seem to prefer the *Hirani* approach.

---

6   Students should always make sure they read the question carefully, and answer what has been set as fully as possible. Here, they are invited to consider all ways of ending the relationship and therefore dissolution should be considered as well as nullity. Note though that nullity has the advantage of being available in the first year.

Applying these tests, is the partnership between Luke and Matthew voidable because of duress? If the *Singh* test is applied Matthew would have to argue that if he did not become Luke's civil partner he faced severe physical harm or homelessness. The facts state that Matthew had borrowed money from a backstreet lender and whilst it might be imagined that he possibly faced some threats if he did not repay, the nature of these threats is not explicit. Moreover, even if Matthew risked physical harm were he not to repay the loan or risked losing his home, it is far from clear that becoming Luke's civil partner was the only solution. On the other hand, Matthew is reasonably young and the fact that he is estranged from his parents may make him more vulnerable and would mean that he could not go to them for financial assistance. In fact, recent precedent suggests that the *Hirani* approach is likely to be preferred and whilst this will be more sympathetic towards Matthew, it is still far from clear that the civil partnership will be held voidable because of duress. The facts state that Matthew was worried about not being able to repay the loan; this, however, is not the same as Matthew's will being overridden and him being forced into the civil partnership.[7]

Another option is for Luke to wait until the partnership is a year old and then apply for the partnership to be dissolved. Although it is clear that the partnership has broken down irretrievably (**Civil Partnership Act s 44(1)**), it can only be dissolved if one of the facts in s 44(5) exists. Matthew has clearly been having relationships with women whilst in a civil partnership with Luke. Although adultery is one of the divorce facts in the **Matrimonial Causes Act 1973**, it is not a fact under the **Civil Partnership Act 2004**; however, it is very probable that Matthew's relationships with women would constitute behaviour under s 44(5)(a). In addition, Matthew states that he finds Luke repulsive and living with these insults would constitute behaviour under s 44(5)(a). Therefore Luke could apply for the partnership to be dissolved once it has lasted a year.[8]

Finally, Luke seems to be better off financially than Matthew and Luke should also be aware that Matthew will be entitled to claim financial relief from him. The fact that the civil partnership has been very brief, and that Matthew is a young man, means that this is likely not to be a significant amount.

........................................................................................................

7   The answer has correctly identified that either spouse can use duress as a grounds for nullity, not just the 'victim' of the duress. The case law on duress is interesting as there is a conflict between the stricter, older cases such as *Singh* and more recent case law which is more subjective. As of yet, there are no leading cases where duress is claimed in a civil partnership, and is probable that a similar approach to that used in *Hirani* would be used.

8   Although there is a great deal of similarity between marriage and civil partnerships, there are some important differences. Notably there is not the same connection between a civil partnership and a sexual relationship as there is between marriage and a civil partnership. One reason for this is that a civil partnership would not be able to satisfy the legal definition of consummation.

## Common Pitfalls ✗

Make sure that you read the question carefully. This question asks how Luke can end his civil partnership with Matthew, therefore whilst you should consider nullity you should also consider dissolution. Weaker students might be nervous about tackling this question as it concerns a civil partnership rather than the more usual marriage and it is important to be clear on the similarities and differences between the two types of relationship. This is especially the case here as the facts clearly state that the relationship between Matthew and Luke has not been sexual.

## Aim Higher ★

Extra marks will be given for a good up to date knowledge and application of the case law relating to duress.

# QUESTION 4

[T]he biological sexual constitution of an individual is fixed at birth (at the latest), and cannot be changed, either by the natural development of organs of the opposite sex, or by medical or surgical means. The respondent's operation, therefore, cannot affect her true sex.

❖    Per Omrod J *Corbett v Corbett* (1971) P 83

Critically examine whether this is still an accurate description of English law.

## How to Answer this Question

The quote is from *Corbett v Corbett* (1971), the leading case establishing the refusal of English law to allow transsexuals to marry in their new sex. Answers should explain how the law has developed. They should include the influence of European case law and the effect that the **Gender Recognition Act 2004** will have.

❖    The approach in *Corbett v Corbett*.
❖    According to *Corbett*, how is gender to be defined?
❖    Transsexuals and consummation.
❖    The European Court allowed national jurisdictions a wide margin of appreciation.
❖    The decision of the European Court of Human Rights in *Goodwin*.
❖    *Bellinger v Bellinger*.
❖    The **Gender Recognition Act 2004**.

## Applying the Law

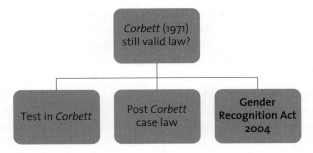

*The main factors affecting how to consider the decision in Corbett v Corbett in relation to current law are shown here.*

# ANSWER

According to the **Matrimonial Causes Act 1973 s 11(c)**, parties to a marriage should be male and female. This requirement has caused problems for transsexuals because unless a transsexual can marry in her acquired gender, her options for marriage are likely to be significantly limited. The leading case for a long time has been that of *Corbett v Corbett* (1971) which is quoted in the question. In this case the petitioner was seeking nullity from his marriage to a male-to-female transsexual. The High Court agreed that the marriage was void. It stated that a person's gender was determined by their biology, that is by the chromosomal, the gonadal and the genital tests, and because by these tests the respondent was a man, her marriage was void. The court in *Corbett* also stated that, in any case, a marriage involving male-to-female transsexual would be voidable because she would be unable to consummate her marriage as a woman. Whether transsexuals can consummate in their new gender is a less significant argument though as, in any case, consummation is merely a grounds for a voidable marriage.[9]

The approach in *Corbett* was for a long time upheld by both the English and the European Courts. For example in *Cossey v UK* (1990), Caroline Cossey's claim to be recognised in her new gender and to be able to marry was rejected and the approach of the English courts was upheld by the European Court. For a long time, the European Court of Human

9   ***Corbett*** is still valid case law and a transsexual would still be defined as their sex at birth using the genital, gonadal and chromosonal tests. The ***Corbett*** test would not, however, apply to an intersexual as in their case the genital, gonadal and chromosonal tests would not give a clear, unambiguous answer, allowing an intersexual to use the psychological test to choose their gender.

Rights viewed the extent to which the acquired gender of transsexuals was recognised to be a matter for national appreciation, allowing individual countries to take different approaches to reflect the different degrees to which transsexualism was accepted by their population. For English law, this changed with the European Court's decision in *Goodwin v UK* (2002). In this case, the European Court decided that denying transsexuals the right to marry was a breach of the **European Convention of Human Rights Article 12**, and that it was no longer appropriate for a person's gender to be determined purely by reference to biological conditions present at their birth.

Whilst the European Court was deciding the *Goodwin* case, the English courts were hearing the claims of Mr and Mrs Bellinger for their marriage to be declared valid. The Court of Appeal in *Bellinger* (2002) was sympathetic to Mrs Bellinger but the majority upheld the decision in *Corbett* that a person's gender was fixed at birth. In his dissenting judgment, Thorpe argued that the law should be changed to take account of changes in social attitudes towards transsexuals and developing medical knowledge. Mrs Bellinger appealed to the House of Lords where despite the decision in *Goodwin* she was unsuccessful. The House of Lords decided that the issue was too important to be decided by a court and that reform would have to come from Parliament. This has now happened through the **Gender Recognition Act 2004**.

The **Gender Recognition Act 2004** enables transsexuals to apply to a Gender Recognition Panel for a certificate recognising their change of gender. This certificate will enable them to marry in their new gender. Perhaps controversially, the Act does not require a transsexual to have undergone surgery before (s)he can obtain a certificate. The reason for this is that if surgery were needed for a gender recognition certificate, an individual who, for medical reasons, was unable to have a full sex change would, perhaps unfairly, be prevented from being recognised in their new gender. Instead a person must show that they have lived for two years in their acquired gender and intend to live in that gender for the rest of their life. If a person is married in their original sex, they can only obtain an interim gender recognition certificate. This interim certificate will make the marriage voidable and once the marriage is dissolved, it can be converted to a full certificate. The Act will not apply retrospectively and individuals like Mrs Bellinger will still find that their existing marriages are void.[10]

The UK approach is interesting because it does not base a person's gender on their biology. It will be possible for an individual to have the sexual characteristics of a man, but be registered by the Gender Recognition Panel as a woman. Furthermore, the fact that a person has to intend to live in their acquired sex does suggest that gender

10  The **GRA 2004** amended the **MCA 1973 s 12** and a marriage will now be voidable either because one of the spouses acquires a new gender under the **GRA 2004** after the marriage (**MCA 1973 s 12(g)**) or because a spouse has only acquired their gender thanks to the **GRA 2004** (**MCA 1973 s 12(h)**). The later provision would enable a person who inadvertently marries a transsexual to end their marriage.

recognition is based, at least in part, on a person's psychological commitment to their new sex. This is a significant development from the approach adopted in *Corbett*.

# QUESTION 5

There is no need for 'Gay Marriage' as civil partnership provides a valid and effective equivalent for Gay and Lesbian couples – discuss.

## How to Answer this Question

❖ Marriage is a lifelong, monogamous relationship between consenting heterosexual partners which is recognised by the State and which carries with it enforceable rights and duties that subsist even after the end of the marriage. Is this also true for a civil partnership?

❖ Marriage is a formal relationship which has special rules for its formation. Is this also true for civil partnership?

❖ Marriage carries with it a duty of support – is this also true for civil partnership?

❖ What is the effect on children of there being a marriage or civil partnership?

❖ When will the law allow a marriage to be ended through divorce? How does this compare to the dissolution of a civil partnership?

❖ What is the effect of the dissolution or divorce?

## Applying the Law

*The legal differences between marriage and civil partnership are illustrated in this flowchart.*

# ANSWER

Under the **Civil Partnership Act 2004**, gay and lesbian couples who choose to, can register their relationship. If they do so, they will have responsibilities towards each other, rights they can claim from each other and their relationship will be recognised by the State. It seems therefore that civil partnership is a homosexual version of marriage, and this is certainly the view that has been taken by the popular media. Moreover, when the Civil Partnership legislation was passed, heterosexual couples were explicitly excluded from civil partnerships as they already were able to marry and therefore did not need civil partnership. Despite this some feel that civil partnership is different, and perhaps lesser, to marriage. In *Wilkinson v Kitzinger* (2006), two lesbians who had contracted a valid marriage in Canada argued that the UK should recognise their Canadian marriage as a marriage rather than as a civil partnership. This argument was however rejected by the High Court.

Marriage has always had significant effects both for the husband and wife and for the State. It is important therefore that anyone who contracts a marriage is able to do so and that anyone who has an interest in blocking an invalid marriage can do so. Partly for these reasons the formation of marriage is a formal process. There are rules on where it can happen, who can conduct the ceremony, on giving notice to enable objections and on who is actually able to agree to be married. Like marriage, civil partnership also has rules on who can validly contract a civil partnership and like marriage, if a civil partnership is formed this has an impact both on civil partners themselves and on other interested parties. It is not surprising therefore that there is a lot of similarity between the rules for forming the two relationships. Both marriage and civil partnership (**Civil Partnership Act 2004 s 8**) require there to be notice of the ceremony and both have to be witnessed to be valid (**Civil Partnership Act 2004 s 2**). They also both have rules on who is actually able to contract a civil partnership or marriage (**Civil Partnership Act 2004 s 3, MCA 1973 s 11**).[11]

One difference between marriage and civil partnership is that marriage has always been able to be formed in a church, whereas civil partnership could not have a religious aspect and could not take place within a church. This was because a homosexual or lesbian relationship could be viewed by some as being against judeo-christian sexual morality. Moreover, the fact that a civil partnership could not take place within a religious building, did not affect the rights and responsibilities it created, and arguably a better comparison with a civil partnership would be a second marriage which would be legal and have full legal effects, but which depending on the church might not be conducted within the church. The problem with this reasoning is that it does deny gay and lesbian couples with religious beliefs the right to have their relationship solemnised in church. This rule

---

11   It is interesting that civil partnership has borrowed the rejection of bigamy and polygamy and like marriage has to be a monogamous relationship given that unlike marriage, civil partnership cannot claim a religious tradition or justification.

is in any case changing, the **Equalities Act 2010 s 202** has removed the bar on civil partnerships being celebrated in church and it is likely that religious civil partnership ceremonies will become an option, albeit one that is left to the conscience of the individual minister.

Both marriage and civil partnership carry with them a duty of financial support and a right to financial support and this survives the ending of the civil partnership or marriage through divorce or dissolution. In marriage the right to financial support during the marriage can be found in either the **Domestic Proceedings and Magistrates Court Act 1973 s 1** or the **Matrimonial Causes Act 1973**. In the **Civil Partnership Act 2004**, the right to support is in **s 72(3)**. This is very different from mere cohabitees, either heterosexual or homosexual, who have no right to financial support from each other and who have no duty to support each other. By formalising their relationship, both spouses and civil partners are deemed to have agreed to this support, whereas the law is unwilling to impose a duty of support on adults who could have chosen to formalise their relationship, but have not and who, despite their living together and perhaps even having children, may not want to have an obligation to financial help their adult partner.

This right to claim support even continues after divorce or dissolution. Although the courts have used different justifications for this, for example compensating a spouse or civil partner for loss they have incurred through the marriage ending, recognising the harm that may be done to a spouse's earning potential through child care (*Miller, McFarlane*), in part the reason why they are able to do this in the case of marriages and civil partners is because the couples at least intended a life long commitment and contracted themselves to that and whilst that commitment may not have actually survived the financial effects of it have.

Another similarity between marriage and civil partnership is how it affects the relationship with children. A husband is presumed to be the father of any child born to his wife during the marriage, he can register the child's birth by himself and automatically obtains parental responsibility for the child (**Children Act 1989 s 2(1)**). In addition he is a step-parent to his wife's children that may predate the marriage. They will be entitled to financial support from him through the **Domestic Proceedings and Magistrates' Courts Act 1978**, the **Matrimonial Causes Act 1973** and the **Children Act 1989**. Although a mother's civil partner cannot be a biological parent to the child, her status as a legal parent is recognised. If a child is conceived as the result of fertility treatment, the mother's civil partner can be included on the child's birth certificate.

One of the biggest differences between marriages and civil partnerships is in relation to them ending. It is clear that marriage has a sexual element which the state supports and upholds, whilst civil partnerships do not. Looking first at the grounds for making a marriage and civil partnership void or voidable, although the reasons why a marriage will be void seem to correspond with the reasons why a civil partnership will be void

(MCA 1973 s 11 and **Civil Partnership Act 2004 s 49**), there is an important difference when looking at when a marriage is voidable compared to when a civil partnership is voidable. A marriage is voidable because of either incapacity to consummate (**MCA 1973 s 12(1)**) or because of wilful refusal to consummate (**MCA 1973 s 12(2)**); however, there are no corresponding provisions for the **Civil Partnership Act 2004**. Lack of a sexual relationship does not make a civil partnership voidable. One explanation for this is the legal definition of consummation which does the require the involvement of both a male and female partner. Drafting a new definition of consummation which would take account of both gay and lesbian relationships as well as heterosexual relationships might have been thought of as potentially too vague or intrusive. Furthermore, a civil partner need not be unhappily trapped in a sexless civil partnership, he or she would always have the option of dissolving the partnership using the behaviour fact.

A similar distinction can be seen when dissolution of civil partnership is compared to divorce. Both relationships can only be ended if they have broken down irretrievably (**MCA 1973 s 1(3)**, **Civil Partnership Act 2004 s 41**) and this irretrievable breakdown is demonstrated by proving the existence of a particular fact. Most of these facts are present in both statutes – behaviour that the petitioner cannot be expected to live with, desertion and separation. However, whilst the **Matrimonial Causes Act 1973 s 1(2)(a)** allows adultery as one of the facts that show that a marriage has broken down irretrievably, the **Civil Partnership Act 2004** does not. One reading of this might be that the law is dismissive of the nature of gay and lesbian relationships and considers monogamy less significant in them; however, it is probably fairer to see that this again stems from the definition of adultery. Furthermore, a civil partner who wishes to end his relationship because of either heterosexual or homosexual infidelity on the part of his civil partner can do so through the behaviour fact.

In April 2012 the Government announced a consultation on same sex marriage. The plan is that same sex civil marriage will be introduced and part of this will be that existing civil partners will be able to convert their civil partnership to a marriage. This does suggest that there is a difference between marriage and civil partnership even if it is largely one of image.

# Divorce and Dissolution of Civil Partnerships

**2**

## INTRODUCTION

Divorce questions frequently feature on examination papers, either as a whole question or linked with other issues. Divorce is increasingly common, with recent statistics showing that around one in three marriages ends in divorce. The law regarding divorce is in confusion. The **Family Law Act 1996** would have fundamentally altered the way in which divorces would be obtained, and abolished the concept of fault-based divorce. The Act was radical, but was rejected as pilot schemes were not successful.

In practice, the vast majority of divorces are uncontested, but examination questions tend to concentrate on whether the basis for divorce exists. Students should ensure that they have a good knowledge of the rules concerning divorce; these are not questions that can be skated over superficially.

## THE MATRIMONIAL CAUSES ACT 1973

Remember that there is only one ground for divorce, that of irretrievable breakdown of marriage: MCA 1973 s 1(1). This must be evidenced by one of the five facts in s 1(2).

## THE FIVE FACTS

- ❖ Section 1(2)(a) provides for the granting of a petition based on the respondent's adultery and the petitioner finding it intolerable to live with the respondent (*Cleary v Cleary* (1974)).
- ❖ Section 1(2)(b) allows divorce if the respondent has behaved in such a way that the petitioner cannot reasonably be expected to live with him/her. This depends on the character of the petitioner (*Ash v Ash* (1972), *Livingstone-Stollard v Gunstone-Stollard* (1974)).
- ❖ Section 1(2)(c) contains the fact of two years desertion by the respondent:
  - ❖ there needs to be a separation, that is, withdrawal from married life;
  - ❖ this needs to be without the consent of the petitioner;
  - ❖ and last for a two-year duration.
- ❖ Section 1(2)(d) deals with two years living apart and the respondent consents to the granting of the petition:

❖ note that living apart can be done within the same house, although this may be difficult (*Mouncer v Mouncer* (1972));

❖ possible delay through s 10.

❖ **Section 1(2)(e)** allows divorce on a no-fault basis, even without consent, if there has been five years living apart:

❖ physical separation into two households;

❖ possible bar under s 5 if grave financial or other hardship.

Remember also that no petition can be presented within one year of marriage.

# BARS TO DIVORCE

The respondent in a divorce based on five years' separation as that context may be able to prevent the divorce if it would cause grave financial or other hardship. This is a difficult test to justify.

# THE FAMILY LAW ACT 1996

Divorce procedure was set out in **Part II**. This is not in force and there are no plans for it to be implemented. The ground for divorce would have remained the irretrievable breakdown of marriage, and this was to be demonstrated by a statement by one or both of the parties that they believed the marriage had irretrievably broken down. The initial marital statement could only be lodged with the court after at least three months after one or both parties had attended an information meeting. Fourteen days after the statement is lodged, the period of reflection and consideration would begin. This would last for a minimum of nine months, although it can be extended by another six months. Once the period for reflection and consideration had ended, then either or both parties could apply for a divorce or separation order. The court would then make the order unless the arrangements for the future are unsatisfactory, or unless one of the parties raises the hardship bar in s 10. No application for a divorce order could be made within one year of the marriage: s 7(6).

# ENDING CIVIL PARTNERSHIPS UNDER THE CIVIL PARTNERSHIP ACT 2004

The **Civil Partnership Act 2004** introduces the possibility for homosexual and lesbian couples to register their relationships. **Chapter 2** of the Act sets out the reasons why a civil partnership may be dissolved. Dissolution under the **Civil Partnership Act 2004** largely corresponds to divorce under the **Matrimonial Causes Act 1973**. The only ground for dissolution is that the partnership has broken down irretrievably. This is shown by proving one of the facts in s 44(5):

❖ That the respondent has behaved in such a way that the petitioner cannot reasonably be expected to live with respondent.

❖ That the applicant and the respondent have lived apart for a continuous period of at least two years immediately preceding the making of the application and the respondent consents to a dissolution order being made.

❖    That the applicant and the respondent have lived apart for a continuous period of at least five years preceding the application.
❖    That the respondent has deserted the applicant for a continuous period of at least two years preceding the making of the application.

The main difference between this and divorce is that a civil partnership cannot be ended because of adultery. This is because of the definition of adultery. If there were infidelity, either with a same or different sex partner, this would come within the definition of behaviour that a civil partner could not be expected to live with.

## EXAM QUESTIONS

Divorce is a popular topic for exams, either on its own, or with financial relief, or where appropriate, domestic violence. Problem questions require the student to advise a spouse whilst essay questions require a critical view of procedure.

## QUESTION 6

Fred and Wilma married ten years ago, and were initially very happy, however, Fred started to go out with his friends every Saturday night, leaving Wilma at home with their daughter, Pebbles. Fred frequently returned home drunk, waking Wilma and Pebbles with his raucous singing. One Saturday, Fred crashed his car, returning home after a night in the pub, and was severely injured and left with permanent paraplegia. Wilma visited Fred every day whilst he was in hospital, but when he returned home she realised that the marriage was effectively at an end. Wilma continued to cook for Fred, and she would help bathe and dress him. She did not tell Fred of her feelings, but she began to have an affair with a neighbour, Barney. Wilma told Barney that she would never leave Fred whilst he still needed her, but five years after the accident Wilma moved out of the matrimonial home, to live with Barney, taking Pebbles with her. Wilma said that Fred's depression and irritability had proved too much for her, and she could no longer cope with the strain of looking after him. Fred has refused to consider divorce, saying that he needs Wilma to look after him and that he misses Pebbles.

▶    Advise Wilma as to whether she has any basis for divorce under the present law.

### How to Answer this Question

Present law

❖    Ensure that you mention the one ground of divorce, irretrievable breakdown.
❖    Check that a petition can be presented, which it can, given the duration of the marriage. Examine:
   ❖    s 1(2)(a) – adultery and intolerability (unlikely on the facts);
   ❖    s 1(2)(b) – behaviour (problem of Fred's condition; consider their characters; is it reasonable to expect them to continue to live together?);
   ❖    s 1(2)(c) – desertion (unlikely);
   ❖    s 1(2)(d) – two years living apart (physical separation; mental element; duration; Fred's consent – seems unlikely);

❖    s 1(2)(e) – five years living apart (physical separation; mental element; duration; possible s 5 application).

## Applying the Law

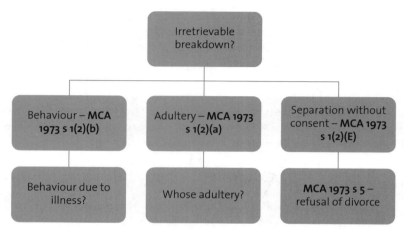

Wilma's basis for divorce under irretrievable breakdown is illustrated here.

# ANSWER

At present, there is one ground for divorce, namely that the marriage between Fred and Wilma has broken down irretrievably: MCA 1973 s 1(1). However, in order to establish irretrievable breakdown, Wilma must establish one of the five facts in the MCA 1973 s 1(2): *Richards v Richards* (1972). From the facts of the question, it seems clear that the marriage has broken down irretrievably; despite Fred's unwillingness to divorce, there seems little realistic prospect for the couple's marriage to revive.

A petition for divorce may only be presented after one year of marriage (MCA 1973 s 3(1)). Since this marriage has lasted ten years, Wilma can petition, provided she can establish one of the five facts.

Adultery is not a relevant fact. Although it is quite clear that Wilma has had voluntary sexual intercourse with Barney, she cannot petition on the basis of her own adultery. Instead this may be relied on by Fred if he were to cross-petition, with the additional requirement of intolerability having to be satisfied.[1]

1    A spouse cannot rely on their own adultery to petition for divorce. Also note that as well as the sexual relationship with a third party (the adultery), the petitioner must also prove that it was intolerable; however, the intolerability does not have to be because of the adultery (*Cleary* (1974)).

A more realistic option for Wilma is to use the fact in the **MCA 1973 s 1(2)(b)** that the respondent has behaved in such a way that the petitioner cannot reasonably be expected to live with the respondent. First, she will need to establish that there has been some behaviour on Fred's part: a mere state of affairs is insufficient (*Katz v Katz* (1972)). Fred's physical condition may cause difficulty if he is merely handicapped; there would need to be a significant strain on Wilma for her petition to succeed: *Thurlow v Thurlow* (1975). If Fred had become difficult, bad tempered or violent, then Wilma's chances of success would increase. It is also possible to maintain a petition based on several incidents, each insufficient in itself, but which have a cumulative effect: *Livingstone-Stallard v Livingstone-Stallard* (1974). Wilma may be able to argue that Fred's Saturday nights out with his friends, his drunkenness, and his disturbing of her and their child amounted to intolerable behaviour. In addition, his action in driving whilst drunk was behaviour that led to his present incapacity.

Once some kind of behaviour has been established, it is then necessary to look at the character of the individual concerned (*Ash v Ash* (1972)), and examine whether it would be reasonable to expect them to continue to live together: *Livingstone-Stallard v Livingstone-Stallard* (1974). Applying that to Wilma and Fred, it could be contended that the strain of looking after Fred, who has been severely incapacitated through his own negligence, is too much for Wilma. Against this it could be argued that Wilma has been having an adulterous relationship with Barney, she has continued to share the same house with Fred for a number of years, stating that she would not leave him, and, although cohabitation of more than six months is not an absolute bar under **s 2(3)** to a successful petition based on behaviour, it does seem that her unwillingness to remain is based more on her developing romance with Barney rather than Fred's behaviour. Nevertheless, in reality it is likely that Wilma would bring her divorce petition using the special procedure. This would mean she would be unlikely to face much opposition or questioning and there would be little examination of whether Fred's behaviour really justified a divorce.[2]

Desertion by the respondent **(MCA 1973 s 1(2)(c)** is rarely used and would not be suitable here. In particular, Wilma would struggle to show that Fred has intended to leave her and this has been without her consent.

It may be more realistic to examine the facts based on separation, namely **s 1(2)(d)** and **(e)**. Both require the petitioner to establish separation in that the parties have lived apart. Living apart is explained in **s 2(6)** by reference to whether the husband and wife live with each other in the same household. If they do, then they are not living apart. In Fred and Wilma's case, they have been living in two households once Wilma left to live with

---

2   Most divorce petitions use the behaviour fact. Thanks to special procedure, few divorces are defended and it is in reality quite easy to establish the behaviour fact. Despite this, it is important that answers do refer to and apply the relevant case law and that they note whether, if this case law were to be applied, the behaviour fact would be made out.

However, there is still the possibility that they lived apart prior to this, whilst in
e house. Although it will not suffice to show merely that there was no intercourse
between them (*Mouncer v Mouncer* (1972)), if it can be shown that they did not share any
married life, then they may be treated as living apart (*Fuller v Fuller* (1973)). From the facts,
it is clear that Fred and Wilma did have some shared life, but Wilma could try to argue
that her case is like *Fuller v Fuller* in that this shared life was in a different capacity of
nursemaid/patient and not husband/wife. However, this case is distinguishable from
*Fuller*, in that in *Fuller* the wife's boyfriend lived in the same household and it was clearly
recognised by all parties that the marriage was at an end. Unfortunately for Wilma, no
third party was present in the household apart from Pebbles, and Fred did not realise that
Wilma no longer cared for him as a spouse.[3]

In addition to living apart, the petitioner must show that at least one of the parties
recognised that the marriage was at an end, even though this does not need to be
communicated: *Santos v Santos* (1972). Clearly this could not have existed until Fred
returned home from the hospital, but Wilma may have difficulty establishing this if Fred
contests the petition. She did not inform anyone of that conclusion, although, when she
told Barney of her unwillingness to leave Fred, she may have communicated the
conclusion that the marriage was at an end.

To petition under **s 1(2)(d)**, Wilma needs to show two years living apart, and that the
respondent consents to the granting of the decree. Given Fred's attitude, it is unlikely
that Wilma will be able to provide the court with Fred's positive consent to the granting
of the divorce.

Therefore, the only other option open to Wilma would seem to be the fact of five years'
separation in **s 1(2)(e)**. As discussed earlier, there needs to be the fact of five years living
apart, coupled with Wilma's recognition that the marriage was at an end. This
necessitates the finding that Fred and Wilma were living apart whilst still in the same
house, something that is not without difficulty. If this were to fail, Wilma would need to
wait for five years after leaving Fred before she petitioned.

Regardless of when her petition based on **s 1(2)(e)** is presented, Fred may oppose the
granting of the decree if the dissolution of the marriage would cause him grave financial
or other hardship, and in all the circumstances it would be unjust to dissolve the
marriage: **MCA s 5(1)**.

Fred's argument would be based on the loss of Wilma's care and the fact that he misses
Pebbles. The court is required to look at all of the circumstances of the case, including the

........................................................................................................................

3  Although it is possible to live apart whilst sharing a house, *Mouncer* shows that this is difficult to do. This
   may in part explain why the separation facts are rarely used.

conduct of the parties, their interests and the interests of any children or other persons: s 5(2). It is unlikely that the court would dismiss the petition as Fred's hardship arises from the breakdown of the relationship with Wilma, not the granting of a divorce: *Parghi v Parghi* (1973). Even if there is no divorce, he will still not have Wilma's care, as she is now having a relationship with Barney. Since both Fred and Wilma seem to be young, and Wilma is involved in another relationship, the court might consider that justice demands the divorce be granted to give Wilma the freedom to start a new life, as in *Parker v Parker* (1972). There is no evidence that Fred would suffer grave financial hardship on divorce, and therefore he is unlikely to succeed in his use of s 5.[4]

## Common Pitfalls

In a problem question on the availability of divorce, it is important to focus on the most relevant facts rather than wasting time discussing each of the five facts.

## Aim Higher

Extra marks will be gained for demonstrating good understanding of the relevant case law and analysing how the controls on the availability of the facts in the case law contrast with the reality of easily available divorce due to the special procedure.

# QUESTION 7

H and W married six months ago after a brief courtship. From the outset, the relationship was fraught with problems. W had led a very sheltered life and found some of the sexual practices H forced her to undergo extremely repugnant. H responded by claiming that W was very cool towards him, unaffectionate and sexually inhibited. W began to shop frequently, often spending enormous amounts of money on luxury items, despite the fact that she and H were not well off. Whilst out shopping last week, W saw H emerging from a restaurant with his arm around X, his secretary. H had been working late recently, and W accused him of an adulterous affair with his secretary. H was furious at this, denied any impropriety and slapped W across the face.

▶ **Advise W, who wishes to obtain a divorce.**

.........................................................................................................

4    Only rarely will a respondent be able to succeed under **s 5**. Most hardships will often be due to the relationship breaking down and the petitioner moving out rather than due to the legal recognition of this through a divorce.

## How to Answer this Question

At the outset, mention the bar on petitioning for divorce within one year of marriage in the MCA 1973 s 3(1). The only possibility would be nullity or judicial separation immediately;

Then go on to consider divorce:

- ❖ irretrievable breakdown as the only ground – s 1(1);
- ❖ evidenced by one of the five facts – in s 1(2);
- ❖ examine s 1(2)(a):
    - ❖ adultery and intolerability;
    - ❖ difficulty in proving;
    - ❖ effect of cohabitation;
- ❖ consider s 1(2)(b):
    - ❖ behaviour and unreasonable to expect her to continue living with him;
    - ❖ repugnant sexual practices;
    - ❖ violence;
    - ❖ examine their characters and the objective test for the reasonableness of cohabitation;
    - ❖ the effect of continued cohabitation;
    - ❖ possible cross-petition by H based on W's behaviour – both sexual and financial;
    - ❖ reject possibility of desertion;
    - ❖ explain possibility of waiting and petitioning under s 1(2)(d) or (e).

## Applying the Law

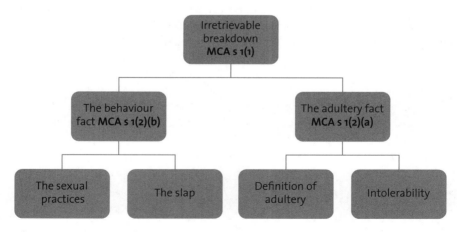

*W's position on applying for a divorce is outlined here under the MCA 1973.*

# ANSWER

In order for W to petition for divorce under the present law, the marriage between her and H must have lasted for at least one year. The MCA 1973 s 3(1) imposes an absolute bar on the presenting of petitions for divorce within one year of marriage, regardless of the hardship or injustice to the petitioner, therefore W cannot petition for divorce until the expiry of one year from the date of the marriage, although incidents within that period may be relied on to support the petition: MCA 1973 s 3(2).[5]

After the expiry of one year from the date of the marriage, W can then petition for divorce on the grounds that the marriage has broken down irretrievably: MCA 1973 s 1(1). This concept of irretrievable breakdown must be established by proving one of the five facts in the MCA s 1(2): *Richards v Richards* (1972). In this case, proof of one of the five facts would give rise to the presumption that the marriage had broken down irretrievably and it seems unlikely that the couple could be reconciled.

The first possible fact that W could rely on is that of adultery and intolerability in the MCA s 1(2)(a). As the petitioner, W would need to establish that H has committed adultery and that she finds it intolerable to live with him. Adultery may be defined as voluntary sexual intercourse between persons of the opposite sex, at least one of whom is married to another. W will need to establish that H had sexual intercourse with his secretary; sexual behaviour that does not amount to intercourse is insufficient to establish adultery (*Sapsford v Sapsford* (1954)). H clearly denies that there has been intercourse and therefore W is faced with the difficulties of proving that intercourse took place. Circumstantial evidence of inclination and opportunity may be used: *Farnham v Farnham* (1925). It seems unlikely that H had the opportunity to indulge in intercourse in the restaurant, even if he did have the inclination. Likewise, the recent excuse of working late is very flimsy evidence, since W does not even know whether the secretary was present or not. Adultery is a serious accusation to make, and the courts have always insisted on strong evidence to support such a weighty accusation: *Serio v Serio* (1983). W may therefore experience difficulty in establishing that H had voluntary intercourse with his secretary. If intercourse can be established, W must then show that she finds it intolerable to live with H. The test is subjective and the intolerability does not have to be caused by the adultery: *Cleary v Cleary* (1974). Thus W could rely on H's sexual practices and his response to her accusation as supporting her claim of intolerability.

The facts do not disclose whether W has ceased to live with H, or whether they are still living together. Periods of cohabitation that total six months or less may be ignored when

---

5    In a divorce question remember to check whether the couple can actually divorce. Here, they have only been married six months so would have to wait. Even though divorce is not immediately available, the facts that could be relied on after the year should still be discussed.

a petition is presented on the basis of adultery: MCA 1973 s 2(1). However, if W continues to live with H for a period in excess of six months from the last act of adultery complained of, the petition will fail.

Another option open to W is to petition relying on the fact in s 1(2)(b) that the respondent has behaved in such a way that the petitioner cannot reasonably be expected to live with him. In this case, H has insisted on sexual practices that W finds embarrassing and degrading. There is no detailed evidence as to what these practices are, and there seems to be a conflict in evidence between W who objects to the practices and H who feels that W is sexually inhibited, given her sheltered upbringing. Behaviour must be some action or conduct by one spouse that affects the other and is referable to the marriage (*Katz v Katz* (1972)), and it may be that if H's actions are really perverted, then this will constitute behaviour such that W cannot reasonably be expected to live with him. However, W could also argue that H's lack of understanding, his taunts and his forcing her to do something she finds repugnant constitute behaviour.[6]

It would also be possible for W to include in her petition the violent response of H, but H would probably argue that this was a one-off incident after extreme provocation, and so should be excluded. H's relationship with his secretary, if not adulterous, could also be used by W to support her petition if it was more than merely platonic, or if H were flaunting this friendship to try to force W to be more sexually accommodating, since such relationships can be very destructive: *Wachtel v Wachtel* (1973). Cumulative incidents can be included in a petition even if each individual incident would be insufficient, since their total effect can be examined: *Livingstone-Stallard v Livingstone-Stallard* (1974). It would then be necessary to look at the character of the petitioner and respondent (*Ash v Ash* (1972)), and ask if it would be reasonable to expect these individuals to live together. This approach combines a subjective and objective approach: *Livingstone-Stallard v Livingstone-Stallard* (1974). Whether it is reasonable to expect W to live with H, given their totally different characters and attitudes to sex, is arguable. Cohabitation is not a bar to petitions based on behaviour (MCA s 2(3)), but it is important for W to remember that the longer she lives with H, the weaker her argument that it is unreasonable for her to have to do so becomes. It is highly likely that H would defend a petition based on behaviour, and W should be advised of the possibility that H will cross-petition based on her behaviour. H may well cite her unaffectionate nature, but since this is a state of affairs rather than deliberate behaviour (*Pheasant v Pheasant* (1972)), he will need more to support his petition. A complete and deliberate refusal to have any kind of sexual intercourse might well be behaviour, but her unsatisfactory sexual performance would not be (*Dowden v Dowden* (1977)). In addition, H might want to cite W's financial

6   The question under **s 1(2)(b)** is whether this particular petitioner can reasonably be expected to live with the behaviour of the respondent, It is therefore important to examine the petitioner's own behaviour as a less than innocent petitioner might be expected to put up with a less than innocent spouse.

irresponsibility in spending large sums of money on luxury items which the family finances could not afford. Such behaviour might well, if very extreme, result in it being unreasonable to expect H to live with W (*Carter-Fea v Carter-Fea* (1987)), especially if H was financially prudent, yet faced debt and financial ruin because of W's habit.[7]

There is no evidence in this case that either party is in desertion, nor have they been living apart as two separate households as required for s 1(2)(d) and s 1(2)(e). Obviously, if W cannot succeed in her petition based on adultery or behaviour, then she must begin to live apart from H, and, after two years, petition for divorce with his consent under s 1(2)(d) or, if H refuses consent, she will have to wait for five years before petitioning under s 1(2)(e).

# QUESTION 8

X and Y were married seven years ago, when they were both 50, but, unknown to Y, X's hobby was the keeping of reptiles, including a snake. Y was terrified of the snake and threatened to leave if X did not get rid of the snake. X was very fond of his snake, and felt Y was being unreasonable in forcing him to choose between her and his snake. X refused to get rid of the snake, offering instead to confine it to the spare room, but six months later Y stormed out of the matrimonial home. X did not hear from Y for several months, and only heard of her whereabouts when he was contacted by a mental hospital where Y was a patient. X visited Y frequently in hospital, but Y was suffering from insane delusions about snakes. After six months in hospital, Y was discharged to be cared for in the community but refused to return home to X whilst he had the snake.

X and Y have not lived in the same house for the past six and a half years, and X now wishes to divorce Y. Y is opposed to the divorce as she is concerned about her financial situation should she lose her widow's pension on X's death.

▶ Advise X on his position under the present law.

## How to Answer this Question

Restate the one ground for divorce, namely irretrievable breakdown, and the requirement for it to be evidenced by one of the five facts. Consider each of these in turn:

- ❖ reject adultery – s 1(2)(a);
- ❖ consider behaviour – s 1(2)(b):
  - ❖ problem of mental illness;
  - ❖ reasonableness of cohabitation;
  - ❖ possible cross-petition;
- ❖ examine desertion in detail (s 1(2)(c));
- ❖ consider living apart – for two years (s 1(2)(d)) and five years (s 1(2)(e)):

---

7   Note how the answer considers the effect of continued cohabitation on a petition using the adultery fact and a petition using the behaviour fact.

❖    problem of s 5 – grave financial and other hardship;
❖    possible postponement under s 10.

## Applying the Law

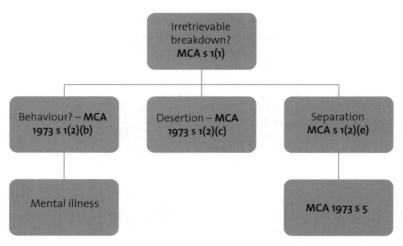

The law to consider here and how it can be understood in relation to s 1(2)(b) and 1(2)(c) of the MCA 1973 is illustrated in this diagram.

# ANSWER

If X wishes to petition for divorce now, he must establish the one ground for divorce in the MCA 1973 s 1(1); that the marriage has broken down irretrievably. Since his marriage to Y has lasted longer than one year, he is not prevented from presenting his petition by the bar in the MCA 1973 s 3(1). However, the petition must do more than allege irretrievable breakdown; it must also specify one of the five facts in the MCA 1973 s 1(2).

There is no evidence that either party to the marriage has committed adultery and so it is unnecessary to consider the application of the MCA 1973 s 1(2)(a). The next fact, contained in s 1(2)(b), is that the respondent has behaved in such a way that the petitioner cannot reasonably be expected to live with her. X will need to point to some behaviour by Y, and there may be difficulty in doing this. The first thing mentioned in the question is Y's insistence that X removes his snake from the house. Whilst X's distress at losing his pet is understandable, a snake is not something that many people would feel easy living with. Much might depend on the kind of snake, how large it is, and the way in which it is confined. Y's simple desertion cannot be evidence of behaviour (*Morgan v Morgan* (1973)) and there would also be problems if X were to try to rely on Y's illness or mental condition. Behaviour needs to be some action or conduct by one spouse that affects the other and is referable to the marriage: *Katz v Katz* (1972). The development of a mental illness by Y, after she left the matrimonial home, is somewhat problematic, especially since the nature of the illness may suggest that it was precipitated by X and his snake. The courts often take the view that marriage involves a certain amount of give and take and understanding for a spouse's illness (*Thurlow v Thurlow* (1975)), and X would probably need to refer to stressful incidents committed by Y in her illness, rather than just her unhappy condition. If her delusions resulted in violence, as in *Thurlow*, or caused him considerable distress as in *Katz*, then he might succeed, but this is doubtful. The nature of Y's behaviour must be such that, taking into account the issues and personalities of the parties (*Ash v Ash* (1972)), it is not reasonable to expect X to live with Y (*Livingstone-Stallard v Livingstone-Stallard* (1974)). It could be argued that a snake-loving husband cannot reasonably be expected to live with a snake-hating wife! It would be open to Y to defend X's petition based on behaviour, and she could always cross-petition on the basis of X's behaviour. He has constantly failed to assuage her fears of the snake, and indeed, it could be argued that his love for and relationship with the snake have been destructive and his deliberate refusal to give the snake away despite his wife's genuine fear is behaviour that makes it unreasonable to expect her to live with him. From the facts, Y does not want a divorce, but, if one appears to be inevitable, it may be that she will seek one on the basis of X's behaviour.

Another possibility available to X is to petition on the basis of Y's desertion of him for a period of two years prior to the presenting of the petition under the **MCA 1973 s 12(c)**. This fact is very rarely relied on in practice and has a number of technical requirements. First, X must establish that there has been factual separation in that there has been a withdrawal from married life: *Pulford v Pulford* (1923). When Y left X, she withdrew from married life, and they have not cohabited together since. X's visits to the hospital probably do not count as periods of living a married life, since they were out of his concern for Y, and there is no evidence that she was in any way responding to him. If, however, there were brief resumptions of married life during these visits, the reconciliation provisions in the **MCA 1973 s 2** provide that such periods totalling six months or less shall be disregarded.

It is then necessary to establish that Y had the intention to desert. At the time she left X, it seems that Y, although distressed, was not insane and her mental illness developed later. If this is so, then she had the intention permanently to desert X, unless she just intended to storm out to teach X a lesson and force him to remove the snake. Subsequently, Y has become mentally ill, and at common law her desertion would cease when she developed the incapacity: *Crowther v Crowther* (1951). This has been affected by the **MCA 1973 s 2(4)**, which provides that the court can treat the period of desertion as continuing through the period of mental incapacity; if the evidence is such that had Y not been incapable, the court would infer that her desertion continued. From the facts, there is no evidence that Y had changed her mind, and so the likelihood is that she would still have the intention to desert even during her period in hospital. It is quite clear that on her discharge, she has no intention of returning to X whilst the snake remains in the house, and so she would continue in desertion.

If, however, at the time of leaving X, Y was suffering from delusions about the snake, then her capacity to form the intention to desert is questionable. In *Perry v Perry* (1964) it was suggested that the respondent be judged on the basis that the delusions were true, and therefore if she has delusions that her husband and the snake would harm her, then she may not be held to have formed the intention to desert. In such a case, X will need to establish at what point Y ceases to suffer from the delusions and is capable of forming the intention to desert.

X must then establish that he did not consent to the desertion; if he did then it is more appropriate to use **s 1(2)(d)** (two years living apart and consent), or **s 1(2)(e)** (five years living apart). The problem X faces here is that Y left only after he refused her ultimatum for staying. A petitioner who refuses a respondent's reasonable offer of reconciliation cannot rely on desertion: *Gallagher v Gallagher* (1965). Much will depend on whether Y's offer of staying with the snake removed was reasonable, in which case she is not in desertion, as in *Slawson v Slawson* (1942). It is by no means clear that X can establish that Y is in desertion; indeed, it may be that if he has refused her reasonable offer of reconciliation, he will be in desertion (*Hall v Hall* (1960)).

If X can show that he did not consent to Y's desertion, then he must finally establish that Y deserted without just cause. The same problem concerning X's relationship with the snake and the fear it caused Y is encountered. Indeed, if it could be said that X's behaviour in refusing to remove the snake, despite the terror it caused his wife, is grave and weighty (*Lang v Lang* (1953)), and has caused Y to leave, this would thereby place X in constructive desertion.

If desertion can be established, it must be for a continuous period of at least two years immediately prior to the presenting of the petition. In X and Y's case, they separated shortly after their marriage seven years ago, and have not really resumed married life since. It seems likely that the two-year period is satisfied, notwithstanding what was said previously regarding the period of Y's mental illness. It is clear from the facts of the case that the couple have been living apart for a considerable time. There have been two separate households (**MCA 1973 s 2(6)**), but it will be necessary to show that one party formed the conclusion that the marriage was at an end, even though this was not communicated to the other: *Santos v Santos* (1972). Looking at X, it is not clear when, if at all, he reached this conclusion. Initially, he offers to confine the snake to ensure Y does not leave; he also visits Y whilst she is in hospital. It may be that on Y's discharge, it becomes clear to X that the marriage has ended, but there is no evidence of this. X did not mention it to anyone, make a note, nor is there evidence of a relationship with anyone else. If Y were to defend this case, she might well contend that X never recognised the marriage was at an end, and this could cause X difficulty in establishing that he did to the court's satisfaction. If living apart can be established, it seems clear that X and Y have lived apart for at least two years. However, Y seems unlikely to consent to the granting of the divorce as required in **s 1(2)(d)**. This would necessitate X relying on the fact of five years living apart in **s 1(2)(e)**. It seems that the couple have lived apart since shortly after their marriage, which is longer than five years, but again the problem of recognition of the ending of the marriage (*Santos*), may mean that the five-year period is not yet established. If it is, then X does not need Y's consent to the divorce, although she may be able to prevent or postpone the divorce through the use of **s 5** or **10** of the **MCA 1973**.[8]

The **MCA 1973 s 5** provides that a respondent may oppose the granting of a divorce on the grounds of grave financial or other hardship, and that, in all the circumstances of the case, it would be wrong to dissolve the marriage. Y has expressed concern about her financial situation if the divorce were to be granted. Hardship is defined to include the loss of the chance of acquiring any benefit (**s 5(3)**), and here Y is concerned at the possible loss of a widow's pension. At present, on divorce, the ex-wife would lose her entitlement to a widow's pension. This would not cause grave financial hardship if only the state widow's pension were lost, as this would be replaced by income support or a retirement pension: *Reiterbund v Reiterbund* (1975). However, if on X's death his widow would be provided with an occupational pension, then this might cause grave financial hardship if it were lost. Much will depend upon Y's personal financial position, since if she has independent means or wealth she is unlikely to be prejudiced. In *Archer v Archer* (1999), the 53-year-old wife risked losing £18,000 per annum on her 55-year-old husband's death if the divorce were granted. However, she had a house valued at £200,000 and her own investments of £300,000, and therefore would not suffer grave hardship through the divorce. If, however, she is in difficult financial circumstances, then grave hardship may be established: *Dorrell v Dorrell* (1972). She is now in her late 50s and is the kind of wife that **s 5** was designed to protect, in that a widow's pension is not a remote possibility, but something that might realistically accrue to her if married, but be denied to her on divorce: *Mathias v Mathias* (1972).

Under the **Pensions Act 1995 s 166**, part of one partner's private pension can be earmarked for the benefit of the other partner. However, this would only be of benefit on the retirement of the partner with the pension. The more radical option of splitting X's pension fund between him and Y has been made possible by the pension sharing provisions of the **Welfare Reform and Pensions Act 1999**. This would arguably remove any argument that the divorce would cause grave hardship. If such a defence is raised, then X may be able to obtain his divorce if he can put forward reasonable proposals that would compensate Y for the loss of pension, such as the provision of an annuity, or insurance

---

8    Desertion is rarely relied on as a fact. It is easier to use behaviour rather than waiting two years, or for the petitioner to consent to the living apart and use **s 1(2)(d)**. There is no advantage to the petitioner in being the wronged party and using desertion rather than living apart.

policy (*Parker v Parker* (1972)). In the circumstances, if X cannot adequately compensate Y, then the court may consider, in all the circumstances, including the conduct of X, that it would be wrong to dissolve the marriage.[9]

Even if Y does not seek to rely on s 5, she may seek to postpone the granting of the decree based on either s 1(2)(d) or (e) until the court has considered her financial position. The **MCA 1973 s 10** provides that on such an application the court must look at all of the circumstances of the case, including the age, health, conduct, needs and resources of the parties. The decree will not be made absolute until the court is satisfied that either no financial provision for Y will be made, or that the financial provision made by X is reasonable and fair or the best that can be made in the circumstances. Therefore, it is important for X to be prepared to outline his proposals for financial provision for Y, if any can be made.

# QUESTION 9

H and W have been married for 30 years, and are now both aged 60. H is a successful businessman and has, for many years, been involved in Freemasonry. H and W have become increasingly estranged over the years, especially since their daughter, J, grew up and left home. When J left home, W joined some adult education classes and has become increasingly involved in women's rights and radical politics. H finds this embarrassing and has had to endure many taunts from his friends about his wife getting 'out of control'. W has become increasingly assertive and will not cook H's meals or wash and iron his clothes, arguing that she is no longer his slave.

W frequently makes jokes about H's involvement with the Freemasons and has refused to accompany H to the annual Freemasons' social event, 'Ladies' Night', saying that it is derogatory to women. This is too much for H who told her to 'shape up or get out'. W responded by changing the locks on the doors to the matrimonial home, whilst H was out at work, to teach him a lesson. W made H wait on the doorstep for two hours before throwing him the new keys. H moved back in, but W refuses to cook and clean for him, and H now wishes to divorce W. W is unwilling to consider divorce as she does not wish to upset her elderly mother, C, who is a staunch Catholic and vehemently opposed to divorce. C has threatened to disinherit any of her children who divorce.

▶ Advise H on whether he can obtain a divorce under the present law in the **MCA 1973**.

## How to Answer this Question
Mention irretrievable breakdown as sole ground for divorce, and requirement for it to be evidenced by one of five facts:

---

9    In this case, one concern is that Y might lose her pension entitlement were her and X to divorce. Because this is a factor, the answer is right in explaining how pensions can now be dealt with as part of ancillary relief and how, therefore, concern about pensions is unlikely to lead to a successful **s 5** application.

- ❖ no evidence of adultery (s 1(2)(a));
- ❖ behaviour (s 1(2)(b)):
  - ❖ what constitutes behaviour?
  - ❖ look at character;
  - ❖ consider reasonableness of cohabitation by *Livingstone-Stallard* test;
- ❖ desertion (s 1(2)(c)):
  - ❖ difficult given no complete withdrawal;
- ❖ living apart (s 1(2)(d)):
  - ❖ two separate households do not exist as yet;
  - ❖ unlikely W would consent after two years;
- ❖ living apart for five years (s 1(2)(e)):
  - ❖ need separation;
  - ❖ five years' duration;
  - ❖ no need for consent;
  - ❖ problem – s 5 – grave financial or other hardship;
  - ❖ possible postponement – s 10.

## Applying the Law

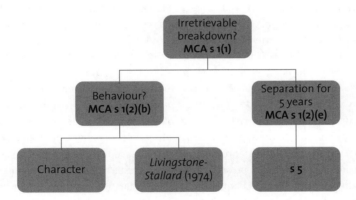

The relationship of this scenario to the relevant section of the MCA 1973 and the key case to consider here are shown above.

# ANSWER

H can petition for divorce if he can show that his marriage has broken down irretrievably: MCA 1973 s 1(1). This must be evidenced by one of the five facts in s 1(2) (*Richards v Richards* (1972)), since irretrievable breakdown in isolation is insufficient to obtain a divorce. The marriage between H and W has obviously encountered difficulties; however, the facts must be such that one of the five facts in s 1(2) can be established. The marriage is of a lengthy nature, and so the bar on presenting petitions within one year of marriage contained in the **MCA 1973 s 3(1)** does not apply. There is no evidence in this case of either H or W committing adultery, and therefore **s 1(2)(a)** is inapplicable. However, there is a need to consider **s 1(2)(b)** whereby a petition may be presented on the basis that the respondent has behaved in such a way that the petitioner cannot reasonably be expected to live with them.[10]

Initially, H will need to specify exactly what constitutes behaviour on W's part. In *Katz v Katz* (1972), behaviour was defined in terms of action or conduct by one spouse that affects the other and is referable to the marriage. It seems that H has been upset by W's new-found interests, and by the jokes made by his friends. It seems harsh to argue that W's desire to gain new interests has somehow constituted behaviour towards H. Many women find the need for new horizons as they grow older and their children leave home. The fact that H feels threatened or embarrassed by this cannot fairly be attributable to W. If, however, W's new interests were very extreme, causing her to completely isolate herself from H, then this might constitute behaviour. She has refused to do any cooking or cleaning for H, and this seems to be a deliberate decision by her. It is not apparent whether both she and H work, or whether only H does; such a factor will determine the reasonableness of the expectation of contribution. W has also begun to ridicule H's involvement with Freemasonry, and has refused to accompany him on one particular occasion. Again, it is unclear whether the ridicule is good-natured joking in private or cruel jibing in public. It seems that W has not withdrawn from all social activities with H, but merely the one 'Ladies' Night' that her conscience found unpalatable. W's changing of the locks was behaviour, albeit of a joking nature, but it is by no means clear that H will succeed on this fact. Then it will be necessary to show that, given the individual parties' characters and conduct (*Ash v Ash* (1972)), it is unreasonable to expect H to live with W. This is a partly subjective approach, and, according to Bagnall J in *Ash v Ash*: 'a violent petitioner can reasonably be expected to live with a violent respondent . . . and if each is equally bad, at any rate in sinister respects, each can reasonably be expected to live with the other'. Applying this to the present case, H seems to be a dedicated chauvinist whilst W seems to be an equally trenchant feminist. There could be an argument that these two extremes could never be expected to live together. The reasonableness of the expectation of contribution is judged objectively, the so-called 'jury test' in *Livingstone-Stallard v Livingstone-Stallard* (1974). Here the parties have had a long marriage, and the readjustment that naturally occurs as the parties adapt in later years will cause problems in most marriages. The disagreements in this case may not be so extreme that it is not

---

10  The only ground for divorce under the **MCA 1973** is irretrievable breakdown but that has to be shown by proving one of the five facts in **s 1(2)**. When writing an answer to a divorce question make sure that the answer is clear that the ground is irretrievable breakdown rather than suggesting that one of the facts is itself the ground for the divorce.

reasonable to expect H to live with W. The changing of the locks was to teach H a lesson after his ultimatum, not a vindictive exclusion of a blameless spouse. Incidents can have a cumulative effect (*Livingstone-Stallard v Livingstone-Stallard* (1974)), but seen in totality it seems that H will have difficulty in establishing behaviour. It seems to be the classic case of 'six of one, half a dozen of the other'.[11]

The fact of desertion in s 1(2)(c) will be difficult to establish for H. W has refused to cook or clean for H, but seems willing to talk to him and share aspects of family life. The fact that H and W are not truly living apart as two households will also make any petition under s 1(2)(d) or (e) unlikely to succeed. The fact that the relationship is strained is insufficient to show the parties are maintaining two households: *Mouncer v Mouncer* (1972). However, if H were to move out or cease to share any common life, then he could petition for divorce after two years with W's consent. This does not seem likely to be forthcoming, in which case H would need to establish five years living apart, in terms of physical living apart coupled with his recognition that the marriage was at an end: *Santos v Santos* (1972).

In such a situation, W may seek to prevent the divorce by relying on the **MCA 1973 s 5**. It could be argued that the granting of the divorce would cause her grave financial or other hardship, and that in all the circumstances it would be wrong to grant the petition. W wishes to avoid upsetting her elderly mother who, for religious reasons, is opposed to divorce. There is no evidence to show whether W herself is opposed to divorce for religious reasons and, in any case, the court will look for strong evidence of social ostracism before refusing the petition, as in *Banik v Banik* (1973). The mere fact that divorce is frowned upon would be insufficiently grave to justify opposing the divorce: *Parghi v Parghi* (1973).

However, W can also argue that divorce would cause her grave financial hardship. This could include the loss of any benefit that the respondent might acquire if the marriage were not dissolved: **MCA 1973 s 5(3)**. This was designed to cover the possible loss of widow's pensions, etc, which could be a severe hardship for a woman of W's age: *Mathias v Mathias* (1972). It is not clear whether this covers the potential loss of inheritance from a third party. The section is widely drafted and could potentially cover it, but it would seem harsh to H to deny him a divorce because of the possible reaction of his elderly mother-in-law. The court is instructed to look at all of the circumstances of the case, including the conduct of the parties and their interests and those of any children or other persons:

---

11  This illustrates the subjective nature of the behaviour fact. The question is not whether the behaviour complained of is objectively unreasonable, but whether it would be reasonable to expect that particular petitioner with their personality, character and habits to put up with the respondent's behaviour.

MCA 1973 s 5(2). If H can make some sort of attempt to mitigate any possible financial hardship for W, then he may be allowed his divorce (*Parker v Parker* (1972)), and since he is a successful businessman it seems likely that he could purchase some kind of annuity or set aside some lump sum to offset the loss of any widow's pension, and possibly any inheritance if that is a valid consideration.[12]

Even if W does not invoke s 5, then she may well use the provisions in the MCA 1973 s 10 to postpone the divorce being made absolute. Where petitions are presented on facts in s 1(2)(d) or (e), the respondent can apply to the court for consideration of her financial position: s 10(2). In such a situation, the court will not award a decree absolute unless no financial provision is to be made, which is unlikely in this case, or unless the financial provision is reasonable and fair or the best that can be made in the circumstances: MCA 1973 s 10(3). After such a long marriage, and given H's standing as a businessman, W is likely to be entitled to financial provision. Therefore H should be prepared to present a clear explanation to the court of the financial provision he is proposing: *Grigson v Grigson* (1974).

# QUESTION 10

Kathy was a devout Christian, and devoted a great deal of her time to charitable works, including prison visits. On one visit to the prison, she met John, who had been convicted of rape and attempted murder. John impressed Kathy with his charm and repentance, and soon she fell in love with him. They were married whilst John was still in jail, some eight years ago, but with Kathy's help John was released early five years ago. Immediately on his release, John's personality changed and he shouted obscenities at Kathy, forcing her to perform degrading acts, but stopping short of actual intercourse. He then hit Kathy, who has been too frightened to tell anyone of what happened. John disappeared and since then there have been numerous reports linking John with rapes throughout the country, but nothing has been heard of him since an incident three years ago, when the victim shot her attacker, who fitted John's description. The attacker had been badly wounded, as much blood was found at the scene and nearby. DNA tests reveal that the blood is almost definitely John's. Kathy does not want to divorce John, for religious reasons, but is most anxious to know what can be done to end her marital obligations to him.

▶ **Advise Kathy.**

---

12  Claims by the respondent that a divorce would lead to grave financial or other hardship under **MCA 1973 s 5** are rarely successful. The hardship has to be due to the divorce, rather than due to the breakdown of the relationship and the couple living separately. Moreover, in relation to financial hardship, this can be mitigated by the financial relief awarded on the divorce.

## How to Answer this Question

In this question, the petitioner does not want divorce, and so you should consider the other options, namely nullity, judicial separation, presumption of death, and dissolution of marriage.

Consider if the marriage is void under the MCA s 11. Explain effect – but no evidence on facts of marriage being void.

Then examine s 12 provisions for voidable marriages:

* s 12(a) and (b):
    * has the marriage been consummated?
    * incapacity or wilful refusal?
* s 12(c):
    * is there lack of consent?
    * only a mistake as to attributes of partner – insufficient;
    * unlikely that John did not understand nature of ceremony;
* s 12(d):
    * mental disorder – on part of John, so as to make him unfit for marriage;
* s 12(e) – venereal disease, and s 12(f) – pregnancy *per alium* is inapplicable.

Consider possible bars in s 13 – approbation and time. Then go on to examine judicial separation which is obtainable by proving one of the five facts in the MCA s 1(2), but without the marriage being ended, merely the obligation to cohabit:

* s 1(2)(a) – adultery:
    * evidence of the rapes;
    * subjective test of intolerability;
* s 1(2)(b) – behaviour:
    * easily established.

Consider also the possibility of applying to have John declared dead and the marriage dissolved:

* absence not long enough for seven-year presumption to operate;
* will need to bring evidence to suggest why dead.

## Applying the Law

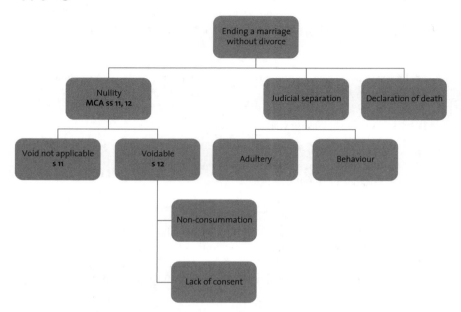

*The relevant considerations for each section of the MCA are illustrated here.*

# ANSWER

Since Kathy is adamantly opposed to the idea of divorcing John, it is necessary to consider the other options available to her if she wishes to end her marital obligations towards John. There are three possibilities, namely nullity, judicial separation, and presumption of death and dissolution of marriage.

Nullity proceedings are available in respect of void marriages by reference to the grounds in the **MCA 1973 s 11** and in respect of voidable marriages by reference to the grounds in the **MCA 1973 s 12**. None of the grounds for a void marriage appear to be present in this scenario and therefore the question is whether this would be a voidable marriage under **section 12** of the **Matrimonial Causes Act 1973**. A voidable marriage is treated as valid unless and until it is voided. This means that a nullity decree is a necessity in order to end Kathy's obligations, but it is only possible for her to petition for nullity during John's lifetime.

The first two grounds in s 12(a) and (b) require the marriage not to have been consummated. Consummation is one act of complete and regular intercourse after the marriage: *D v A* (1845). It is unclear whether Kathy and John had the opportunity to have sexual intercourse whilst John was in prison. If they did not do so, then the incident after

John's release does not amount to consummation. There must be full penetration of the vagina by the penis; sexual activities other than this do not suffice (*W v W* (1967)). If the marriage has not been consummated, then the reason for this must be examined. **Section 12(a)** requires incapacity to consummate on the part of the petitioner or the respondent. There is no evidence that Kathy or John is incapable of consummating the relationship; rather it seems that John has deliberately chosen not to. This may be evidence of wilful refusal to consummate by John, thereby enabling Kathy to petition. In *Horton v Horton* (1947), it was necessary to show 'a settled and definite decision come to without just cause', and such a situation would seem to be indicated here by John's treatment of Kathy and his immediate departure.[13]

The **MCA 1973 s 12(c)** makes a marriage voidable through lack of consent through mistake, duress, unsoundness of mind, or otherwise. In Kathy's case, she could try to argue that she had made a mistake about John's reformed character. However, mistake must be as to the nature of the ceremony (*Mehta v Mehta* (1945)) or the identity of the party, but a mistake as to a quality of the party does not render the marriage voidable (*Puttick v AG* (1979)).

The facts seem to indicate that John is unbalanced, to say the least, but in order for the marriage to be invalid it must be shown that at the time of the ceremony he was suffering from such an unsoundness of mind that he could not understand the nature of the ceremony (*Sheffield City Council v E and Another* (2004)). This rarely succeeds, and, in the present case, John seems to have exploited the prospects that marriage brings in terms of early release, and, therefore was unlikely to have satisfied the test of unsoundness of mind.

There is no evidence of duress or any other factor to vitiate consent, and there is no evidence of the grounds in **s 12(e)** (venereal disease) or **s 12(f)** (pregnancy *per alium*). The only other option available to Kathy is to rely on **s 12(d)** and argue that although John was capable of consenting to the marriage, he was suffering at the time from a mental disorder, within the meaning of the **Mental Health Act 1983**, of such a kind or extent as to be unfit for marriage. The test is whether the party was capable of carrying out the ordinary duties and obligations of marriage (*Bennett v Bennett* (1968)), and, despite his criminal tendencies and cunning, it would seem that John was not suffering from some such disorder.

If the petition is presented on the basis of non-consummation, then the possible bars to the granting of the decree need to be considered. Kathy has not behaved in any way to

---

13   Note that Kathy would not be able to rely on the fact that the marriage was not consummated during John's prison sentence as at that time John would have had a 'just cause' for not consummating the relationship.

lead John to believe that she would not annul the marriage and so statutory approbation does not apply: MCA 1973 s 13(1). There are no time bars to petitions based on non-consummation, although a petition based on any other ground must be presented within three years of the marriage: MCA s 13(2). The only possible waiver of this time limit is a discretionary one if at any time the petitioner has been suffering from a mental disorder. Kathy's wedding took place eight years ago, and since she has never suffered such a defect, she could not petition on any basis other than s 12(b) (wilful refusal to consummate).

If the marriage has been consummated, then Kathy's other option is to seek a decree of judicial separation. The decree does not end the marriage, but it does end the duty to cohabit: MCA 1973 s 18(1). There is no need to establish that the marriage has irretrievably broken down, but the petitioner must establish one of the five facts in the MCA s 1(2). John has committed rape, and this will amount to adultery since he has voluntarily had sexual intercourse with a woman whilst he was married to Kathy. Section 1(2)(a) further requires the petitioner to show that she finds it intolerable to live with the respondent, and there is little doubt, given what has happened, that this subjective test can be satisfied. The intolerability need not arise from the adultery (*Cleary v Cleary* (1974)), and therefore John's treatment of Kathy will help satisfy the fact in s 1(2)(b). In addition, there is little doubt also that John has behaved in such a way that it is not reasonable to expect Kathy to continue to live with him: MCA s 1(2)(b). Therefore Kathy will be able to obtain a decree of judicial separation.

There is the additional possibility here that John may be dead. The forensic and identification evidence seems to indicate that he was shot and badly wounded, and as nothing has been heard of him by friends, relatives, or victims of his crimes, it may be possible to apply to the court for a decree of presumption of death and dissolution of marriage: s 19 MCA. Section 19(1) provides that any married person who has reasonable grounds for supposing that his or her spouse is dead may present a petition to the court to have the spouse presumed dead and the marriage dissolved. Section 19(3) provides a presumption that a person is dead if he or she has been absent for seven years or more, but this does not apply to John. Therefore, Kathy will need to provide the court with details as to why she believes John to be dead. She seems to have made enquiries about him (*Bullock v Bullock* (1960)), and despite a huge police search for him, he has not been found. His last known appearance was in circumstances to suggest he had been fatally wounded and so Kathy could succeed in her application under s 19. If she does, and John reappears, then the decree nisi will be rescinded, but if the decree has been made absolute, the marriage remains ended.

Therefore, it can be seen that despite her unwillingness to divorce, Kathy has several options available to her to end her obligations towards John.

# QUESTION 11

The present procedures for ending a marriage fail both the parties and society, generally.
Something radical must be done.

▶  Discuss.

## How to Answer this Question

❖  Look at irretrievable breakdown and the need to prove one of five facts;

❖  no-fault divorce facts;

❖  fault-based facts – commonly used;

❖  bitterness inherent in present system;

❖  Booth Committee, Law Commission and Government proposals;

❖  conciliation and its role – criticisms and reforms.

With a question like this, it is easier for the poorer student to write all he has
remembered about divorce. This should be avoided; instead he should be focused and
analytical.

## Applying the Law

*The procedures for ending a marriage are illustrated here.*

# ANSWER

A marriage may end in divorce if one of the parties successfully presents a petition
alleging that the marriage has irretrievably broken down (**MCA 1973 s 1(1)**), and proves
this by establishing one of the five facts in the **MCA 1973 s 1(2)**. Very few petitions are
contested (less than 1%), and the vast majority of divorces are granted by way of the
special procedure whereby the petition is read and approved without oral hearing.
However, for many couples, divorce is a bitter process, and does not end their problems,

but merely leads to further dispute and antagonism. It is therefore necessary to examine the current divorce procedures and see how far, if at all, they serve the parties' and society's interests.

Historically, marriage has been regarded as an institution that should be firmly supported and not undermined by the State. However, increasing numbers have found their marriages intolerable and have sought an end to their marital obligations. Initially, it was only possible to divorce a partner who could be shown to be at fault. This inevitably leads to bitter accusations about past indiscretions and conduct and is hardly conducive to civilised conduct after the divorce. This bitterness can have repercussions on the welfare of any children as well as the parties' willingness to co-operate in other matters, such as financial agreements.[14]

Despite much opposition, especially from vocal clergy, the **Divorce Reform Act 1969** introduced the concept of a no-fault divorce. This is now to be found in the **MCA 1973** s 1(2)(d) and (e), namely divorce after two years' separation with the respondent's consent to the granting of the petition, and five years' separation if there is no such consent. The idea behind a no-fault divorce is that it would reduce bitterness and antagonism and improve the ongoing relationship between the parties and their children. However, the provisions of **s 1(2)(e)** have been objected to by those who opposed the idea of an 'innocent' spouse being divorced against his or her wishes.

The **Matrimonial Causes Act 1973** does not provide for a completely no-fault divorce system, and it retains fault-based facts of adultery, behaviour and desertion. Despite the availability of no-fault divorce, more than 80 per cent of petitions allege adultery or behaviour, which enables immediate divorce and obviates the need to live apart for a lengthy period. Thus, in reality, no-fault divorce exists in less than one-fifth of cases, and the requirement of physical separation is often difficult to achieve for families on low incomes. Presently, therefore, most divorces do involve the petitioner alleging fault on the part of the respondent. This encourages petitioners to rake over incidents in the past, often exaggerating them, in order to obtain a speedy divorce. This can increase the respondent's resentment, lead to cross-petitions, antagonism and lasting conflict that can be very damaging to the welfare of the children.

Once it is recognised that divorce is inevitable in many cases, good divorce law should ensure that it provides an effective method of ending marriages that have not worked with the minimum of bitterness, leaving the parties in a position where future co-operation in financial matters and the upbringing of the children can be achieved. The present law does not do that because of the tendency for most divorces to be fault-based.

---

14   There is, however, a contrary argument that an 'innocent' spouse may feel bitter if (s)he is not able to cite the other spouse's fault in claiming a divorce.

In 1985, the Booth Committee on Matrimonial Causes Procedures recommended that all divorce should be fault-free, since the fault element increases bitterness and stops sensible discussion about crucial future issues. The only basis of divorce should, according to the Committee, be irretrievable breakdown of marriage without specifying any further facts. This has been criticised, but in reality the lack of investigation in the special procedure adopted by the courts for most divorces means that this could be happening already if the parties agree not to contest the petition. There is little evidence that fault-based divorce reduces the divorce rate or saves marriages from failure and, from society's point of view, the bitterness of fault-based divorce spills over into ancillary matters and children issues, which are costly in terms of legal aid and human misery.

The Law Commission reported in 1990 (The Ground for Divorce) and agreed that the way forward lay in no-fault divorce. Its report suggested that irretrievable breakdown without any further fact should be the basis of divorce. Once a person felt that their marriage had broken down, they should be able to lodge a sworn statement in court to that effect. The Law Commission thought that a joint application could also be made, and that, once this had happened, the parties should be given an information pack outlining what should happen next and the need to sort out financial arrangements and arrangements for the children. Mediation would be available to assist the parties to reach agreement on these matters, and then after 11 months it would be open to either party to apply for a divorce stating that the marriage had in fact irretrievably broken down. Thus, the important practical issues would be sorted out before the divorce was granted, and hopefully the no-fault nature of proceedings would ensure the minimum of bitterness. The Law Commission wanted the court to retain the power to refuse divorce on the basis of grave financial or other hardship. Critics argued that this would further undermine the institution of marriage, make divorce easier to obtain and could lead to parties instigating proceedings as a threat, thereby setting the process in motion. There would also be no method of ending a marriage sooner than 12 months, and the statistics presently show that many petitioners prefer not to wait once they have decided the marriage is at an end.

The Lord Chancellor published a Green Paper on divorce reform at the end of 1993, which mirrored the Law Commission's view that the way ahead might well be no-fault divorce on the basis of irretrievable breakdown. A period of reflection once the initial application was made was considered a good idea. There has been considerable public debate on this matter, with opinion divided upon whether the proposals would make divorce too easy and undermine marriage. Most commentators felt, however, that reform was long overdue and hoped that the provisions of the **Family Law Act 1996** were going to address the problems of the past.

Further criticism of the present system concerns the enormous financial cost of protracted litigation for the public purse, and there are those who have suggested that legal aid should be withdrawn in contested divorce cases and ancillary relief applications. Others suggest that it should only be available if the parties agree to conciliation.

Mediation is a process whereby an impartial and trained individual meets with the parties and encourages them to reach an agreement on areas of dispute such as financial provision and arrangements for the children. This hopefully reduces bitterness, saves costs and has an important role in making divorce less traumatic and adversarial. Mediation may take place in court, and in 1971 a Practice Direction allowed courts to refer cases to the court's welfare officer if it was thought he could help with the process. Initially, pilot schemes were established, but they have spread throughout the country and allow emotional and possibly confrontational issues to be handled in a constructive manner. Criticisms have been made, in that the parties often feel under pressure to reach an agreement in a short time, and it is very important that the parties are legally represented and kept fully informed. The Law Commission and the Green Paper did not suggest making mediation compulsory in all divorces, as it is its voluntary nature that ensures co-operation and a willingness to reach agreement.

Out-of-court mediation schemes also exist whereby trained personnel offer assistance to parties to reach agreement independently of the court system. Some people believe that these schemes are more successful since they are not so involved in the legal process and can be used before the parties' positions become too entrenched. However, there has been concern that such schemes can be dominated by the more forceful partner and that information may be withheld.

The **Family Law Act 1996** tried in statutory format to provide a mechanism which recognised that divorce was a social reality, but at the same time tried to get the couple concerned to properly consider whether their relationship was at an end. The no-fault concept attempted to reduce bitterness if divorce was to occur, but the information meetings and period for reflection and consideration were designed to encourage parties to think about reconciliation. Assistance was provided to parties by giving information about organisations helping resolve difficulties, as well as funding for conciliation services and marriage support services.

The Act also sought to reduce bitterness and encourage future co-operation by requiring the couples to seek to negotiate their own arrangements regarding finance and their children where possible. The option of mediation was available in the hope that expensive adversarial litigation could be avoided. However, the pilot schemes have shown that the Government's expectations for mediation have not been met. Fewer than one in 10 couples were prepared to mediate rather than litigate, and the vast majority felt better protected by lawyers. Mediation can be expensive and time-consuming, and requires a certain willingness on the part of those involved. Mediation can often be thwarted by the attitude and actions of one of the parties. In addition the Government failed to fund and train sufficient mediators to provide a nationwide service.

The most serious flaw shown by the pilot schemes is that it is a mistake to think that legislation can control human emotions at such a traumatic time. The information meetings were badly thought out, and whilst objective information is desirable, the compulsory nature of the meetings antagonised and humiliated some participants. The nature of these meetings was also not properly thought through, and it is unrealistic to think that parties really do spend the period for reflection and consideration doing these two things.

The complex statutory provisions, far from reducing conflict, actually increased the potential for an obstructive party to delay the divorce and obstruct resolution of issues regarding the children and finances. Whilst the current law is far from ideal, and although the **Family Law Act 1996** had many laudable aims, the practical experience of the pilot schemes has led to the conclusion that the law would be 'jumping from the frying pan into the fire'. Consequently, the Government has abandoned plans to implement the far-reaching provisions of the **Family Law Act 1996** relating to divorce, and decided to stick with 'the devil we know', the **Matrimonial Causes Act 1973**.

In conclusion, therefore, it does appear that the present system and procedures for obtaining divorce fail the parties, their children and society generally. Whilst no reform seems perfect, a move towards no-fault divorce in the **Family Law Act 1996**, with an emphasis on conciliation, would go some way to ensuring that failed marriages end with the minimum of animosity and that future relationships between family members are not irrevocably soured. However, a completely no-fault scheme may leave those who have been grievously upset by the behaviour of their spouses feeling badly treated. Whatever reform is made, there will always be those who feel let down at the ending of their relationship.

## Common Pitfalls

You will never be given an essay question that invites you to, for instance, tell the examiner everything that you can remember about divorce, so please do not do it! Here the question clearly asks you to identify the problems with current divorce law for the spouses *and* for society as a whole *and* to discuss whether something radical needs to be done. Your answer should consider all these points.

## Aim Higher ★

Good answers which show critical thought will be backed up by good knowledge of the statute and case law.

# Financial Provision for Adult Partners

## INTRODUCTION

The following two chapters consider financial provision. This chapter looks at financial relief for adult partners both during the relationship and when the relationship has ended, and Chapter 4 considers financial support for children. Whilst spouses can claim financial support from each other, both during and after the marriage, adult partners who have not married have no right to maintenance.

## FINANCIAL RELIEF DURING MARRIAGE

Financial provision for spouses may be sought from the Magistrates' Court under the **Domestic Proceedings and Magistrates' Courts Act (DPMCA) 1978**, or from the County Court under the provisions in the **MCA 1973 s 27**.

Applications to the Magistrates' Court are generally quicker and cheaper, but their powers are more limited. The County Court has more extensive powers and its orders are not automatically affected by cohabitation of the parties. This makes it suitable for those married to financially irresponsible spouses who they may want to force into providing more regular financial support, without necessarily separating.

## FINANCIAL RELIEF ON DIVORCE

When a couple divorce, there are often very complex financial implications. The court has wide powers to order maintenance pending suit (**MCA 1973 s 22**), although it is usually quicker and cheaper to go to the Magistrates' Court under the **DPMCA 1978** until the ancillary relief can be sorted. The long-term financial solutions are provided by the powers in the **MCA 1973 ss 23 and 24**, which are exercised in accordance with the principles in the **MCA 1973 s 25**. Section 23 allows the making of secured or unsecured periodic payments and lump sum orders, whereas **s 24** permits various orders in relation to transfer, settlement and variation of settlements of property. The factors in **s 25** allow the court to take into account all the circumstances of the case, and, as each family is different, subtle variations of the facts can lead to very different conclusions.

The **MCA 1973 s 21** defines financial provision orders and property adjustment orders. The Act introduces the concept of interim financial provision and lump sum orders for a party to a marriage or child of the family (**MCA 1973 s 22(4)**).

Section 25(2)(a) has been amended by the **Pensions Act 1995 s 166**, to allow the court to take into account any benefit under a pension scheme that a party has or is likely to have. There is no need for this to be in the foreseeable future, and part (h) is amended to allow consideration of the loss of pension scheme benefits. The **Pensions Act 1995** also allows for earmarking of pension scheme funds, so that when the pension becomes payable the receiving party can receive income from the pension fund of the yielding party and a lump sum. This represents an improvement on the old position, but still has disadvantages in that it forces the receiving party to wait for payment and may be defeated by the early death of the yielding party. A more far-reaching reform is the concept of pension splitting, introduced in the **Family Law Act 1996 s 16**, amending the **MCA 1973 s 25**. The pension adjustment order will enable the court to order the immediate division of a pension fund, thus facilitating a clean break and avoiding the need for the receiving party to wait. The complex statutory provisions governing this are contained in the **Welfare Reform and Pensions Act 1999**.

Division of property is governed by the **MCA 1973 s 25**. First consideration is given to the welfare of the children of the family, and you should bear in mind the provisions designed to ensure that the court considers whether to impose a clean break between the parties. Ensure that all of the factors that are relevant to the case are explored in turn. These include the following:

❖ the income, earning capacity and financial resources of the parties – this is a realistic assessment of what the parties have and what they can reasonably be expected to acquire in the future;

❖ the financial needs and obligations of the parties – bearing in mind housing needs, children's costs, and so on;

❖ the standard of living enjoyed by the family, trying to ensure that any resulting drop in standards because of the divorce is borne equally;

❖ the age of the parties and duration of the marriage – the usual argument here is that greater provision is needed for an elderly spouse who has been disadvantaged after a long marriage, whereas a young, childless spouse, when the marriage has been short, should quickly adjust. However, it may still be possible for a short marriage to lead to considerable financial relief – *Miller v Miller* (2006). Whilst traditionally courts have ignored premarital cohabitation, they now seem to be taking a more liberal approach (*GW v RW* (2003));

❖ any physical or mental disability – looking at the effect this has on the spouses' needs and ability to provide for themselves;

❖ any contributions made or likely to be made in the future to the welfare of the family – this includes financial and other contributions such as care and housekeeping;

❖ any conduct, if it would be inequitable to disregard it. It will be exceptional for conduct to be taken into account. This factor can be used to enable courts to apply a pre-nuptial agreement (*Radmacher v Grantino* (2009));

❖ any loss of benefit in the future, such as lost pension rights, which often need to be compensated for.

In 2000 the House of Lords gave judgment in *White v White*. This was an important re-evaluation of **s 25** and how it should operate. In that case the couple had been married for over 30 years, had four children and had built up a successful farming business. Their assets were considerable. Their Lordships were critical of the trend that had grown up in high value cases to limit the wife's award to her reasonable needs, especially where the marriage was a long one. The factors in **s 25** did not have an order of precedence, and there was no authority for limiting a wife to a sum for her reasonable needs. **Section 25** required that the parties be treated fairly, without discrimination between husband and wife, wage earner and home care provider. Although the House of Lords made it quite clear that they were not creating a presumption of equal division, it was stated that the judge should use the factors in **s 25** to form a tentative view of the level of provision called for and then check that against 'the yardstick of equality'.

Since the decision in *White* there has been much judicial discussion of when the yardstick of equality can be avoided.

❖ One possibility is that it can be avoided if a spouse is deemed to have made a particular extra, special contribution to the couple's resources entitling him/her to greater share on divorce – *Cowan v Cowan* (2001). The court in *Lambert v Lambert* (2002) was less keen on this approach.
❖ Another option is to consider what property is included within the matrimonial property and what property belongs solely to one of the spouses – *Miller v Miller* (2006), *Charman v Charman* (2007), *N v F* (2011), *S v AG Financial Remedy Lottery Prize* (2011).
❖ Courts will also consider whether a spouse needs to be compensated for the end of the marriage (*Charman v Charman* (2007), *Mills v McCartney* (2008)).
❖ Another issue where there has been recent judicial development is that of pre-nuptial agreements. Whilst these are not binding, courts may take them into account as far as it seems reasonable and fair to do so (*M v M (Pre-nuptial agreement)* (2002), *K v K (Ancillary relief: pre-nuptial agreement)* (2003), *Radmacher v Grantino* (2009), *Z v Z* (2011)).

# FINANCIAL RELIEF FOR CIVIL PARTNERS DURING THE CIVIL PARTNERSHIP

Civil partners are also entitled to claim financial support from each other during the civil partnership – **Civil Partnership Act 2004 s 72(3)**.

# FINANCIAL RELIEF FOR CIVIL PARTNERS AFTER THE DISSOLUTION OF THE CIVIL PARTNERSHIP

The **Civil Partnerships Act 2004 s 72** and **Sched 5** provide for civil partnerships to receive financial relief on the dissolution of the civil partnership (*Lawrence v Gallagher* (2012)).

# FINANCIAL RELIEF FOR ADULT PARTNERS

Adult cohabitees do not have any duty to support each other, either during the relationship, or after the relationship has ended. Property matters are dealt with using the rules of Land Law.

## EXAM QUESTION

This is a popular topic. It may be combined with a divorce, child maintenance or property. Problem questions focus on advising individual spouses whilst essay questions may look at recent judicial developments.

# QUESTION 12

Abigail and Ben have been married for eight years. They have no children, and both of them have worked throughout the marriage. Abigail has had a successful career as a solicitor, but recently lost her job when the firm she worked with closed their local office. However, she was offered a job in an office with an associated firm of solicitors, some 250 miles away, and as the job situation was bleak, Abigail accepted the position. She rented a small flat near her new job, and returned home to Ben each weekend. However, her visits became more infrequent, and now she hardly ever returns home.

When Abigail and Ben married, Ben was a school teacher with a passion for composing music. With Abigail's encouragement, he gave up his job and has concentrated on composing. However, not many pieces attracted the music companies' approval, and his earnings have averaged £6,000 per annum. Abigail's earnings are in the region of £30,000 per annum, but she only sends money to Ben occasionally. Ben does not want to get a divorce, but needs money to cover the mortgage and other bills.

▶ **Advise Ben as to any remedy he may pursue in the Magistrates' Court or County Court.**

## How to Answer this Question

Again, a question on financial support of spouses within a marriage, but from the somewhat unusual standpoint of the husband seeking the support. The powers of the Magistrates' Court under the **DPMCA 1978** and the County Court under the **MCA 1973** **s 27** must be examined, with mention being made of the relative advantages of each.

Consider **s 2** application:

- ❖ proof of a **s 1** ground necessary;
- ❖ failure to provide reasonable maintenance more applicable than behaviour or desertion;
- ❖ how this is assessed;
- ❖ look at **s 3** factors.

Examine the possibility of **s 6** or **s 7** orders. Describe the **MCA 1973 s 27** powers of the County Court.

## Applying the Law

*The key factors to consider in relation to financial support for spouses are outlined here.*

# ANSWER

The parties in this case do not wish to divorce, and therefore the wide powers available for ancillary relief applications are inapplicable. Ben is experiencing financial difficulty in maintaining his lifestyle and the former matrimonial home in the absence of regular financial support from Abigail. In order to remedy this situation, Ben must either seek a court order requiring Abigail to provide him with financial assistance, or negotiate some kind of separation or maintenance agreement with Abigail. The present case is somewhat unusual in that the wife is in the dominant financial position, but the courts treat applications by husbands and wives on property and financial matters on the 'basis of complete equality': *Calderbank v Calderbank* (1975). Therefore it is possible for Ben to apply either to the Magistrates' Court under the **DPMCA 1978** or to the County Court under the **MCA 1973**.

Most applications are made to the Magistrates' Court since it is a quicker and cheaper process. Often spouses who rely on legal aid will only receive legal aid for proceedings in the Magistrates' Court. The **DPMCA** only provides financial relief for spouses, and this may be available by virtue of **ss 2, 6** or **7** of the Act.

In order to apply under **s 2**, the applicant, Ben, must establish one of the grounds in **s 1**, namely that the respondent has failed to provide reasonable maintenance for the applicant, or failed to provide or make proper contribution to the maintenance of a child of the family, or has behaved in such a way that the applicant cannot reasonably be expected to live with them, or has deserted the applicant. It is certainly arguable that, on the facts, Abigail has failed to make reasonable provision for Ben. Whether Abigail has been making reasonable provision for Ben will be determined by the Magistrates' Court. They will first consider what level of maintenance they would have ordered and this is compared with what Abigail is in fact paying. If, as seems likely in this case, Abigail is paying less than the court would have ordered, the ground of failure to maintain will be established. There is no need to show that Abigail was deliberately depriving Ben of support; she may genuinely have thought he was managing, yet still find the s 1 ground established.

There are no children of the family and behaviour does not seem an issue. Desertion is a complex concept, and although there is no requirement for a specific time it could be difficult to establish that Abigail is in desertion. Whilst there is physical separation, it would seem that the job situation would give just cause for the initial separation, and so, consequently, Ben would be best advised to use the failure to maintain ground. **Section 2** gives the court the power to make periodical payment orders, and to award lump sums up to a maximum of £1,000 per application. The lump sum can be awarded to cover debts or expenses already incurred by the applicant, so if Ben has incurred such expenditure he could seek a lump sum. The periodical payments will be unsecured, and in determining Ben's entitlement, the court will have regard to the factors in **s 3(1)** of the Act. These factors are similar to those contained in the **MCA 1973 s 25**, and the court will look at all the circumstances of the case.

First consideration is given to the welfare of any children of the family, but there is none in the present case. The court will then look at the income, earning capacity and financial resources of the parties: **DPMCA s 3(2)(a)**. Abigail's income is considerably greater than Ben's, but he may be earning at a lower level than his earning capacity. Consideration must be given to whether Ben can reasonably be expected to take steps to increase his earning. Ben is a qualified teacher, who would normally earn in excess of £6,000 per annum. His composing was undertaken with Abigail's encouragement, and so it is likely that the court would agree that he needs financial assistance for the immediate future. However, the policy of encouraging spousal self-sufficiency would mean that Ben would not be able to expect support to continue indefinitely.

By examining the needs and obligations of the parties (**DPMCA s 3(2)(b)**), it is obvious that Ben's resources will not stretch to maintaining himself and the mortgage on the matrimonial home, whereas Abigail's needs can easily be met by her resources. It seems likely therefore that Abigail will be ordered to pay some kind of periodical payment to Ben. The court will try, where possible, to have regard to the standard of living enjoyed by the couple previously, and ensure that any drop in standard does not fall inequitably on one party: *Scott v Scott* (1978). At present, Ben seems to be struggling to live frugally, whilst Abigail's income is enabling her to enjoy a much higher standard of living. The age of the parties is unknown, but there is no indication that they are particularly old, and the marriage has lasted eight years, so cannot be regarded as short. There are no known disabilities (DPMCA s 3(2)(e)), and so the only other relevant factors are the parties' contributions (s 3(2)(f)), and conduct (s 3(2)(g)). Each party seems to have contributed in his/her own way to the marriage; each has worked and there is no evidence of any conduct that it would be inequitable to disregard. This seems to be a case where the couple have unfortunately drifted apart, without any blame to be attached.

Consequently, it seems apparent that a periodical payment order would be made. The court could also award Ben a lump sum up to a maximum of £1,000, and since Abigail has been away for some time, it is likely that he could have accumulated debts and a lump sum payment would enable him to pay off the debts. However, the order ends if the parties cohabit for more than six months.

It is also possible to make an application under the DPMCA s 7 where the parties have been separated for a continuous period of more than three months, with neither being in desertion. (The reference to neither being in desertion would have been removed once the appropriate parts of the Family Law Act 1996 were in force.) This would seem to be the case here and so if Ben can show that Abigail has been making payments to him, albeit sporadically and differing sums, he can apply for an order placing those payments on a permanent and compulsory basis. However, he must specify to the court the total or aggregate amount of these payments in the three months prior to the application. The court is then limited to making a periodical payment order that does not exceed the aggregate amount. This may not help Ben, as it seems that Abigail's contributions over the past three months have been inadequate for his needs, and so the court will not make an order if it does not provide reasonable maintenance, and will treat the application as if it had been made under s 2: s 7(4). Section 7 also does not provide for lump sums, so would be inappropriate where Ben needs help to repay debts, etc.

If Ben and Abigail can agree a level of financial provision, then such an agreement can be embodied in a court order by virtue of the DPMCA 1978 s 6. The court would still need to be satisfied that the level of provision is adequate and fair, and can refuse the order if the parties refuse to agree to amendments required by the court: DPMCA 1978 s 6(5).

If a periodical payment order is made, it can be payable weekly or monthly, and the Maintenance Enforcement Act 1991 s 2 enables the Magistrates to specify how the payments should be made, for example standing orders or attachment of earnings orders. The order would end on the death of either party or if they cohabit for more than six months: DPMCA 1978 s 25(1).

The other possibility available to Ben is to make an application to the County Court under the MCA 1973 s 27. The ground for applying is that Abigail has failed to provide reasonable maintenance for Ben. This is established in the same way as the Magistrates' Court would, and reference is made to the factors in the MCA 1973 s 25 in determining the level of maintenance. These factors mirror those already discussed in relation to the **DPMCA 1978 s 3**. Although application to the County Court is more costly, its powers are somewhat wider than those of the Magistrates' Court are in that it can order both secured and unsecured periodical payments, and lump sums of unlimited amounts.

# QUESTION 13

The clean break – fact or fiction? Discuss with reference to the concept of a clean break and how the **Matrimonial Causes Act 1973** achieves it.

## How to Answer this Question

Policy of encouraging spousal self-sufficiency:

❖ difficulties experienced by spouses;
❖ explain new **s 25** and factors to encourage self-sufficiency;
❖ duty to consider clean break or to limit payments to period;
❖ power to end obligations on application to vary.

## Applying the Law

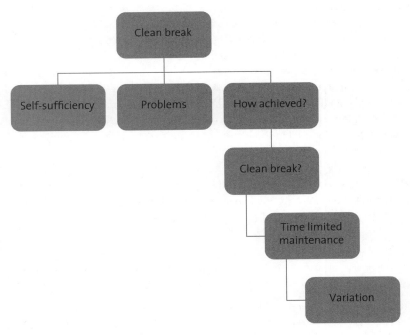

*The concept of the clean break is illustrated here.*

# ANSWER

The **Matrimonial and Family Proceedings Act 1984** amended the **Matrimonial Causes Act 1973** in a number of respects designed to encourage greater spousal self-sufficiency on divorce. It would be a mistake, however, to assume that these provisions make a clean break a routine result in ancillary relief proceedings. This was never the intention of the legislation and, in an economically uncertain climate, it is an unrealistic expectation in most cases.[1]

The Law Commission issued a discussion paper in 1980 to seek views on the financial consequences of divorce and as a result in 1981 they issued a report proposing change. It was felt that the change in the basis of divorce from fault based divorce to that based on irretrievable breakdown meant that it was no longer appropriate to provide continuing lifelong maintenance for an ex-spouse. There had also been a dramatic increase in the number of divorces over the years, and so many divorced people go on to remarry and incur new financial commitments. There was considerable pressure from so-called second families to be relieved of the financial pressures caused by the first family. Many women also worked or had the opportunity to do so, and the concept of man as a lifelong provider for his ex-wife was the subject of much criticism.[2]

The Law Commission did not, however, feel able to recommend a radical alteration to financial provision on divorce and a complete shift to total spousal self-sufficiency in all cases was ruled out. In many families this would not be possible. Women frequently are disadvantaged in employment matters, as they often give up work, or take less demanding work to fit in with family commitments. Where there are children, it is usually the woman who gives up or adapts her career to look after them, and after a divorce most children continue to live with their mother. The demands of child care, and the difficulty of finding flexible employment, provide considerable handicaps to a woman's earning capacity. Many women could only work for school hours or must pay considerable costs for child care, and it is unrealistic to expect her to be able to support herself in such circumstances.[3]

Likewise, a woman who has been married for a considerable time and who has been absent from the workplace would find it difficult to be self supporting. There is

---

1 As with all essay questions, it is important to answer the question set, rather than just spewing out everything remembered about clean breaks. Here the issues are the statutory basis for clean breaks and how likely and how effective they are in reality.

2 This introduction explains how changes in society have led to legal changes designed to encourage clean break divorces. In an essay question where the student is called to evaluate the reasons behind a provision or how effective it is, it is often useful to discuss the context within which the provision works.

3 The first consideration in financial relief is the welfare of children of the family and therefore a clean break would not be ordered if it was detrimental to their welfare.

considerable age discrimination and an elderly or middle-aged woman would experience difficulty in acquiring a job or retraining and acquiring relevant skills. Nevertheless, there are spouses who could readjust quickly on the termination of marriage and support themselves, and the lack of continuing support obligations may help reduce animosity. The young, childless wife could arguably adjust without hardship, so could a spouse whose family resources are considerable and can be divided and invested to provide an income. Consequently, it was felt desirable that in appropriate cases self-sufficiency should be encouraged.

The desirability of a clean break is highlighted in **s 25A(1)** where the court is given a duty to consider whether it would be appropriate to order that the financial obligations of the parties towards each other be terminated as soon as is just and equitable. This is a duty to consider a clean break, not to impose it routinely (*Clutton v Clutton* (1991)), where the Court of Appeal recognised that a clean break is often inappropriate and unfair. It was thought initially that the presence of children would make a clean break impossible (*Suter v Suter and Jones* (1987)), and this has been highlighted by the controversy surrounding the **Child Support Act 1991**, whereby any arrangements made, including generous clean break provisions, were disregarded in assessing the father's financial liability for his children. Although the **Child Support Act 1995** allows the payer to apply for a departure direction, such payments will not automatically be taken into account; it will depend on whether it would be just and equitable to do so. Consequently, consent orders enacting clean breaks will be more infrequent, and the court will no doubt bear this in mind in considering whether to impose a clean break. The older wife is also in a precarious financial position and is often an unsuitable candidate for a clean break (*Scallon v Scallon* (1990)) unless there is sufficient family wealth to settle some capital to provide an income (*Duxbury v Duxbury* (1987)).

If the court decides to provide maintenance for a spouse, then it is given an additional duty under **s 25A(2)** to consider whether it would be appropriate to award maintenance for a limited period only (*Parlour v Parlour* (2004)). This would then in theory allow the spouse to adjust without undue financial hardship. In practice, however, there are still many women who could not readjust with any degree of certainty because, for example, they are too old (*Morris v Morris* (1985)), or because there are very young children (*Suter v Suter and Jones* (1987)). It is arguably dangerous to make a limited order in respect of a woman with no job, and for whom the future is uncertain. However, a limited order might be advantageous to a man, who could then plan his own future, and possibly a second family, with more certainty. Thus a limited order might be desirable where the woman has reasonable prospects of readjusting, but with the safety net of applying for a variation by way of an extension if her plans do not work out.

The final power that the court has is under **s 25A(3)**, which is to completely end all further financial obligations of the spouses to one another, including applications under the Inheritance (Provision for Family and Dependants) Act 1975. This power could be used where it is considered desirable to remove the possibility of a spouse claiming increased provision in the future. It will be exercised rarely, for instance, in cases where a generous financial solution has already been agreed or in special cases, such as *Seaton v Seaton* (1986), where the severe disability of one spouse and the inability of the other to improve his quality of life led to a termination of obligations.

The Law also encourages a clean break by its introduction of the concept of pension splitting, which will divide up pension assets at the time, rather than earmarking provisions as contained in the Pensions Act 1995, which will still link the parties to one another. This has been enacted in the Welfare Reform and Pensions Act 1999, but the complex procedures and the financial reality of pension splitting mean this is only worthwhile where the pension holder has built up a sizeable pension fund.

Emotionally, most divorcing couples would prefer a clean break. However, the financial uncertainty of the present economic climate has left many spouses in difficult financial positions, with future predictability very unclear (*Lyons v Lyons* (2010)). Although the clean break is desirable in that it encourages self-sufficiency and, arguably, reduces animosity, it is not the solution for most divorcing couples. The English system is following that of some American States where spousal support is not awarded.

In most situations the clean break will be an unattainable ideal, rendered even more unlikely by the provisions of the Child Support legislation, which acts as a disincentive for many men.

# QUESTION 14

Ursula and Vincent have been married for 32 years. Six years ago Vincent began a relationship with his secretary, Wendy, and after six months he moved in with her. Vincent and Wendy now have two children, Yvonne and Zachery, aged four and two. Vincent has decided that he would like to divorce Ursula and marry Wendy. Ursula is opposed to the divorce. She is Roman Catholic and feels that divorce is wrong. She also believes that eventually Vincent will tire of Wendy and return to her.

When Ursula and Vincent got married, she was a primary school teacher and he worked as a photographer. Vincent wanted to set up on his own and the couple rented a small shop. At weekends and during the evenings, Ursula would help him as his assistant and she would drive him to assignments. After two years, Vincent decided to enter some of his photographs in a national competition. He won and suddenly became a very sought-after and fashionable photographer. He was able to move to better premises in a more exclusive area and to take on staff. About this time, the couple also had the first of their six children. Ursula decided to leave her job and become a full-time housewife and mother. She was often on her own as Vincent spent a lot of time abroad on fashion shoots. The couple's youngest child, currently aged eight, is autistic.

Over the years, Vincent's career has gone from strength to strength. He not only makes a lot of money from photography itself but he is now in demand as a celebrity himself. In all, his income per annum is £450,000. Fifteen years ago, Vincent bought a penthouse flat in London, which is now worth £2.5 million. Ursula and the children still live in the family home, which has been valued at £3.5 million.

▶ Advise Ursula on the divorce and the ancillary relief for her.

## How to Answer this Question
Can Ursula prevent the divorce?

If they do get divorced, what sort of financial relief will she be entitled to? The welfare of any children of the family would be the court's first consideration. What contributions have Vincent and Ursula made to the marriage? In particular the answer should consider the impact of cases such as *White, Parlour* and *Lambert*. Why is a clean break not appropriate? Note, the question is about financial relief for Ursula, therefore child maintenance does not need to be discussed.

## Applying the Law

This diagram illustrates how to advise Ursula on the financial relief in relation to *MCA 1973*.

# ANSWER
In order to obtain a divorce, Vincent will have to prove that his marriage to Ursula has broken down irretrievably and that one of the five facts in the **Matrimonial Causes Act 1973 s 1** is satisfied. On the facts it seems that Vincent has been living with Wendy for five and half years, and therefore he could use five years' separation without consent. However, Ursula may try and prevent the divorce under the **Matrimonial**

Causes Act 1973 s 5 claiming that, as a Roman Catholic, it would cause her grave hardship to be divorced. It is unlikely, though, that her claim would be successful. Cases such as *Rukat v Rukat* (1975) suggest that claims under s 5 are rarely successful. It is probable that the court would allow the divorce and therefore the next issue to discuss is financial relief.[4]

The court will use the **MCA s 25** to determine financial relief. According to s 25(1), the court's main consideration is the welfare of the children. Given that the couple have been married for over 30 years it is likely that some of their children are now adults and would no longer be a consideration for the court, but their youngest child (and possibly some others) are still minors and therefore they would be the court's first consideration. Furthermore, the fact that the youngest child is autistic is likely to be significant. Having a disabled child may make it more difficult for Ursula to obtain work outside the home. In addition, it might be that Ursula could argue that she and her children need the stability of being able to remain in the family home.

The court will look at the couple's contributions to the marriage – **Matrimonial Causes Act 1973 s 25(2)(f)**. Vincent has been the breadwinner. Thanks to his hugely successful photography business he has been able to provide the couple with a very high standard of living. Ursula has been the homemaker and mother. In the leading case of *White* (2000), the House of Lords were clear that there should be no distinction between the two types of contribution. Applied to the facts this would mean that Ursula's contribution could be assessed as being as valuable as that of Vincent. However, in *Cowan* (2001) the Court of Appeal allowed the husband a greater share of the couple's wealth because his business acumen and design skills meant that he had made an extraordinary contribution. Applied to the facts, perhaps Vincent could argue that his particular skills should mean that he be allowed a greater share. On the other hand, Ursula could argue that she showed particular talent as a homemaker during the times when Vincent was absent, and that her contribution also included helping with the business in the early days. In any case, the later case of *Lambert v Lambert* (2002) suggests that contributions should be assessed equally in part because looking for a special contribution is unfair on the spouse who looks after the home and children as it is more difficult to show a special contribution doing these than being an entrepreneur or employed. It is also worth noting that Ursula will not be restricted to her reasonable requirements.

The facts state that Vincent now has two children with Wendy. Although these children will not be the court's main consideration under s 25(1), under s 25(2)(b) the court will

---

4    Watch out for **s 5** of the **MCA 1973** in divorce and financial relief questions. Although a **s 5** application is rarely successful, in reality it is important to consider whether it does apply in cases where the petitioner is relying on five years' separation without consent.

take account of Vincent's need to maintain these children. Another important factor is the earning capacity of Vincent and Ursula. Thanks to his talent and high profile, Vincent looks to enjoy continued professional success. Ursula, on the other hand, has had her more modest career interrupted, and it is likely that it would prove more difficult for her to find financially rewarding employment that would fit around the demands of caring for a disabled child. The court would take into account the fact that this has been a long marriage. The court may also consider whether Ursula should be compensated for the end of the marriage (*Charman v Charman* No 4 (2007)). Although Ursula has not given up a lucrative career, she would be less well off because the marriage has ended.[5]

Having identified relevant factors in the **MCA 1973 s 25**, it is now possible to suggest how a court might deal with ancillary relief in this question. The facts state that Ursula and the children are currently living in the family home. It would be appropriate to transfer this home outright to Ursula. This provides the children with security and it is not unduly harsh on Vincent as he could keep the penthouse.

Under the **Matrimonial Causes Act 1973 s 25A**, the court would also have to consider whether a clean break would be appropriate. In this case, it is unlikely that a clean break would be appropriate because the marriage has lasted a long time and because the couple still have children who need care. As a clean break is not appropriate, it is likely that the court would also award Ursula periodic payments.

## Common Pitfalls

Watch out! Before even thinking about financial relief you need to discuss whether **MCA 1973 s 5** will apply to prevent the divorce. As for financial relief, make sure that your answer has a clear, logical structure. Because there are often so many things to consider in financial relief problem questions it is easy to get confused (and confuse the examiner).

## Aim Higher ★

This is an area where there have been some recent, important cases and therefore extra marks can be gained through being able to apply these appropriately and analytically.

---

5    The principle of compensation was discussed in both *Miller* and *Charman*. The idea is that a spouse may need to be compensated by financial relief either because they took decisions during the marriage which have benefited the family as a whole but have cost them personally, for example, giving up work to care for children, or because they would lose out by the marriage ending, for example, due to loss of a pension.

# QUESTION 15

Quentin is 45 and has been married to Polly, aged 35, for three years. Quentin is a very successful businessman. He started his company when he was 20 and it is now worth £25 million. When Quentin met Polly she was a technical translator and earned £35000 per annum. One year after they were married, Polly gave up her job. Polly had to work abroad a lot and Quentin persuaded her that this was making it more difficult for them to settle into married life. Polly also wanted to start a family and believed this would be easier without the stress of a busy job. Sadly, this has not proved successful. The couple have drifted apart and Polly has become very unhappy. She had a short affair with a friend from university and Quentin has found out about this and decided to divorce her. Before the couple married, Quentin's solicitor drew up an agreement which restricted any claim that Polly might have if the marriage were to end to £500,000. Polly signed this as she was afraid that otherwise Quentin would pull out of the marriage.

▶ Advise Quentin on the financial consequences of ending his marriage to Polly.

## How to Answer this Question

❖ MCA 1973 s 25(1) does not apply so financial relief will depend on factors in s 25(2).

❖ The court may decide to apply the pre-nuptial agreement under s 25(2)(g). Much will depend on whether Polly was properly advised before signing it.

❖ Quentin may be able to claim that most of his wealth was accumulated before the marriage and therefore should not form part of the marriage settlement.

❖ Should Polly be compensated for giving up her job?

This question looks at financial relief. It is important therefore that the student identifies and discusses the relevant factors and is able to apply the appropriate statute and case law.

## Applying the Law

*How financial relief relates to the relevant cases and legislation in this scenario is illustrated here.*

# ANSWER

Quentin will claim that his marriage to Polly has irretrievably broken down (MCA 1973 s 1(1)) and will rely on the fact of her adultery in order to obtain a divorce (MCA s 1(2)(a)). As there are no children of the family, s 25(1) of the **Matrimonial Causes Act 1973** does not apply, therefore the division of property will be based on the factors in s 25(2). It is also important to remember that when dividing the property the aim of the court will be to be fair (*White v White* (2000)). Furthermore, the courts are likely to view an equal division of the property as the starting point, only to be departed from if there are good reasons for doing so (*Miller* (2006), *Charman* (2008)).

Quentin is a very wealthy man. At one time, claims by very wealthy spouses were restricted to their reasonable needs. In *White v White*, the Court of Appeal and House of Lords recognised that this approach was unfair. It gave insufficient recognition to the contribution of a spouse whose role had been as home maker and led to a very unequal division of wealth. In *White* itself the wife did not receive a half share of the couple's wealth, but this was because some of the investment had originally come from the husband's family and therefore an equal split would not have been fair. This approach was followed in *Lambert v Lambert* (2002) where the wife of a wealthy and successful businessman was entitled to half the assets. Quentin and Polly's case is however distinguishable. Unlike the spouses in *White* and *Lambert*, Polly and Quentin's marriage is a short one and under s 25(2)(d) of the **Matrimonial Causes Act 1973** this will be relevant and will reduce her award.

Furthermore, Quentin may well argue that any award that Polly receives should be limited to funds from matrimonial assets. He would argue that although the business is valued at £25 million, most of this wealth was accumulated before he was married to Polly and therefore it would not be fair for her to benefit from this. This was the approach taken in *Miller v Miller* (2006) and *Mills v McCartney* (2009). In both these cases, very wealthy men were able to restrict the claims of their wives by arguing that the greater portion of their wealth should not be included as a matrimonial asset as it had been earned before the marriage.

One of the factors in s 25(2) is each spouse's earning capacity (s 25(2)(a)). Quentin would seem to have a very large earning capacity, whilst Polly's is far smaller. She did have a career as a technical translator, but she gave that up. Fortunately for Polly she has only been out of work for a couple of years and therefore it is unlikely that her skills will have grown out of date; nevertheless, she is currently out of work and has lost a couple of years of career development. Recent cases such as *McFarlane* (2004) and *Charman* (2008) have recognised that a spouse may need to be compensated for the loss (s)he has incurred both because of the marriage through giving up work and because the marriage has not lasted and therefore she has not benefited as she might expect to.

Whatever settlement the court orders, their aim will be to be fair. However, the court may find its discretion fettered if it decides to follow the pre-nuptial agreement between

Quentin and Polly. Although courts used to refuse to follow pre-nuptial agreements, recent decisions have shown that they may be taken into account under **s 25(2)(g)**. This was seen as favouring the parties' autonomy and their ability to determine for themselves how best to order their finances. In the leading case of *Radmacher v Grantino* (2009), the Supreme Court decided that the court would normally apply a pre-nuptial agreement if the couple had received proper independent legal advice. This approach has since been followed In *V v V* (2011) and *Z v Z (No 2)* (2011). There is little information here on the circumstances in which the agreement was signed and whether Polly was properly legally advised. There is, however, a good chance that the pre-nuptial will be binding.

On balance, therefore, whilst Polly will certainly be entitled to financial relief, her award is likely to be limited to a small part of Quentin's wealth. Much of his wealth will be excluded as not part of the matrimonial wealth and it is possible that the pre-nuptial agreement will be applied.

# QUESTION 16
Discuss the extent to which English law upholds pre-nuptial agreements.

## How to Answer this Question

❖ Traditional approach – pre-nuptial agreements rejected as against public policy – contemplating end of marriage, fetter of judicial discretion.

❖ Increasing recognition in limited circumstances as a relevant factor under **s 25(2)(g)**.

❖ Decision of Supreme Court in *Radmacher v Grantino.*

❖ Post *Radmacher* case law.

❖ Law Commission consultation.

## Applying the Law

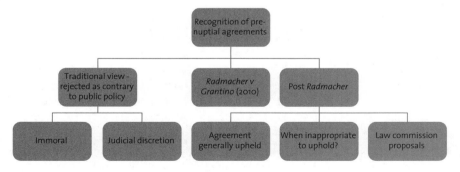

*Key cases and legislation at play in the recognition of pre-nuptial agreements are illustrated here.*

# ANSWER

As their name suggests, pre-nuptial agreements are contracts agreed between the future husband and wife setting out how they want their property to be divided in the event of a divorce. Until recently, these agreements were of very limited effectiveness in English law. The traditional view of the English judges had been to reject them as immoral and contrary to public policy. It was seen as immoral to contemplate and plan for the end of the marriage before it had even been celebrated and against the very character of marriage as a lifelong commitment. Furthermore the **Matrimonial Causes Act 1973** is clear the awarding of financial relief is a matter for judicial discretion and sets out in **section 25** the factors that need to be carefully weighed and balanced in determining it. A pre-nuptial agreement will not always consider these factors and in any case would restrict the judges in the exercise of their discretion.[6]

The argument that a pre-nuptial agreement is immoral because it discusses the possible ending of the marriage in divorce is not wholly convincing. The reality is that a significant minority of marriages will end in divorce and especially for people celebrating a second or even third marriage discussing a pre-nuptial agreement will not be seen as shocking or immoral but sensible and realistic. Certainly it is arguable that pre-nuptial agreements are a result of increasing marriage fragility rather than the cause. As for judicial discretion, it should perhaps be noted that there is an increasing willingness and indeed encouragement to couples to settle their own affairs. Mediation must at least be considered and will, unless there are compelling factors, for example domestic violence, be used, with the result that divorcing couples are deciding their own financial arrangements which are then ratified by the courts. Consequently, the idea that pre-nuptial agreements are a unique strike against complete judicial discretion is perhaps far fetched.

In more recent years, the traditional total rejection of pre-nuptial agreements has softened. The fact that a spouse has signed a pre-nuptial agreement has, provided that they have been properly advised, been viewed as conduct that should be considered when deciding on financial relief under **s 25(2)(g)** of the **MCA 1973**. This increasing judicial willingness to apply pre-nuptial agreements was confirmed by the Supreme Court in the leading case of *Radmacher v Grantino*. In *Radmacher*, a husband was unsuccessful in arguing that his award should not be limited by the pre-nuptial agreement. In particular he argued that the pre-nuptial agreement was irrelevant as it had made no allowance for children to be born and had been signed without proper legal advice. Despite these factors both the Court of Appeal and the Supreme Court decided that the pre-nuptial agreement should be followed and that a pre-nuptial

---

6   **Matrimonial Causes Act 1973 s 25(1)** states that the welfare of the children of the family is the court's first consideration in determining the financial relief. **Section 25(2)** sets out the other factors to be considered.

agreement that was entered into freely would be applied unless, in all the circumstances of the case, it would be unfair to apply the agreement. In *Radmacher* itself, it was fair to use the agreement to limit the husband's award because his wife's considerable wealth had been gained prior to the marriage and therefore he had not contributed towards it, he did not need to be compensated for having given up his career in order to support the family, and his needs were adequately met by the terms of the pre-nuptial agreement.[7]

The idea that a pre-nuptial agreement will be followed unless it would not be fair to do so has been applied in the post *Radmacher* case law. It is helpful therefore to consider what circumstances might make it unfair to apply a pre-nuptial agreement. One possibility is that the needs of children of the family might overrule the pre-nuptial agreement. This seems a reasonable interpretation given that under s 25(1) of the MCA 1973, the needs of children of the family are the first consideration in determining financial relief. On the other hand, it is worth remembering that in *Radmacher* itself, the couple had children but this did not prevent the agreement being applied. On the other hand, in *Radmacher*, applying the agreement did not disadvantage the children as they were to spend the majority of their time with their mother.

Another possibility is that an agreement will not be binding if the spouse does not have competent and independent legal advice. This would make sense as the justification for upholding pre-nuptial agreements is that it would support autonomy, but this rationale is undermined if the spouse is not properly informed. Furthermore, in *B v S (financial remedy matrimonial property regime)* [2012] EWHC 235 the fact that the wife had not received independent legal advice meant that the court did not follow the pre-nuptial agreement. Again though, it is possible that even without legal advice, a pre-nuptial agreement might still be applied. One of the husband's arguments against applying the agreement in *Radmacher* was that he had not been properly legally advised. In his case, however, this argument was rejected, in part because he was expected, due to his nationality, to be more aware of the purpose and the effects of a pre-nuptial agreement.

The issue of pre-nuptial agreements has recently been considered by the Law Commission. Unsurprisingly their discussions have reflected the issues in the recent cases, namely whether and to what extent pre-nuptial agreements should be enforceable and in particular what legal advice should be necessary and what effect children should have on the enforceability of the pre-nuptial agreement.

7    It is interesting to read *Radmacher* alongside cases such as *Miller* where issues such as compensation and what is matrimonial property for the purposes of financial relief are discussed.

# QUESTION 17

Discuss the extent to which English law promotes the equal division of property on divorce.

## How to Answer this Question

❖ Matrimonial Causes Act 1973 s 25 – especially s 25(1).
❖ Impact of *White* (2000).
❖ Special contributions – *Cowan* (2001), *Lambert* (2002).
❖ What is matrimonial property – *Miller* (2006), *Chaman* (2007)?

## Answer Structure

# ANSWER

Upon the breakdown of a marriage, the couple's property needs to be divided and potentially one spouse will be claiming maintenance from the other. The statutory rules for how this division should be achieved are set out in the **Matrimonial Causes Act 1973 s 25**. It seems from case law that the main aim of the division is to be fair to both spouses and therefore the question is whether fairness has been, and is being, interpreted as an equal division.

Looking first at the statute, this does not seem to support an equal division. The starting point for a couple with minor children is that the needs of those minor children are the court's first consideration (**MCA 1973 s 25(1)**). For many couples, the most important asset will be the family home and this provision will often mean that the spouse who has care of the child after the divorce will either get a greater share of this family home, or be able to stay in it. In reality, therefore, economic pressures mean that for many divorcing couples an equal split is not an option (*Lyons v Lyons* (2010)). It will arguably only be in the big money cases where there are sufficient resources to enable the needs of the children to be met with property left over so that an equal division may be possible. After **s 25(1)**, **s 25(2)** sets out a list of factors which should direct the division of property. Whilst these will not be relevant in every case, when applied they could mean that depending on the facts and the history of the marriage, one spouse gets a greater share.

Although there is clearly no statutory presumption in favour of an equal division and there are factors in **s 25** which argue against equality, in the leading case of *White v*

*White* (2000), the House of Lords stated that equality should only be departed from if there were compelling reasons to do so. In *White* the couple were millionaires and were divorcing after over 30 years of marriage. At that time, the wife's claim would have been restricted by her reasonable requirements to £800,000. The House of Lords decided that this was unfair and did not adequately recognise her contribution to the marriage and her award was significantly increased. Although *White* is a hugely important decision, it is very questionable whether it did favour equal division for most divorcing couples. There is a difference between equality, i.e. the contributions of a housewife and mother being rated equally to those of a wage earner and equal division, which means that the couple's property has to be equally divided. Secondly, *White* was a big money case involving multi-millionaires. In more modest households, a different division may be necessary.

Notwithstanding this, post-*White* courts have discussed when an equal division is appropriate. Initially, the focus was on determining when a spouse was entitled to a greater share of the matrimonial assets. In *Cowan v Cowan* (2001), the husband successfully argued that his contribution exceeded that of his wife and therefore he was entitled to a greater share. In *Lambert v Lambert* (2002), this approach was rejected as being unfair to the non-earning spouse.

More recently the issue has changed and the discussion has instead centred around what is meant by matrimonial property. In *Miller v Miller* (2006), the House of Lords were concerned with a very short marriage involving a very wealthy husband. The husband argued that some of his property should not be included in the division as it was his personal property rather than matrimonial property. Although the House of Lords did not accept the husband's definition of matrimonial property, they did agree that equal division could only apply to the matrimonial property and therefore not all the husband's assets were included. Similarly in *McCartney v Mills* (2008), the wife received significantly less than 50% as most of the husband's fortune had been accumulated before the marriage. *Miller* was a very short marriage and in *Charman v Charman* (2007) the court decided that a similarly restrictive definition of matrimonial property was not appropriate in a longer marriage. The court in *Charman v Charman* (2007) also determined that financial relief could be used to compensate a spouse for giving up his or her career, or for the cost of ending the marriage.

Finally, the extent to which English law favours an equal division is going to be largely influenced by the wishes of the spouses themselves. Much financial relief is determined not by the courts, but by the couples themselves, either through agreements during the process of the divorce or through premarital agreements. The latter may not be binding but could be the decisive factor to persuade the court that a non-equal division is fair.

## Common Pitfalls

Read the question. It is about the court's approach towards equal division of property and therefore it is that, rather than financial relief in general, that your answer should focus on.

## Aim Higher

Extra marks will be gained through up to date knowledge of the case law and through being able to explain the reasons for the courts' decisions and to critically discuss these decisions.

# Maintenance for Children

This chapter looks at maintenance for children. A person can be liable for a child either because he or she is their birth parent or adoptive parent, or because they have married the child's parent and have assumed responsibility for them.

## CHILD MAINTENANCE BASED ON BLOOD RELATIONSHIP

The main provisions for claiming maintenance from a child's biological mother or father or an adoptive parent are found in the **Child Support Act 1991** and the **Child Support Act 1995** as amended by the **Child Support Pensions and Social Security Act 2000** and the **Child Maintenance and Other Payments Act 2008**. These provisions enable a person with care (this could be a parent or another adult) to claim maintenance from the non-resident parent(s). A parent with care who is claiming State benefits has to make an application under the **Child Support Act**; a parent with care who is not in receipt of benefits or a non-parent carer has a choice whether to make such an application.

The amount of maintenance payable is calculated using a formula – **The Child Maintenance and Other Payments Act 2008** changed the formula so that it is now based on gross rather than net income. The non-resident parent will have to pay 12% for one child, 15% for two children and 19% for more than two children. The formula uses the non-resident parent's income, which can be problematic if this is very low or if it is irregular. There are also problems with collecting the maintenance (*R (Kehoe) v Sec. of State for Works and Pensions* (2005), *Kehoe v UK* (2008)), whilst on the other hand, the non-resident parent may feel that it is unfair that the income and capital of the parent with care is not taken account of or that there is no link between payment of maintenance and contact.

Maintenance can also be claimed from a biological parent under the **Children Act 1989 Sched 2** and if the biological parent is married to the other biological parent then maintenance can also be claimed under the **Matrimonial Causes Act 1973** and the **Domestic Proceedings and Magistrates' Court Act 1978**.

## CHILD MAINTENANCE FOR A CHILD OF THE FAMILY

Financial responsibility towards children who are not biological offspring is incurred under the **Domestic Proceedings and Magistrates' Courts Act (DPMCA) 1978** and

Matrimonial Causes Act (MCA) 1973. The DPMCA ss 2, 6 and 7 allow orders to be made in respect of children of the family. A **section 2** order is governed by additional criteria in s 3(3) which include the financial resources and needs of the child, and the manner in which it was expected to be educated. **Section 3(4)** further provides that in the case of a non-biological child of the family, regard must be paid to whether the respondent assumed responsibility for the child, on what basis and for how long; whether the respondent knew that this was not his child; and the liability of others to maintain the child must also be considered. This is mirrored in the County Court under s 27. Another option for claiming child maintenance is the **Children Act 1989**. Under this Act, maintenance can be claimed from step-parents as well as the child's birth parents. Furthermore, this Act can be used by children of unmarried as well as married parents. The **Children Act 1989** is also quite broad in terms of the maintenance available; as well as periodic payments and lump sums, property settlements are also available provided that they are for the benefit of the child (*A v A (A minor: Financial Provision)* (1994)).

# QUESTION 18

Philip and Rosy married six years ago, and have two children, Holly and Molly, aged four and two respectively. After the birth of the children, Rosy suffered from severe post-natal depression and, much to Philip's concern, she began to neglect the children. He frequently came home to find the children locked in the house, and Rosy nowhere to be seen. Matters came to a head three months ago when the couple had a heated argument, during which Philip slapped Rosy once after she made unfounded allegations that he had abused the children. Rosy stormed out of the house and since then has not visited Philip or the children. Philip has sent Rosy money on occasions, but he has found it very difficult to meet the bills and pay for child care from his modest income. Philip has now received a letter from Rosy threatening to take him to court unless he sends her £100 each week. Philip says he cannot afford to pay anything like this sum, as he earns £120 per week, out of which he must pay child care costs of £60 as well as other household bills.

▶ Advise Philip.

## How to Answer this Question

Another question concerning financial provision for spouses who are not divorcing. Rosy is not seeking provision for the children, as they are in Philip's care, so it is only necessary to consider the level of provision for her as a spouse under the **DPMCA 1978** and the **MCA 1973**. Ensure that some mention is made of the advantages of each method.

Examine the **DPMCA 1978 s 2** powers:

❖ proof of one of s 1 grounds;
❖ failure to provide reasonable maintenance and how it is assessed;
❖ the s 3 factors as they apply to the facts of the case;
❖ consider the s 7 power and how it would operate;

❖    mention s **6** power to embody any agreement into court order;
❖    outline the **MCA 1973 s 27** option in the County Court;
❖    briefly mention Philip's option of seeking maintenance under the **Child Support Act 1991**.

Please note the spouses in this question are not divorcing. Older students will incorrectly discuss divorce.

## Applying the Law

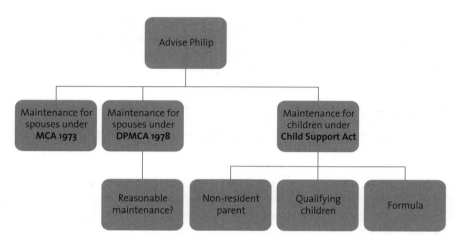

*How the law relating the maintenance applies in Philip's situation is illustrated here.*

## ANSWER

The courts have wide powers to order ancillary relief if the parties divorce, but it seems in this case that the issue of financial provision must be resolved without recourse to such powers. If, in the future, Philip and Rosy are unable to reconcile, then financial provision can be reorganised on divorce. In the meantime, there is the possibility that Rosy could seek financial provision from Philip by applying to either the Magistrates' Court or the County Court. Since Philip is caring for the children, she will be seeking maintenance for herself only.

An application may be made to the Magistrates' Court under the **DPMCA 1978**, and this is a somewhat cheaper and quicker process than an application to the County Court under the **Matrimonial Causes Act 1973**. Only spouses may use the Magistrates' Court, and Rosy may seek relief under s **2**, or possibly s **6** or **7**. If she applies for an order under s **2** for periodical payments and/or a lump sum, then Rosy must establish one of the grounds in s 1. **Section 1** provides jurisdiction for the court to make a **section 2** order if the respondent has failed to provide reasonable maintenance for the applicant or a child of the family or has behaved in such a way that the applicant cannot reasonably be expected to live with him or has deserted the applicant.[1]

The most likely ground is that the respondent has failed to provide reasonable maintenance. The behaviour ground may be difficult to establish for Rosy, as it mirrors the test for behaviour in the **MCA 1973 s 1(2)(b)**. The only behaviour by Philip was when he struck Rosy after her accusations of child abuse. This is an isolated act of violence, and whilst violence should not be condoned, Rosy's behaviour had been extremely provocative. There is also no substance to an allegation of desertion.

Consequently, the court will consider whether the level of maintenance provided by Philip was reasonable in the circumstances of the case. First, the court will consider what level of maintenance it would be minded to award, given the factors in **DPMCA 1978 s 3**. This will be compared with the level of maintenance paid by Philip, and if Philip is paying less than the court would have awarded, the s 1 ground will be established. It is immaterial whether Philip was deliberately depriving Rosy of support, or whether he was innocently believing she was managing.

The level of maintenance is determined by the facts in the **DPMCA 1978 s 3(1)**, which are broadly similar to those contained in the **MCA 1973 s 25**. All the circumstances of the case will be examined, giving first consideration to the welfare of the two children of the family, Holly and Molly. These children are staying with their father, who is struggling to care for them and pay for child care whilst he works. This means that whilst Philip may have financial resources in terms of his income of £120 per week, he has considerable financial obligations of child care and housing as well as feeding and clothing the children. It is not clear, on the facts, whether Rosy is earning any money; if she does have income it would seem that she only has herself to support on it. Even if she has no income, the court is required to consider any earning capacity she has or can reasonably be expected to acquire. Whilst she may not have worked when the children were so small, now that she no longer cares for them, she should be able to seek work.

Usually, the court will not take into account the availability of State benefits as a resource for the applicant. However, this family does not appear to have sufficient resources for Philip to be able to support the children himself and still send money to Rosy. The net-effect method (*Stockford v Stockford* (1981)) whereby the court looks at what each

---

1    It is important to decide which Act to apply under as both have advantages. The Magistrates' Court is quicker and cheaper. On the other hand, the **Matrimonial Causes Act 1973** offers a wider range of remedies and larger awards.

party has, rather than the one-third rule, would be appropriate here, but it is unlikely that the court would want to make any order that would take Philip below subsistence level (*Barnes v Barnes* (1972)).

The court will also look at the other factors in **s 3**, namely the standard of living enjoyed by the family, the age of the parties and the duration of the marriage. Any drop in the standard of living should be equally borne if possible: *Scott v Scott* (1978). Physical and mental disability also requires consideration and here Rosy is suffering from severe post-natal depression. This may affect her ability to support herself.

In terms of contributions made by the parties, initially both contributed, one by working, the other by looking after the home and children. However, as Rosy has deteriorated in health, so Philip's contribution to the welfare of the family has increased, with him ultimately bearing responsibility for child care. This further contribution must be taken into account, thereby, possibly, reducing his obligation to maintain Rosy. Conduct will also be taken into account if it would be inequitable to disregard it. Philip has been violent towards Rosy on one occasion; however, the violence was not extreme, nor was it repeated (*Bateman v Bateman* (1979)), nor did it affect Rosy's earning capacity (*Jones v Jones* (1975)).

Indeed the violence was provoked by Rosy's unfounded suggestion of abuse, and by her chronic neglect of the children. It may be that this could amount to conduct on her part, but if it is involuntary and caused by mental illness, as in *J (HD) v J (AM)* (1980), then it may not result in an immediate ending of Philip's obligations to Rosy.

In conclusion, it would seem that there are very few resources in this family, and if Rosy is well enough to work, it is unlikely she would receive much, if anything, by way of financial support from Philip. However, if she is too ill to work, it may be pointless making anything more than a nominal order, because to do otherwise would reduce Philip and the children to below subsistence level. Instead, Rosy would need to claim State benefits. Given the unavailability of resources, it would not be possible to order Philip to pay any lump sum to Rosy either.

An application could be made by Rosy under the **DPMCA 1978 s 7**, if the parties have been separated for a continuous period exceeding three months, with neither in desertion. Rosy would need to show that Philip has been making payments to her, and this is so, even though the payments have been made irregularly and infrequently. However, the court only has power to make a periodical payment order that does not exceed the aggregate value of payments made by Philip over the previous three months: **s 7(3)(2)**. If the court considers that this is insufficient for Rosy's reasonable maintenance needs, it can treat the application under **s 7** as an application for a **s 2** order: **s 7(4)**. Given the relatively small sums Philip has paid to Rosy, it is unlikely that a **s 7** order would be sought or ordered.

If Philip and Rosy could come to some reasonable arrangement about financial provision, then this arrangement can be formalised by court order under the **DPMCA 1978 s 6**. Again, the court would need to be satisfied that the level of maintenance was fair, and, given the circumstances, a **s 6** order does not seem likely. Rosy could also make an application to the County Court for financial provision. The County Court has powers to make secured or unsecured periodical payments for the applicant and/or a child of the family, and lump sum orders of unlimited amounts. The basis for financial provision in the **MCA s 27** is that the respondent has failed to provide reasonable maintenance for the applicant and/or a child of the family. This would be determined in much the same way as in the Magistrates' Courts, with reference being made to the factors in **s 25**. Again, the County Court is unlikely to make any order that would reduce Philip to below subsistence level.

If Rosy were in employment there is the possibility that Philip could seek financial assistance in the upkeep of the children under the **Child Support Act 1991**. Rosy would be a 'non-resident parent' within the meaning of the Act, and both Holly and Molly would be 'qualifying children'. Philip is a 'person with care' and therefore a maintenance requirement would be established. That maintenance requirement would then need to be discharged in part by Rosy and in part by Philip's income.[2]

If Rosy moves back to live with Philip, then any **s 2** or **s 6** order that had been made would terminate after six months' cohabitation: **DPMCA s 25(1)** and **(2)**. A **s 7** order would terminate on resumption of cohabitation: **DPMCA 1978 s 25(3)**. A County Court order is not affected automatically by a resumption of cohabitation, although this would be a change in circumstances that would entitle the respondent to apply for variation or discharge of the order: **MCA 1973 s 31**.

In conclusion, it would seem that whilst Rosy may apply to the courts for financial provision, the precarious financial position the family are in may make it unlikely that she will receive any, or any substantial, financial provision from Philip.

# QUESTION 19

Rebecca and Sam married three years ago after cohabiting for two years previously. Rebecca has a daughter from a previous relationship, and this daughter, Tilly, is now eight. Rebecca and Sam's relationship has encountered problems, mainly over his insistence that she remains at home as a full-time wife and mother. Rebecca feels increasingly isolated, especially now that Tilly, an exceptionally intelligent child, is at

---

2   The **Child Support Act 1991** originally used the term 'absent parent'. Non-resident parent replaced this as being more neutral.

school. Sam has threatened to withdraw all financial support from Rebecca and Tilly if Rebecca insists on finding herself a part-time job.

This situation concerns Rebecca, who does not want to divorce but wishes to be advised of her position and possible options if Sam were to withdraw support.

▶ **Advise Rebecca.**

## How to Answer this Question

The question requires an examination of financial provision for spouses and for children of the family, who are not the natural children of the payer. Both the **DPMCA 1978** and the **MCA 1973** must be considered. The **Child Support Act 1991** does not apply here but, since Tilly is a child of the family, she is covered by the **DPMCA 1978** and the **MCA 1973**.

Explain **s 2** orders:

- ❖ the need to satisfy the **s 1** grounds;
- ❖ failure to provide reasonable maintenance;
- ❖ how this is assessed;
- ❖ factors in **s 3**;
- ❖ additional factors for child of family;
- ❖ effect of cohabitation.

Not appropriate for **ss 6** and **7**. Explain the **MCA 1973 s 27** as it applies to spouses and children of family.

## Answer Structure

## ANSWER

Rebecca is married to Sam, and, as a spouse, is entitled to a reasonable level of financial support. If Sam withdraws that, then she may apply to the Magistrates' Court under the **DPMCA 1978**, or to the County Court under the **MCA 1973**, to obtain financial provision for herself. Tilly is not Sam's natural child, and consequently the provisions of the **Child Support Act 1991** do not apply. There is the possibility of seeking maintenance under the

Child Support Act from Tilly's natural father, but on the facts, it is unclear whether he is identifiable, alive and traceable.

Consequently, financial support from Sam for Tilly can be sought under the **DPMCA 1978** or the **MCA 1973** as Tilly is a 'child of the family'. This concept is defined in the **MCA s 52** to include a child who has been treated by both parties as a child of their family. Tilly has been with Sam and Rebecca for five years, and it seems likely that she is a child of the family.

Applications to the Magistrates' Courts are generally quicker and cheaper than those made to the County Court, although the County Court's powers are somewhat wider. In this case, Tilly and Rebecca's financial support has not yet been withdrawn, and there is no indication that at present there are any grounds for applying. However, if Sam were to withdraw support then Rebecca may apply to either court.

An application to the Magistrates' Court may be made for an order under the **DPMCA 1978 s 2**. Under **s 2**, the Magistrates' Court has power to order unsecured periodical payments for the applicant and child of the family in addition to lump sums up to a maximum of £1,000 per application. The applicant must satisfy, however, one of the grounds in **s 1** of the Act: namely, that the respondent has failed to provide reasonable maintenance; or the respondent has behaved in such a way that the applicant cannot reasonably be expected to live with him; or that the respondent has deserted the applicant. An application under **s 2** may be made even if the parties are still living together (**DPMCA 1978 s 25**), but it will cease to have effect if they cohabit for more than six months. This is important, since it means that Rebecca can seek financial support without having to leave Sam.

The first possibility is that the respondent has failed to provide reasonable maintenance for the applicant. Clearly, if Sam provides no money for Rebecca, since she has no way of immediately supporting herself, then there will be no reasonable maintenance. The court looks at the level of maintenance it would usually order to the applicant and compares it with that being provided by the respondent. If, as in this case, the respondent is providing less than the court would order, the ground is established. It is no defence for Sam to argue that he did not realise this, or that he had good reason for not paying Rebecca. Once this ground is satisfied, the court has the power under **s 2(1)** to make an order for periodical payments for both Rebecca and Tilly.

If Sam were to continue to provide for Rebecca, but stop paying for Tilly, it would be necessary to show that one of the other **s 1** grounds exists. In determining whether reasonable maintenance is being provided or contributed to, the court will again have regard to what it would normally order.

It would not be possible to argue that Sam was in desertion, and the behaviour point would also be difficult to establish. It might be argued that Sam's overbearing and dictatorial treatment of the family would suffice, but the application is most easily established by arguing a failure to provide reasonable maintenance.

In determining what level to award, the court will take into account the factors in the DPMCA 1978 s 3(1), which are based on the factors in the MCA 1973 s 25. Looking initially at the income, earning capacity and financial resources of the parties, it seems that Sam works and earns an income. Rebecca has not worked during the relationship at Sam's insistence; therefore, she will be in need of financial support initially. However, the court will have regard to her earning capacity and whether she can reasonably be expected to work to support herself. Rebecca's qualifications or occupation before she met Sam are unknown, and although she is willing to work, it may not be easy for her to obtain employment immediately such that it enables her to support herself and care for Tilly. The court will encourage spouses to become self-sufficient and it can place a limit on the time that the financial support will continue for: DPMCA 1978 s 4. However, given the uncertainties of Rebecca's position, it is more realistic to make an unlimited order, indicating to Rebecca that she should seek employment, and then Sam can apply for variation of the order if she does this, or if she should have achieved self-sufficiency: DPMCA 1978 s 20(1). The financial needs and obligations of the parties must be considered (s 3(1)(b)), and clearly both Rebecca and Sam need housing and Tilly must be cared for. The standard of living enjoyed by the parties prior to the conduct alleged as the ground for the application should be considered to ensure that any drop in standards does not fall inequitably on one party. There is nothing exceptional about the age of the parties, but the marriage has been relatively short. The marriage followed a period of cohabitation, and there has been a child for whom Sam has assumed responsibility. Although cohabitation before marriage is usually irrelevant (*Campbell v Campbell* (1977)), in *Day v Day* (1988), on similar facts to this, the court did accept that cohabitation could in certain cases be a factor to take into account as part of the circumstances of the case. Sam and Rebecca have had a long-term relationship during which he has assumed responsibility for Tilly, and has prevented Rebecca from working. It would not be right for him to be able to argue that as it was a relatively short marriage, he should avoid financial obligation towards Rebecca. There is no disability to take into account (DPMCA s 3(1)(e)), and both parties appear to have contributed to the marriage, Sam by working and Rebecca by being a wife and mother. Conduct under the DPMCA s 3(1)(g) is only taken into account if it would be inequitable to disregard it. Rebecca has done nothing that would amount to conduct sufficient to deny her financial support. In determining the level of financial support, regard must be had to the family resources. When the court looks at making an award in respect of Tilly, they will take into account not only the parties' resources and obligations, but also those of the child: DPMCA 1978 s 3(3). Tilly is not disabled in any way; in fact she is particularly intelligent. If this affects the way she was being educated, or the way the parties intended to educate her, possibly sending her to a private school, for example, then this is a factor affecting the level of maintenance awarded. The standard of living of the family is examined, and the court would obviously be concerned to ensure that Tilly does not suffer enormous disruption by the removal of financial support by her stepfather, Sam.

The amount payable in respect of Tilly will further be affected by the fact that she is not Sam's natural child. The **DPMCA 1978 s 3(4)** requires consideration of certain factors when the child of the family is not the child of the respondent. First, it is necessary to examine whether Sam ever assumed responsibility for Tilly. On the facts, it seems as if he did since they have lived together for five years, and he has financially supported her. Then it is necessary to consider the basis and extent of the assumption of responsibility. Sam appears to have acted as a father figure during this time, and he did so realising that Tilly was not his child. Finally, the liability of any other person to maintain the child should be considered, and it may be that Sam's liability will be reduced if Tilly's father can be traced and made to pay under the **Child Support Act 1991**.

It is not appropriate to consider the **DPMCA 1978 ss 6** or **7** here, and so the other possible action for Rebecca is to apply to the County Court under the **MCA 1973 s 27**. It would seem that if Sam refuses financial support, he would have failed to provide reasonable maintenance for Rebecca, the applicant, and Tilly, the child of the family. The factors to be taken into account in assessing the measure of support are those in the **MCA 1973 s 25**, and operate in the same way as those discussed earlier in reference to the **DPMCA 1978 s 3**. In addition, since Tilly is a child of the family, but not Sam's natural child, the additional factors in **s 25(4)** will need to be considered. These provisions reflect those in the **DPMCA 1978 s 3(4)** and have been discussed above.

The County Court can order secured or unsecured periodical payments, and there is no upper limit on the amount of a lump sum order. The order can be sought even though the parties are still living together, and, unlike the Magistrates' Court order, the order is not terminated by continued cohabitation, although there is always the possibility of variation.

Thus, it can be seen that if Sam were to withdraw financial support, Rebecca could pursue her remedy in either the County Court or the Magistrates' Court, and she does not need to seek a divorce in order to do so.

# QUESTION 20

Angela, aged 25, has four children: Bobby, aged eight; Cindy, aged six; Darren, aged four; and Elzine, aged two. Bobby and Cindy are children from her relationship with Frank, whom she never married. Darren and Elzine were born during her marriage to Greg. Greg does not think Elzine is his daughter, as her colouring is totally different from either his or Angela's. Greg has petitioned for divorce on the basis of Angela's adultery, and Angela does not intend to defend this divorce. However, she is concerned about the financial consequences of this for herself and her children. She is living, at present, in the former matrimonial home, a council flat, and Greg is quite happy for her to remain there.

▶ Advise Angela.

## How to Answer this Question

A question primarily concerned with financial provision on divorce for children and the spouse.

Explain the powers under the **Matrimonial Causes Act 1973 ss 23** and **24** and the factors in **s 25** of the Act and their applicability to spouses and children of the family. Mention the **Child Support Act 1991** and its principles as they apply to natural biological children. Before conducting any detailed examination, decide which provisions apply to whom.

Two children, Bobby and Cindy, are natural children of Frank who has **Child Support Act** liability, and children of the family for Greg who could have **MCA** liability. One child, Darren, is Greg's natural child and therefore the **Child Support Act 1991** applies.

Elzine is of questionable parentage and the presumption of legitimacy should be considered. If she is Greg's natural child, then **Child Support Act** liability will follow; if not, there will be MCA liability if she is a child of the family.

Angela will receive provision as a spouse under the provisions of the **MCA 1973**.

In relation to children of the family, look at the factors that relate to the financial needs and obligations of the parties and children. Examine the special provisions in **s 25(3)** for children of the family. Further attention must be paid to **s 25(4)** and the way in which Greg assumed responsibility for the children.

For the natural child or children, the **Child Support Act 1991** must be considered. Explain how the absent and caring parent would apply to each qualifying child. Also detail the statutory formula.

Mention the impact of the **Child Support, Pensions and Social Security Act 2000**. For the spouse, Angela, only Greg has responsibility under the **MCA 1973**. A general discussion only is possible since no details are known of the financial position of the parties.

## Applying the Law

*How the relevant legislation relates to maintenance in this scenario is illustrated here.*

# ANSWER

Angela's entitlement to ancillary relief from her husband Greg will be determined by reference to the court's powers in the **MCA 1973 ss 23** and **24** and the guidelines in the **MCA s 25**. However, the issues of financial provision for the children are complex.

There are four children involved here and they need to be considered in turn. Bobby and Cindy are the natural children of Frank, who would be liable to provide maintenance under the **Child Support Act 1991**. In addition, they may be children of the family of Angela and Greg if they have been treated by Angela and Greg as such: **MCA s 52**. Greg could then incur financial responsibility towards the children under the **MCA 1973**. There is no **Child Support Act** liability since they are not his natural children.[3]

Darren is the natural child of Angela and Greg and therefore Greg could incur **Child Support Act** liability towards Darren. The other possibility is that the **Child Support Act** can be avoided at present by the making of a consent order.

Elzine was born during the marriage of Greg and Angela and there is a presumption of legitimacy, which may be rebutted on the balance of probabilities: **Family Law Reform Act 1969 s 26**. It will therefore be presumed that Elzine is the natural child of Greg unless this can be rebutted. A confession of adultery does not necessarily establish that the child is not Greg's but it is likely that DNA testing, which can be directed by the court (**Family Law Reform Act 1969 s 20(1)**), would establish Elzine's parentage. It is usually in the child's interests for such testing to be ordered: *S v S* (1972).

---

3   Liability for children can either be based on being their natural parent or on assuming responsibility for them through marriage. Sometimes a child will qualify for maintenance both through blood and through marriage.

If Elzine is Greg's natural child, and this is not impossible even though her colouring may differ, then Greg's liability to maintain will again be under the **Child Support Act 1991**. If, however, Elzine is not Greg's child, then her natural father, if identifiable and traceable, would have **Child Support Act** liability. Greg's obligations would be incurred under the **MCA 1973**, if he had treated her as a child of the family.

It is unclear whether Greg and Angela continued to live together after Elzine's birth. If they separated shortly afterwards because of Greg's suspicions, then he may be able to show that he never treated Elzine as a child of the family. However, if there was a shared family life, when Greg and Angela lived together and acted as Elzine's parents, then Greg, despite his misgivings, will have treated her as a child of the family.

Liability to maintain a child of the family is determined by the provisions of the **MCA 1973** s 25(3), if the child is not Greg's natural child. Thus Bobby, Cindy and possibly Elzine will be provided for under the **MCA 1973**. The financial resources and needs of the parties and the children will be considered, together with any disability the child may have. This does not seem to be an issue here, nor is there evidence that the parties were educating children privately, or intended to do so: **s 25(3)(d)**. Thus it will essentially be a question of considering Greg's available resources.

Since the children are not Greg's own children, it is necessary (**s 25(4)**) to consider whether he assumed responsibility for them, and on what basis. The extent of his liability and whether he did so knowing that they were not his children, must be examined, as must the liability of anyone else to maintain the children. From the facts, it is clear that he knew Bobby and Cindy were not his children, but it is unclear what, if any, liability for their maintenance is being borne by their natural father, Frank. If the Child Support Agency can track him down and succeed in obtaining child support from him, then this could reduce Greg's liability. It does seem, however, that Greg has borne some financial responsibility for both children, and so some periodical payments for their benefit will be ordered. If Elzine is not his natural child, then his liability towards her as a child of the family will be determined as above. Essentially, much will depend on how he behaved after her birth and on the possible liability of her as yet unnamed father.

Angela can also seek financial provision from the natural father of her children under the **Child Support Act 1991**. If Angela is in receipt of State benefits, she will have no choice; the Agency is automatically involved in benefit cases. A parent receiving benefit is required to provide information identifying the father of her child and authorise the Child Support Agency to pursue him for child support. Thus, Frank, Greg and the as yet unnamed father of Elzine could all be pursued by the Agency. If Angela is not in receipt of benefits, Greg could agree a consent order with Angela regarding financial provision for his natural child or children, but would be advised to ensure that the level of maintenance is equivalent to that which would be ordered under the **Child Support Act**.

The Child Support Agency will impose liability on an absent parent, that is, a natural parent not living in the same household as his or her children. The children all have their home with Angela, the caring parent, and since each child is under 16 with one parent absent, they are all qualifying children. Each child's natural father will have his liability assessed by reference to the statutory formula for calculating the maintenance requirement. This formula is applied automatically and without discretion, giving rise to considerable criticism. Frank, who may have played little role until now in his children's lives, will find that he will incur financial liability.

Angela's income would be ignored and there are no allowances for Frank's housing costs and so on. However, this figure may be adjusted downwards, if Frank acquires a second family, or if the children spend time living with him.

This calculation would also be made in respect of the other biological fathers of Angela's children. However, only Greg, the man she married, could incur any direct financial obligations to Angela herself. This obligation could possibly be by way of periodical payments, either secured or unsecured, a lump sum order (s 23), or property transfer, or variations under s 24. The factors in the MCA s 25 must be considered, including the welfare of any children of the family as a first consideration (s 25(1)). Here there are a number of children of the family and their welfare requires them to be adequately housed. There does not seem to be any controversy over what should happen to the former matrimonial home, as Greg is happy for Angela to remain there with the children. The court has power to order the transfer of council house tenancies and although the local authority has no right to prevent this, they are entitled to be present and to voice their opinion, as in *Lee v Lee* (1984).

In relation to financial provision, the court must consider the desirability of a clean break between the parties (s 25A(1)), but is under no obligation to impose one (*Clutton v Clutton* (1991)). Clearly, it is difficult to have a clean break if there are young children (*Suter v Suter and Jones* (1987)), or if the wife has been out to work for some time. However, the court may consider that whilst Angela may need immediate support, it could be desirable to limit maintenance for a fixed period: s 25A(2). *Parlour v Parlour* (2004). This could give Angela time to adjust without undue hardship, but it might not be appropriate if her future is too uncertain, as in *Suter v Suter and Jones* (1987). Only if the future is sufficiently predictable should limited maintenance be imposed: *Barrett v Barrett* (1988).[4]

It seems likely that if maintenance is awarded by way of periodical payments, they will not be limited but will terminate on Angela's death or remarriage (MCA s 28) or if Greg successfully applies to vary or terminate his obligations (MCA s 31).

---

4   Courts have a duty to consider whether a clean break is appropriate; however, the fact that the welfare of children of the family is the court's first consideration means that in the case of minor children a clean break will not often be appropriate.

The amount of maintenance will be determined by reference to the financial resources, income and earning capacity of the parties. It is not clear how much Greg earns, if at all. If Greg is in receipt of State benefits himself, he will not usually be ordered to pay substantial sums to Angela, although an order may still nevertheless be made (*Freeman v Swatridge* (1984)); usually, however, it is a nominal order (*Berry v Berry* (1986)). If Greg does have earnings, it is likely that he will have to pay something to Angela. She is not earning at present, and with young children it may be difficult for her to realise or acquire earning capacity. Nevertheless, she should be advised that the court will not countenance a 'meal ticket for life' and, since she seems to be young, she will need to take steps towards self-sufficiency in the future. No order will usually be made that would take Greg below subsistence level (*Barnes v Barnes* (1972)), and to that extent the court will take into account the safety net of welfare benefits available to Angela.

The drop in standard of living (**s 25(2)(c)**) should be equally borne (*Preston v Preston* (1982)), but the fact that this seems to be a relatively short marriage is offset by the fact that two more children were born, and that there were two other children for whom Greg assumed responsibility. In those circumstances, Angela would find it impossible to adjust immediately to her changed circumstances. The parties are not particularly old, nor are they disabled, and they both appear to have contributed to the marriage and welfare of the family: **s 25(2)(f)**. The only other factor that may have a relevance is conduct under **s 25(2)(g)**. This is not routinely a consideration (*Wachtel v Wachtel* (1973)), and should only be used if it would be inequitable to disregard it. Generally speaking, adultery is not conduct (*Duxbury v Duxbury* (1987)), and it does not appear that there are any additional factors that make Angela's behaviour repugnant and indefensible.

Consequently, it seems likely that some financial provision will be awarded to Angela. The exact amount depends upon Greg's resources and will be affected by his obligations to maintain the various children of the family. In addition, Angela may seek child support from the natural fathers of her children.

## Common Pitfalls

In a question such as this with a number of children all needing maintenance it is important to be clear which children are claiming as natural children and which as children of the family and therefore what the relevant statutes are. Remember too that there have been recent changes in this area through the **Child Maintenance and Other Payments Act 2008**.

## Aim Higher

Extra marks could be gained through explaining any difficulties with using these Acts.

# QUESTION 21

Caroline, aged 30, met David, aged 35, at a school nativity play some eight years ago. Both Caroline and David had recently divorced their respective partners and both were looking after their children from their marriages. Caroline's children were Emma and Freddie, aged six and three, and David's son, George, was also six. After a whirlwind romance, David and Caroline married, and for a while they were blissfully happy. Caroline had worked as a legal secretary prior to marrying David but with her child care expenses, she had not been well off. David was a wealthy businessman and he had been keen for Caroline to stay at home, looking after the children and hosting various social events for his clients. Caroline also helped David in his business during busy times. A year ago, Caroline discovered that David had been having an affair with her sister, Harriet. This so infuriated Caroline that she cut up all of David's clothes with the garden shears, including his expensive suits. She also threw acid over his recently restored antique Rolls-Royce, causing £10,000 of damage. Caroline is divorcing David on the basis of his adultery but seeks financial provision for herself and the children. George, David's son by his first marriage, will live with his father but it has been agreed that he will spend every second weekend with Caroline, Emma and Freddie.

The matrimonial home is currently worth £600,000 and there is no mortgage. David's business has a considerable turnover, and last year his drawings were in excess of £200,000. Caroline used to receive £35,000 per annum from the company but David stopped this when she discovered about his affair. Caroline has remained in the matrimonial home but is keen to buy herself another house, free from painful memories of David.

▶ **Advise Caroline as to what financial provision, if any, she is entitled to on her divorce from David.**

## How to Answer this Question

This question requires a detailed analysis of the **MCA 1973 s 25** factors as they affect entitlement to financial provision for spouses. There is no **Child Support Act 1991** liability as the children involved are not the biological offspring of the payer. Instead, the **MCA 1973** provisions for children of the family must be detailed.

First, consideration must be paid to the welfare of the children and the clean break provisions should be outlined. Then the relevant factors of **s 25(2)** should be examined as they apply to the parties.

Consider the overall package, the home and financial provision. Then outline the special provisions in the **MCA 1973 ss 25(3)** and **25(4)** as they relate to children of the family.

## Applying the Law

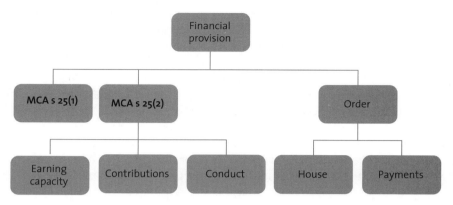

*MCA 1973's significance to financial provision in divorce in this scenario is illustrated here.*

# ANSWER

On divorce, the court has wide powers to order financial provision under the **MCA 1973 s 23** by way of periodical payments and/or lump sum orders as well as property orders under **s 24**. These powers will be exercised by reference to the principles in the **MCA s 25** in order to achieve a just and equitable financial solution.

In this case, Caroline, as a spouse, would be entitled to seek financial provision from David. She can also seek financial provision for her two children, Emma and Freddie. Since Emma and Freddie are not David's natural children, there can be no application under the **Child Support Act 1991**. Instead provision for the children will be under the **MCA 1973**, as they are children of the family. The concept of 'child of the family' is defined in the **MCA 1973 s 52** to include a child treated by the parties as a child of the family. Caroline and David treated all three children as children of the family.

In determining financial solutions, the court will first have regard to the welfare of children of the family whilst they are under 18. George and Emma are presently 14 and Freddie is 11; consequently their welfare is very important when reaching a solution to Caroline and David's financial problem. All the children need suitable homes, and in a wealthy family such as theirs, there should be no problem ensuring that both Caroline and David have homes in which their children can live and visit.

The court is then required by virtue of **s 25A(1)** to consider whether it may be possible to achieve a clean break between the parties, either immediately or as soon as possible after the divorce. This should not be taken to mean that a clean break will be imposed routinely; the duty is for the court to consider, not necessarily impose, a clean break (*Clutton v Clutton* (1991)). A clean break may be difficult where there are children, but it is not impossible

(*Suter v Suter and Jones* (1987)) and it is often easier to achieve if there is substantial wealth (*Duxbury v Duxbury* (1987)). Even if no immediate clean break is ordered, the court is required to consider whether it would be appropriate to limit maintenance to a particular period to enable adjustment (**s 25A(2)**, *Parlour v Parlour* (2004)).

Bearing this in mind, the court will first examine the parties' income, earning capacity and financial resources, including what each can reasonably be expected to acquire. In this case, David is a wealthy businessman with considerable income; there is a valuable matrimonial home and the business itself represents a capital asset for David. It is likely that David is earning to the limit of his earning capacity and therefore care will need to be taken to ensure that David's true worth in terms of savings, investments and assets, such as his antique car, are properly taken into account. As far as Caroline is concerned, she, at present, has no income. Throughout the marriage she was encouraged by David to remain at home, and she has worked only by contributing to the business. In the light of the acrimonious nature of the divorce, this income-generating avenue is not open to her and so the court will need to consider what earning capacity she has. Prior to the marriage, she worked as a legal secretary, but after eight years, technological developments may mean she was outdated and would need retraining. The children are all of school age and old enough for her to work and since she is in her late 30s, she should not expect to be maintained by her husband indefinitely. Therefore, whilst initially Caroline has no income, the likelihood is that she would be expected to retrain and begin to bear more of the burden of supporting herself.[5]

The needs and obligations of the parties will need to be considered: **s 25(2)(b)**. The basic needs of both parties are to provide homes and support their lifestyles and those of the children. There is no mortgage on the matrimonial home, nor do there appear to be any debts. Although David has formed a relationship with Harriet, it is unclear whether that will continue. If David was cohabiting with Harriet or even having children with her, then the needs of that second family would need to be taken into account: *Barnes v Barnes* (1972). In this case, it does seem that David will need to provide some assistance to his wife and the children given that she does not have the ability to be immediately self-sufficient.

Since this is a relatively wealthy family, it should be possible to avoid a drastic reduction in the standard of living (*Foley v Foley* (1981)) and the court will have regard to the standard of living enjoyed by the parties (**s 23(2)(c)**). The age of the parties and duration of marriage must also be considered under **s 25(1)(d)** but since both parties are approaching early middle age, this should not be an influence. There is no disability to be considered under **s 25(2)(e)** and so the consideration of contributions (**s 25(2)(f)**), and conduct (**s 25(2)(g)**) must be made.

---

5    Courts now recognise that financial relief may in part be to compensate a spouse either because they have given up employment or prospects through being married or because the marriage coming to an end has deprived them of an expected benefit (*Miller* (2006)).

David has obviously worked hard to provide the family with the comfortable lifestyle they have enjoyed. However, Caroline has contributed in terms of being a wife and mother (*Wachtel v Wachtel* (1973)) and there are also her contributions to the running of the business (*O'Donnell v O'Donnell* (1975)). This should be reflected in the level of financial relief awarded (*White v White* (2000)).

Conduct should be taken into account only if it would be inequitable to disregard it: **s 25(2)(g)**. Generally conduct should not be a consideration (*Wachtel v Wachtel* (1973)) but, in this case, Caroline's conduct has resulted in a dissipation of the family assets, when she deliberately destroyed or damaged David's clothes and car: *Martin v Martin* (1976) establishes that deliberate dissipation can be taken into account if excessive. However, Caroline's behaviour was a response to discovering David's affair with her sister. Mere adultery is not usually conduct (*Duxbury v Duxbury* (1987)) but the fact that it is with Caroline's sister might possibly be equated with cases like *Bailey v Tolliday* (1983) or *Dixon v Dixon* (1974). However, in those cases the adultery was with a parent-in-law or daughter-in-law, which might be more repugnant than with a sister-in-law. It is possible that David and Caroline's bad behaviour could cancel each other out (*Leadbeater v Leadbeater* (1985)) with no financial consequences on the level of maintenance.[6]

Last, the court will consider whether any benefit will be lost on divorce: **s 25(2)(h)**. This usually involves benefits such as pension rights but could include the loss of a share in the business if one had been promised by David: *Trippas v Trippas* (1973). The **Pensions Act 1995 s 166** alters the **s 25** factors to ensure that any pension entitlement that David might have acquired is considered as an asset of his and that any loss of pension rights by Caroline is also considered, even though this might not be for some considerable time. The court has the power under the Act to earmark some or all of the pension assets, so that when the pension matures and becomes payable to David, it is possible to order that some of the income and/or the lump sum are paid to Caroline. Obviously, this is a deferred benefit to her, which she may or may not live to realise. A preferable option may be the **Welfare Reform and Pensions Act 1999**, which allows the court to make an order splitting a pension fund and ordering part of the fund to be made available for the other party to the marriage.

It would seem, therefore, that this case will require some kind of redistribution of the family assets, as well as some financial provision, at least initially, by David. A lump sum may be ordered if David has the means to pay (*Davis v Davis* (1967)) but it should not be ordered if he would only be able to raise it by selling shares in his company (*Smith v*

....................................................................................................................

6    Under the **MCA 1973** divorce is no longer dependent upon fault. Focusing on blame is seen as unhelpful and antagonistic, therefore it is not surprising that conduct will only rarely be admitted as a relevant factor under **s 25(2)**.

*Smith*) and the proceeds used to rehouse the parties. It would seem appropriate to give Caroline a greater share than David, to take into account both her need for housing and her contributions to the business and loss of any share in it: *Trippas v Trippas* (1973). This would not be unjust to David, who could still use his capital as a deposit on a new home and raise the remainder on mortgage from his income. Caroline will also need an income, therefore, periodical payments will be ordered, unless David is able to settle a large lump sum, obviating the need for periodical payments and achieving a clean break: *Duxbury v Duxbury* (1987).

Any order made for Caroline will terminate on her death or remarriage: s 28(1). It will also terminate on David's death unless secured. If the court does not make a limited-term periodical payment order then David can apply to vary or extinguish his obligation to Caroline under s 31 if circumstances change.

David will also need to provide some kind of maintenance for Emma and Freddie. The court will take into account the financial resources and obligations of the parties and then examine what the needs of the children are: s 25(3). This takes into account how the children were being, or expected to be, educated and so David's liability may be greater if the children were at fee-paying schools: *O'Donnell v O'Donnell* (1976). Since Emma and Freddie are not David's natural children, the court will further consider whether David assumed responsibility for their maintenance, to what extent and on what basis, and whether he knew that this was not his child. On the facts, it seems clear that David did assume responsibility for Emma and Freddie, knowing that they were not his children. However, s 29(4) requires the court to consider the liability of anyone else to maintain the child. Therefore, David's liability may be reduced if their natural father is alive and can be traced. However, it seems likely that some order will be made.

The order in respect of the children will end when they reach 17 years of age (MCA s 29), unless they are in full-time education and their needs require an extended order.

# QUESTION 22

Edward and Fiona met whilst at university 15 years ago. They lived together for a while, but then married after the birth of their child, George, now aged 12. Subsequently, two daughters were born, Isobel, aged six and Jessica, aged two. Unfortunately, Jessica was born severely disabled and requires constant care and attention. The strain on the couple has been enormous, and there have been several rows. Fiona, in desperation, had a brief affair with Jessica's physiotherapist, Kevin, but felt so guilty about it that she confessed to Edward and begged forgiveness. Edward reacted violently at the news and seriously injured Fiona, leaving her also severely disabled.

Fiona had worked as a teacher throughout the marriage, taking maternity leave when she had the children. Since Jessica's birth, she had found it increasingly difficult to work and care for Jessica, but since Edward attacked her she has been unable to work.

Fiona is divorcing Edward, citing his behaviour, and it seems that Edward will not contest the petition. However, it is proving difficult to get agreement about the financial aspects of divorce. The former matrimonial home is valued at £250,000 with an outstanding mortgage of £50,000. Edward earns £40,000 per year as a manager of a small supermarket and the couple have no other assets, save for a small car, valued at £2,000, that Edward uses to go to work, and £3,000 in a building society account. Advise Fiona on her prospects of obtaining ancillary relief for herself and the children.

### How to Answer this Question

Details required of the parties under the **MCA 1973 ss 23** and **24** and what orders will be made in the light of the **MCA s 25** factors for the spouse. Further discussion is required in respect of the **Child Support Act 1991** provisions for the support of the payer's biological children and the possibility of this being bypassed by a consent order.

It is probably safest to consider the **Child Support Act** liability first. Explain the concepts of the qualifying child, and the absent and caring parent.

Then consider the **MCA** provisions for spouses.

### Applying the Law

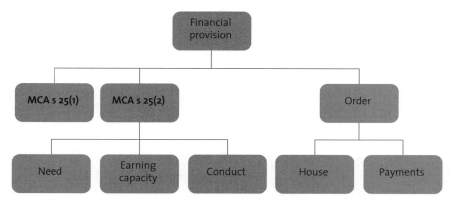

*How the **MCA** provision applies in Fiona's situation is illustrated here.*

# ANSWER

If Edward and Fiona divorce, then the court has wide powers to achieve a just and reasonable financial settlement. The **MCA 1973 s 23** permits awards of secured or unsecured periodical payments as well as lump sum orders, whereas **s 24** permits property orders, including sale, transfer and settlement of property. These powers are exercised with reference to the guiding principles in the **MCA s 25**, and allow for provision for spouses.

As far as provision for children is concerned, it is necessary to examine whether the children involved are the natural children of the parties. If so, their provision will be ordered by reference to the **Child Support Act 1991**. This Act will always apply where the caring parent is in receipt of State welfare benefits and it will apply in other cases at present where the parents are unable to agree the level of financial provision. The court has no jurisdiction to make orders for natural children of the parties under the **MCA 1973** in a disputed case. However, the parties can bypass the provisions of the **Child Support Act** by way of an agreed consent order. Both possibilities will be examined since all three children are the natural children of Edward and Fiona.

If provision is ordered under the **Child Support Act 1991**, it will be made by reference to the statutory formula for child support. Fiona is the parent with care, as the children have their home with her, and she usually provides their everyday care. Edward is the non-resident parent, as he does not live in the same household as the children. All three children are qualifying children in that they are under the age of 16, and one of their parents is non-resident. Once these preliminaries are established, it will be necessary to calculate the maintenance requirement by reference to the statutory formula.[7]

Once provision for the children is determined, it will then be possible to consider the level and nature of provision for the spouses. This is a reversal of the old position, where there was a tendency to deal with provision for children as an afterthought.

First consideration will be the welfare of any children of the family under the age of 18. The three children here will need secure accommodation with their mother, and it is important to ensure that, whatever financial arrangements are reached, the children have a roof over their heads: *Harman v Glencross* (1986).

The court must then bear in mind the desirability of a clean break and the policy of encouraging spouses' self-sufficiency: **MCA 1973 ss 25A (1)** and **25A (2)**. However, it is clear on these facts that, because of Fiona's disability which was inflicted by Edward, a clean

---

7   The **Child Support Act** originally used the term 'absent parent'. This was changed to non-resident parent to be less judgment laden.

break is unlikely. The obligation is for the court to consider, not necessarily impose, a clean break (*Clutton v Clutton* (1991)) and, consequently, in a case such as this where the presence of the children and other factors make a clean break unsatisfactory, it will not be imposed (*Suter v Suter and Jones* (1987)).

First, the court will examine the income, earning capacity and other resources of the parties: s 25(2)(a). Edward earns an average income of £40,000 per annum, and there is no evidence that he could reasonably be expected to earn more. He is not deliberately under-earning: *Hardy v Hardy* (1981). There are few assets here; only the house which is in joint names, one car and modest savings. Fiona, on the other hand, has no financial resources beyond these assets. She has no income, and her earning capacity as a teacher has been destroyed by her disability. Although the facts disclose that she was having difficulty coping with the demands of Jessica, she did have income and now she can earn nothing. It is unclear what would happen if she were to receive compensation for her injuries, for example from the Criminal Injuries Compensation Scheme, or from an insurance policy. Traditionally, damages for pain and suffering were not included as a spouse's assets (*Daubney v Daubney* (1976)), and this case is similar to that of *Jones v Jones* (1975) where the husband could not include damages as part of his wife's assets when he himself had been responsible for inflicting the injury. However, this policy has been criticised in *Wagstaff v Wagstaff* (1992) and it is possible that if Fiona were receiving substantial income from an insurance policy, for example, it might be taken into account.

From the facts, it seems obvious that whilst Edward's means are reasonable, Fiona has no means of supporting herself. There is a safety net of State benefits, but generally the courts are unwilling to take this into account, as it enables a husband to avoid his obligation to his wife by having the State maintain her: *Barnes v Barnes* (1972). The courts try to protect public funds by refusing to take such benefits into account (*Ashley v Blackman* (1988)), unless the husband's means were so limited that any order would take him below subsistence level (*Stockford v Stockford* (1981)). In the present case, Edward's means are such that he would be expected to support his wife without her recourse to State benefits.

It is then necessary to examine the financial needs and obligations of the parties. Edward clearly needs to be able to house himself, and provide accommodation for his children when they visit him: *Calderbank v Calderbank* (1975). However, Fiona needs to provide the children with a permanent home, and Fiona's disability and Jessica's disability are special considerations that increase her needs: *Smith v Smith* (1975). Fiona would have difficulty in housing herself and it seems likely that she will need to remain in the former matrimonial house.

The standard of living enjoyed before the breakdown of the marriage is not often maintained on divorce, but the court will be concerned to ensure that the drop in standard is not borne unequally: *Preston v Preston* (1982). The parties are not particularly old, nor has the marriage been particularly short (s 25(2)(d)), but clearly Fiona's disability is a relevant factor under s 25(2)(e): *Jones v Jones* (1975).

In terms of contributions made by the parties or likely to be made in the future (s 25(2)(f)), both parties have worked to support the family, and Fiona has been a wife and mother. *White v White* (2000) suggests there should be no discrimination between the contribution of the wage earner and the contribution of the home-maker. Looking at future contributions, Fiona will have day-to-day care of the children, which will involve her in added responsibility, in that she will have to supervise the children and obtain physical assistance for tasks she and they cannot perform.

The court will also consider conduct if it would be inequitable to disregard it: s 25(2)(g). Usually conduct is irrelevant (*Wachtel v Wachtel* (1973)), and ordinary adultery is irrelevant (*Duxbury v Duxbury* (1987)). However, Edward's extremely violent response is likely to count against him (*Jones v Jones* (1975)) since it has effectively destroyed Fiona's financial prospects.

The facts do not disclose whether Fiona will lose any benefit because of the divorce: s 25(2)(h). Consequently, it seems that the facts require some kind of financial provision for Fiona, as well as her being allowed to remain in the matrimonial home. The home in this case is jointly owned, but if it were sold there would be inadequate proceeds to rehouse the parties. It is relatively easier for a single person to obtain accommodation than for a disabled woman with three children, and so Fiona would be able to remain in the home. It could be argued that whilst it is not usually desirable to deprive a husband of his equity in the home, it may be sensible to do so in instances of extremely bad conduct (*Bryant v Bryant* (1976)) or where there may be problems enforcing maintenance. Here it may be desirable to order Edward to transfer his interest in the home to Fiona, but this may cause difficulty, given the outstanding mortgage. Fiona would then need to receive sufficient financial provision from Edward to enable her to pay the mortgage and it must be borne in mind that the **Child Support Act** will impose additional requirements on Edward by way of child support.

Another option is to allow Fiona to remain in the matrimonial home until her death or remarriage. Since both she and Jessica have disabilities, any shorter period is inappropriate. This is a variation on the Mesher order (*Mesher v Mesher* (1980)), which postpones sale indefinitely, but which will not necessarily deprive Edward of his capital interest in the home. It is also possible for Edward to pay the mortgage, by making an undertaking.

The parties would be well advised to try to reach some kind of agreement and avoid the need for litigation. A party receiving legal representation under the **Access to Justice Act 1999** may well find that the statutory charge cuts into the value of any property recovered or retained by the proceedings. This must be borne in mind as expensive litigation could dissipate the parties' assets, as in *Piglowska v Piglowski* (1999), where lengthy litigation left the couple with virtually no assets once their legal bills were paid.

# QUESTION 23 ----------------------------------------

Henry and Wanda married five years ago, after the death of Henry's first wife, Bronwen. Henry and Bronwen had two children, Scott, now aged 14, and Charlene, now aged 12. Henry and Wanda have one child, Jimmy, aged three. Henry owns the matrimonial home, which is a large four-bedroomed executive house, valued at £350,000 with a mortgage of £50,000 outstanding. When Jimmy was born, Wanda used her entire savings of £12,000 to build an extension to the house, which included a playroom and 'den' for the children. Wanda has no further savings, and has not worked since before Jimmy was born. Henry earns £40,000 per annum. The marriage has encountered difficulties, and both parties agree that a divorce is the best option for them. Scott and Charlene will remain with their father, and Wanda will care for Jimmy. Wanda wishes to obtain periodical payments for herself and Jimmy, and a lump sum to enable her to buy a new home. Wanda is legally aided and has heard horror stories about what can happen if the dispute drags on. Henry is being quite reasonable and his lawyer has indicated to Wanda that he feels a compromise can be negotiated and agreed by way of a consent order.

▶  **Advise Wanda.**

## How to Answer this Question

Explain the provisions of the **MCA 1973** as they relate to spouses and children of the family. However, the biological child, Jimmy, would be a qualifying child for the **Child Support Act 1991** and the statutory formula will apply unless the parties make a consent order.

❖  Explain how a consent order operates and how the parties are often influenced by the **s 25** factors.

❖  Detail the **Child Support Act** provisions and the need for maintenance to be agreed at least at this level.

❖  Give a general discussion of what the parties might agree vis-à-vis the home and continuing financial provision.

## Applying the Law

*How the relevant legislation relates to Wanda's entitlement to maintenance is illustrated here.*

# ANSWER

If the parties divorce, then the court has wide powers to order ancillary relief in the form of secured or unsecured periodical payments or lump sum orders (MCA 1973 s 23), and property orders under the MCA s 24, which will be determined by reference to the factors in the MCA s 25. However, this case is one of the few relatively amicable 'divorces' and the parties are keen to agree the level of ancillary relief rather than have it imposed on them by the courts. If the parties are able to reach agreement then the various aspects of the agreement are embodied in a consent order. This order is then formally presented to the court which can approve it under the MCA 1973 s 33A. The order will then be as enforceable as any other order, and will mean that any maintenance payments made under it are 'qualifying maintenance payments' for the purposes of the Finance Act 1988, thereby attracting additional tax allowances for the payer and being tax free in the hands of the payee. The parties are often influenced in reaching agreement by the realisation of what a court is likely to order on the s 25 guidelines.[8]

It is necessary to ensure that a consent order embodies all aspects of ancillary relief, as such an order is usually regarded as full and final, and consequently difficult to vary or

---

8    Consent orders are encouraged as the couple are more likely to understand what will best suit their circumstances and are more likely to follow the terms of an agreement that they have reached.

appeal against. Wanda should therefore ensure that the consent order properly reflects any agreed financial provision for Jimmy, herself and any lump sum that Henry is agreeable to paying. In terms of financial provision for Jimmy, he is the natural child of both Henry and Wanda. Henry, as a non-resident parent, would be liable financially to support Jimmy under the **Child Support Act 1991**. Jimmy is a qualifying child, that is, aged under 16, who has his home with a parent with care, Wanda. Henry would be liable to pay 12 per cent of his income to support Jimmy. However, because Henry has care of Scott and Charlene, their needs will first be taken into account so this will reduce the income available to Jimmy.

The two children of Henry's former marriage, Scott and Charlene, may well qualify as children of the family (**MCA 1973 s 52**), as they have been treated by both Henry and Wanda as such, even though they are not Wanda's natural children. Wanda will have no **Child Support Act** liability towards them as they are not her natural children, but she could potentially have to contribute to their maintenance under the **MCA 1973**. However, she has no job or obvious resources and it would seem inappropriate for her to have to support them. Therefore the consent order should reflect this.

In terms of periodical payments for Wanda, it is clear that she will at least initially require them. She has no job, nor any savings, and would find it difficult to get work given the young age of her child and the fact that she has not worked for a number of years. Consequently, she will need to look to Henry for such support but as she is relatively young, she cannot expect this to continue indefinitely. Assuming that substantial sums can be agreed upon, it will then be necessary to agree the period during which these will be paid. An immediate clean break would be unfair to Wanda; even if the clean break were to be deferred, as it would not be possible to predict her future accurately, therefore, it might be best to agree that the order can be varied or discharged later in relation to periodical payments for Wanda.

Wanda also needs a home for herself and Jimmy and it does not seem unreasonable to suggest that, whilst Henry can remain in the matrimonial home with his two children, he should raise a lump sum to enable Wanda to buy a small home for herself. Although the home is owned absolutely by Henry, Wanda has contributed during the marriage by paying for the extension, looking after the house and children, and it is right that she should have some share of the family assets. It is also in Henry's interest that his son, Jimmy, should be properly and securely housed. In *White v White* (2000) the House of Lords suggested that any financial resolution considered by the judge should be measured against the yardstick of equality and that equal division should only be departed from if there were good reason, which should be explained by the judge. This should enable her to buy a modest home and is within the range of what Henry could borrow by way of mortgage on his home. However, this increase in Henry's borrowing may mean he is less able to make periodical payments at the level suggested earlier, and so Wanda must be prepared to make some sort of compromise here. It should be pointed out to Henry that by paying for the extension, Wanda could acquire an interest in the house by virtue of her contribution, under the **Matrimonial Proceedings and Property Act 1970 s 37**.

# QUESTION 24

Peter and Wendy were divorced eight years ago, when they were both aged 36. Peter was ordered to pay periodical payments of £200 per month for Wendy and £100 per month for each of the couple's two children, Michael, then aged eight and John, aged six. The former matrimonial home was jointly owned, and an order was made permitting Wendy to remain there until John, the youngest child, was 17. At that point, the house was to be sold and the proceeds divided equally between Peter and Wendy.

At the time of the divorce, Wendy worked part-time, earning £12,000 per year, but one year later Peter was made redundant, and Wendy was forced to work full-time to make ends meet. Peter applied to the court for variation of the order, and the court substituted a nominal order for Wendy and reduced the payments for the children to £50 per month each. Peter worked only occasionally for the following five years and did not obtain employment until he met and married Belle, a wealthy widow. Peter now lives with Belle, and earns £50,000 per year in a job Belle got for him with her father's company. Wendy earns £18,000 per year and has now applied to the court for the last order to be varied so as to obtain substantial periodical payments from Peter. Wendy is also reluctant to sell the matrimonial home, which is worth £240,000 with a £20,000 mortgage.

Peter is annoyed at the prospect of having to continue to support Wendy, and seeks advice as to whether he can be free of future obligations to her.

▶ **Advise Peter.**

## How to Answer this Question

In this case, the original orders for ancillary relief on divorce were made some years ago, and advice is sought on variation. Variation is possible under **s 31**, but the court can also limit the term for future provision or terminate obligations entirely.

    ❖    Examine exactly what can and cannot be varied. Only periodical payments in the case.

    ❖    Examine those in relation to the children and their father's changing circumstances.

    ❖    Then examine the case in relation to the spouses and their circumstances.

## Applying the Law

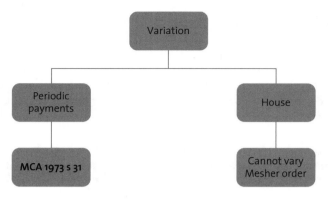

*The circumstances in which payment can vary are shown here.*

# ANSWER

This question requires an analysis of the powers of the courts to vary orders that have been made for ancillary relief. The original order, made on divorce, provided for periodical payments for Wendy and the children under the MCA 1973 s 23, and a settlement of property order, the so-called Mesher order, under the MCA 1973 s 24.[9]

These orders would have been made after a consideration of the factors in the MCA 1973 s 25 and have already been varied once when Peter became redundant. In order to alter arrangements once more, Wendy has made an application for variation under the MCA 1973 s 31. The court has power under s 31 to vary periodical payments for a spouse or children of the family, and this may involve increasing or reducing the amount payable. The court must also consider under s 31(7) whether to impose a fixed term for which the order will be paid, thereby enabling the payee to readjust before terminating the payer's obligations. It is also possible on variation that the court will terminate the order.

The court cannot order that periodical payments be replaced by a lump sum order for a spouse, although this is possible for a child: s 31(5). This means that the court cannot force Peter to pay a lump sum to Wendy in lieu of periodical payments, although he could, if he wished, negotiate this with Wendy, and their agreement could then be conveyed to the court, who would terminate the periodical payment order after the lump sum is paid, as

9    The advantage of variation is that it enables an order to be changed if circumstances alter and therefore could be seen as fairer. The disadvantage is that it is against the clean break principle.

in *Peacock v Peacock* (1991). He would be ill-advised to pay a lump sum in lieu of his periodical payments for the children, as there is always the possibility that the Child Support Agency may intervene later. There is no absolute entitlement to have prior financial generosity taken into account. Instead the payer must apply for a departure direction under the reforms introduced by the **Child Support Act 1995**.

There is no power to vary what are seen by the courts as one-off final settlements, such as lump sums (s 31(2)), unless to vary the instalments, or property transfer orders. An order for sale of any property can, however, be varied: ss 24(A)(1) and 31(2)(f). In this case, there were no lump sum orders, and the property was dealt with by way of a Mesher order. Therefore, as there is no power to vary this, both Peter and Wendy will have to wait until John reaches 17 for the house to be sold and proceeds divided. There is no way that the court can order the sale to be postponed or for Wendy's share in the proceeds to be increased: *Carson v Carson* (1981). Nor can the court order the sale to be brought forward. It would seem that the only variation here would be by consent of both parties.

Consequently, the only aspect of the order that can be varied is the periodical payment part. It seems clear that Wendy wishes to increase this, whereas Peter would like to reduce, and hopefully extinguish, his obligation. The periodical payments for children usually do not extend beyond their seventeenth birthday: **MCA 1973 s 29**. Michael is now aged 16 and John aged 14, therefore, the order in relation to Michael will end shortly. If Michael is working and supporting himself, then Peter could ask the court to end the order earlier than Michael's seventeenth birthday. This increase in his son's income and financial resources would satisfy the change in circumstances normally required for variation: s 31(7). However, if Michael has remained in full-time education, it may be that Peter's liability to maintain him will be extended up to 18, or beyond: s 29(3). The amount payable in respect of Michael and John may also be increased. The court will examine any change in circumstances (s 31(7)), taking into account any change in the **MCA 1973 s 25** factors.

Since the last order was made, Peter has obtained a job, and therefore his income and financial resources have increased. In addition, he has married Belle, who is wealthy in her own right. Although a court will not make a periodical payment order that would have to be paid by a second spouse (*Macey v Macey* (1981)), the second spouse's resources are relevant in that they free up Peter's income to meet the needs of his first family. Thus, it seems likely that the court would take the view that Peter could afford to increase the periodical payments for his sons who, as they have grown older, have increased needs and costs.

Insofar as Peter's obligations to Wendy are concerned, again his income and resources have improved since the last order. In addition, during the period of his redundancy, Wendy has had to make increased contributions to the welfare of the family by looking after both boys, working full-time and trying to make ends meet in difficult financial circumstances. The court might well feel that, now Peter's prospects have improved, he should do something to mitigate the drop in Wendy's standard of living.

Peter's main argument would lie in the fact that Wendy is now working full-time and that since the children are older, she can support herself. The court must consider the desirability of limiting periodical payments to a fixed period of time (s 31(7)), to enable the payee, Wendy, to adjust without undue hardship. In the circumstances, it would be harsh to immediately terminate Wendy's order and, in *Whiting v Whiting* (1988), the Court of Appeal said that a wife's order could be her guarantee against ill health or redundancy in the future. Given that she has shouldered responsibility for financially maintaining the family for the five years of Peter's redundancy, it would not be equitable to allow him to terminate her order now that he has improved his financial position. Even the imposition of a fixed term may not occur, as the courts have shown a marked reluctance to do this: *Hepburn v Hepburn* (1989); *Fisher v Fisher* (1989).

In conclusion, it would seem that there is no prospect of varying the Mesher order, but the periodical payments may well be varied. Peter's chances of terminating his obligations seem to be slim.

# QUESTION 25

Robert and Susan were divorced after 15 years of marriage. They had four children, now aged 14, 12, 10 and 8 respectively. It was agreed between the parties that the two older children, both boys, would live with Robert, and the two younger children, both girls, would live with Susan. Robert has agreed that Susan can remain in the former matrimonial home, now worth £150,000, with an equity of redemption of £120,000. He is also agreeable to paying £800 per month for the support of the two younger children.

However, Robert is unhappy about having to support Susan, who, he feels, could support herself. Susan is now aged 36, and although she has never worked since the marriage, she has developed her own interior design business over the past two years, during which time she has earned £10,000 for the first year and £14,000 for the second year. Susan is sharing the former matrimonial home with Tony, a freelance photographer, but she says they have no intention of marrying. Robert is somewhat suspicious as his youngest daughter has spoken excitedly of when she will be 'Mummy's bridesmaid'. Tony does not contribute anything towards the household expenses and Susan has said that he only earns £5,000 per year. Again, Robert is suspicious as he has often seen Tony's photographs in magazines and newspapers, and Tony also drives an expensive new car.

Robert is 40, and earns £50,000 per year as a surveyor. He has set up home in rented accommodation with Vicky and his two sons, as well as her child from a previous relationship. Robert intends to marry Vicky.

▶ Advise Robert on his potential financial responsibilities towards Susan, and how these may be met in the most tax-efficient way.

## How to Answer this Question

The question relates to maintenance following the breakdown of a marriage.

❖ This will be governed by the **Matrimonial Causes Act 1973 s 25**.
❖ Consequently the needs of children of the family are the first consideration.
❖ The earning capacity of both spouses should be considered – can Susan earn more?
❖ The impact of new relationships. What about Robert's responsibility for Vicky's children?
❖ What should happen to the family home?
❖ What about pensions?

## Applying the Law

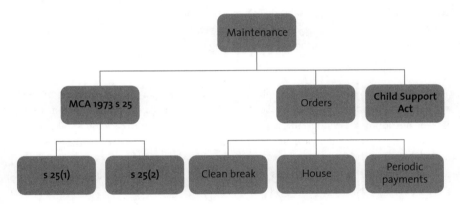

*Factors to consider in relation to Robert's financial responsibilities are outlined here.*

## ANSWER

On divorce, the courts have wide powers to order ancillary relief for the parties to the marriage. This can take the form of secured or unsecured periodical payments, lump sum orders (MCA 1973 s 23), and property orders (MCA 1973 s 24). In deciding what kind of order to make, the court will have regard to all the circumstances of the case and the factors mentioned in the MCA s 25. In this case, the parties have reached agreement on certain matters, which will be taken into account when advising Robert as to his potential liability.

The children in this case are the natural children of both parties, and, as such, Robert's liability to maintain them will be subject to the provisions of the **Child Support Act 1991**.

The provisions of this Act can be avoided at present by the parties reaching agreement by way of consent order, but Robert would be advised to ensure that the level of maintenance he agrees to is broadly that which would be awarded under the Act. In addition, if the Child Support Agency does become involved, for example because Susan is in receipt of State benefits, there is no guarantee that account will be taken of any generous financial provision he may have made to Susan on the divorce. It is possible, by virtue of the **Child Support Act 1995** amendments, to seek a departure direction requiring any transfer of assets to be taken into account. The making of the direction depends upon whether it would be just and equitable in all the circumstances to reduce the payment. It would seem that the £800 per month is reasonably generous, especially since he is maintaining the two older children without contribution from Susan.

The needs of the children of the family are a first consideration under the **MCA 1973 s 25(1)**. Whilst this is not an overriding consideration, it will be necessary to ensure that, in the redistribution of family assets following divorce, the interests of the children are well served. Both parties need to be able to house themselves and the children in their care, as well as have suitable accommodation for the other children of the family to visit: *Calderbank v Calderbank* (1976). It seems that the parties have agreed that Susan should remain in the former matrimonial home, although the basis of that occupation has not been determined.[10]

The court will also consider the desirability of a clean break (**s 25A(1)**), although it will not strive to impose one in unsuitable cases (*Clutton v Clutton* (1991)). Spousal self-sufficiency is to be encouraged, although this can be difficult with children to care for: *Suter v Suter and Jones* (1987). In Susan's case, her children are of school age and she could well become self-sufficient in the future. The court can impose a limit to the time for which she would receive support although this should only occur where her future independence can be predicted with a degree of certainty (*Barrett v Barrett* (1988)).

Looking at the income, earning capacity and financial resources that the parties have or can reasonably be expected to acquire, it can be seen that Robert earns a salary of some £50,000 per year. This seems to be the limit of his earning capacity and is not being artificially depressed. In terms of assets, he has his share in the matrimonial home, but it is unclear whether there are any other substantial assets. The home he shares with Vicky is rented, and there are no apparent savings. Vicky's resources are irrelevant in that the court will not make an order that would need to be paid out of a third party's resources. However, her resources may release more of Robert's income to meet the needs of his first family: *Macey v Macey* (1981).

---

10  The welfare of children of the family is the court's first consideration. This is different from them being the paramount consideration.

The **Pensions Act 1995 s 166** alters the **s 25** factors to ensure that any pension entitlement that Robert might have acquired is considered as an asset of his, and that any loss of pension rights by Susan is also considered, even though this might not be for some considerable time. The court has the power under the Act to earmark some or all of the pension assets, so that when the pension matures and becomes payable to Robert, it is possible to order that some of the income and/or the lump sum be paid to Susan. Obviously this is a deferred benefit to her, which she may or may not live to realise. More radical provision is also possible using the pension-splitting provisions of the **Welfare Reform and Pensions Act 1999**. This will enable an order to be made effecting the immediate division of the pension assets between the parties, although such assets will need to be reinvested in new individual pensions.[11]

In examining Susan's means, it is obvious that she is capable of earning money to help support herself; however, the income generated thus far has been modest. It may be that she has only been working part-time; if so, she might be expected to work longer hours. She is also cohabiting with Tony, and whilst she claims he makes no contribution, his lifestyle would indicate that he is capable of contributing to household expenses, thus freeing more of her income.

Both parties have housing needs that will need to be considered under **s 25(2)(b)**, as well as costs involved in caring for the children. It seems that Robert will be taking on additional obligations if he marries for the second time, and these obligations must be recognised: *Barnes v Barnes* (1972). Fortunately, Robert earns a lot of money and should be able to provide for both families.

The standard of living enjoyed by the parties must be considered, and in very wealthy families it may be possible to avoid any drop in such standards: *Calderbank v Calderbank* (1976). If there is a drop, it should not be borne inequitably: *Preston v Preston* (1982). This marriage is not of short duration, nor are the parties particularly old or suffering from any disability: **s 25(2)(d)** and **(e)**. However, the court will look at the contributions each has made, and is likely to make, to the welfare of the family: **s 25(2)(f)**. Robert has worked throughout the marriage, and Susan has been a supportive wife and mother (*Wachtel v Wachtel* (1973)), and so both have contributed (*White v White* (2000)). Susan has also made a financial contribution in recent years, and the child care burden will fall on them both in the future.

As far as conduct is concerned, only behaviour that it would be inequitable to disregard will be taken into account: **s 25(2)(g)**. This means that most conduct is irrelevant: *Wachtel v Wachtel* (1973). The parties seem to have drifted apart, and there is little by way of

---

11    Because courts are able to deal with pension arrangements as part of financial relief, it is less likely that a claim that the divorce should be prevented under **s 5** of the **Matrimonial Causes Act 1973** will succeed.

conduct. However, it may be argued that, by allowing Tony into the matrimonial home without requiring him to contribute to costs, Susan establishes the requirement of conduct, as in *Suter v Suter and Jones* (1987). This could have the effect of reducing Susan's entitlement.

Susan is cohabiting with Tony and has indicated that she has no intention of remarrying. Remarriage is an important consideration when making a consent order or a court order, and a party who remarries having previously indicated that they have no plans to do so, may well find the order being set aside: *H v H* (1975); *Livesey v Jenkins* (1985). Robert should be alerted by his daughter's comments and should not be too keen to make generous property orders in exchange for reduced financial provision, as periodical payments would terminate on Susan's remarriage: **MCA 1973 s 28(1)**.

The matrimonial home is jointly owned, and Robert has agreed that Susan can remain there. Robert has not behaved in such a repugnant or financially irresponsible way that the court would consider depriving him of his interest: *Bryant v Bryant* (1976). Nor, given the possibility of Susan remarrying, would it be sensible for him to agree to transfer his interest in return for terminating or reducing his periodical payments. Therefore, it would seem appropriate to allow Susan to remain in the house under a Mesher order, that is until she remarries, dies or the youngest child reaches 17, or, more generously, until she dies or remarries (*Martin BH v Martin BW* (1978)). If Susan did remarry, the house would be sold and the proceeds of sale divided between her and Robert.

This would still mean that Robert may need to make periodical payments, at least initially, to enable Susan to readjust, become more financially self-sufficient or remarry. Robert is earning £50,000 per annum, but has agreed to provide £9,600 for the children. He is also looking after his other two children, Vicky and her daughter, and renting accommodation whilst Susan remains in the matrimonial home. In these circumstances, the one-third guideline, whereby Susan would be awarded periodical payments to bring her up to one-third of their joint incomes, would seem overgenerous. Instead, it may be more appropriate to assess Susan's reasonable needs: *Preston v Preston* (1982), although the House of Lords was cited on this approach in relation to capital (*White v White* (2000)).

In the past there was a tax allowance in respect of qualifying maintenance payments. However, this has been abolished in the **Finance Act 2000** and from 5 April 2000 there is no tax relief in respect of maintenance orders made after 5 March 1988.

# Property Disputes

## INTRODUCTION

It is necessary for students of family law to be able to use their knowledge of property law principles to resolve disputes between people over ownership of property. If the people are not divorcing, then the court has no discretionary powers under the **Matrimonial Causes Act (MCA) 1973**; instead, the dispute must be resolved according to normal property law rules.

Many disputes centre on the home. In examination questions this is often owned by one party yet the other party claims to be entitled to a share. In this situation, mention should be made of the legal interests and then the case should be examined to see if there is any valid declaration of a trust which would give a beneficial entitlement. Usually, however, there will be none, and it will be necessary to see if there is an implied, resulting or constructive trust.

Essentially, there needs to be evidence of a common intention to share, and detrimental acts by the party seeking an interest. After *Lloyds Bank v Rosset* (1991), you must examine critically what will amount to evidence of a common intention to share, although a slightly more flexible approach to quantifying the amount of such an interest is suggested in the case of *Midland Bank v Cooke* (1995). Courts have now decided that when determining the proportion of the share they should look to all the circumstances (*Oxley v Hiscock* (2004), *Cox v Jones* (2004)). If the property has been conveyed into joint names, this will not be ignored just because of unequal contributions (*Stack v Dowden* (2007)). In *Jones v Kernott* (2011), the Supreme Court decided that although the starting point was that property would be held in equal shares, this could be rebutted. In *Jones v Kernott* itself, this was because it was clear that the common intention of the parties had changed and they clearly did not intend the property to be held equally. There is also the possibility that an interest may be acquired or enlarged by virtue of the **Matrimonial Proceedings and Property Act 1970 s 37**.

Some examination questions may also require you to consider equitable estoppel and contractual licences. Many questions require students to consider what protection, if any, the law gives to a party who has a beneficial entitlement. The **Land Registration Act 1925** and the concept of overriding interest in **s 70(1)(g)** should be considered, as well as the provisions in the **Trusts of Land and Appointment of Trustees Act 1996 s 14** for ordering a sale when there is a dispute.

The **Married Women's Property Act 1964 s 1**, concerning things bought and savings made from housekeeping allowances, provides that such property belongs to both parties equally. There is also the **Law Reform (Miscellaneous Provisions) Act 1970**, which deals with engagement rings.

# QUESTION 26

The marriage between Michael and Sarah has encountered difficulties, and the couple have decided to part amicably. They are both keen to go their separate ways with no financial responsibilities towards each other, and so they propose to divide their assets according to their beneficial entitlements in property law. They do not want the court to impose an arrangement under the **MCA 1973**.

Advise Michael and Sarah on their beneficial entitlement to the following:

(a)    On their engagement, Michael gave Sarah an antique diamond ring, worth £5,000, that belonged to his grandmother.

(b)    £20,000 invested in a building society savings account, which is held in joint names.

(c)    Shares to the value of £6,000 registered in Michael's name, but paid for with a cheque drawn on the couple's joint bank account.

(d)    The matrimonial home, registered in Sarah's name. The initial deposit of £20,000 was paid by Sarah with money from an inheritance, but the mortgage instalments have been met from the joint bank account. Michael spent every weekend for a whole year renovating the property and carrying out all the interior design. The house was purchased for £100,000 five years ago, and is now worth £150,000. The outstanding mortgage is £20,000.

## How to Answer this Question

It is clear that the couple do not want an **MCA 1973** solution to their problems, and so normal property law rules apply.

❖    The engagement ring: look at the **Law Reform (Miscellaneous Provisions) Act 1970 s 3** – likely that she will keep it.

❖    The money invested in a joint account: arguably used as a common fund – presumption that jointly owned.

❖    The shares bought from the account: conflict between presumption that jointly owned and argument that both individuals can buy for themselves.

❖    The matrimonial home is registered in Sarah's name only – she has legal entitlements. Examine if beneficial entitlement by way of implied, resulting or constructive trust, and consider the **Matrimonial Proceedings and Property Act 1970 s 37.**[1]

## Applying the Law

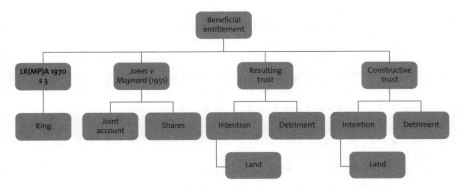

*How the couple's beneficial entitlement is understood in relation to their land and property is shown here in relation to the relevant cases and legislation.*

## ANSWER

(a)   The position of engagement rings is often determined by reference to the **Law Reform (Miscellaneous Provisions) Act 1970 s 3.** This section provides that the gift of an engagement ring should be assumed to be an absolute gift but the presumption may be rebutted by proving that the ring was given on the implied condition that it should be returned if the marriage did not take place for any reason. In the instant case Michael and Sarah have gone on to marry. However, the presumption that a man has given a woman a gift in such a situation would be very strong. The diamond ring, however, is quite valuable and has been a family heirloom; so in order for it to belong to Michael rather than Sarah it would be necessary for Michael to show that the presumption of advancement has been rebutted by a contrary intention. This contrary intention needs to be that he only intended the ring to be a conditional gift upon the marriage subsisting. It is easier to show in the case of a valuable family heirloom but nonetheless, the presumption that this is a gift appears to be quite strong and on balance it would seem that Sarah is entitled to keep the ring.[1]

---

1   When a question is divided into parts, it makes sense to also clearly divide your answer. This way both you and the examiner can be sure that you have dealt with all the issues.

(b)  Money invested in a joint savings account may cause difficulty in that it will often depend on the intention of the parties and their respective contributions as to who is entitled and in what proportion. In this case, the parties have contributed to the savings account but little is known about what arrangements they made for withdrawing from the savings account. Where money is invested in a joint account there is an argument that the money should be regarded as jointly owned. In *Jones v Maynard* (1951) both husband and wife contributed to the account just as Michael and Sarah have done. In that case, as in the present, both paid in their various earnings and funds and, although the husband paid in more than the wife, it did seem that they viewed the account as a common savings account. The argument would be that this is a joint account and that they are therefore both equally entitled since they viewed it as a common pool. There is no evidence that they merely intended the shares to reflect their contributions.

(c)  The shares purchased for £6,000 which are registered in Michael's name only were purchased with a cheque drawn on the couple's joint account. If the case of *Jones v Maynard* (1951) were to be followed then the shares would be jointly owned since the investments could be regarded as joint investments and merely a continuance of their arrangements for the joint account. However, there is an argument that if both were entitled to draw on the account to purchase whatever they wished to by way of investments or chattels, then each separate investment or chattel should be regarded as belonging to the person who made the investment or purchase of the chattel as in *Re Bishop (Deceased)* (1965). If that were the case then the shares would be owned by Michael absolutely since they are registered and purchased in his name. If, however, they could regard it as an extension of the joint account then the shares would be jointly owned.

(d)  The former matrimonial home is registered in Sarah's name only. This declaration of legal title in the conveyance would conclusively establish that Sarah is the sole legal owner unless it can be established that there is fraud or mistake (*Goodman v Gallant* (1986)). There is no evidence that there has been any separate declaration of a beneficial entitlement in favour of Michael and an interest under a trust must be created and evidenced in writing. However, it is possible that Michael may have an interest in the home by way of some resulting implied or constructive trust. The initial deposit of £20,000 was paid by Sarah and the mortgage instalments have been met from the joint account. Michael has renovated the property and carried out interior design. It is necessary to examine to what extent, if any, Michael has acquired or enlarged his interest in the home.

To acquire an interest under a resulting, implied or constructive trust it will be necessary to show that there is a common intention between the parties that, although Sarah has the legal entitlement, Michael has a beneficial interest in the home. It will also be necessary to show that Michael, as the owner of the beneficial interest, has acted to his detriment based on this common intention. Michael has not made any direct contribution towards the deposit; however, it is arguable that he has made contributions towards the mortgage instalments. The couple have had a joint bank account which they have regarded as a common pool; both have paid their salaries into the account and both have made various drawings on the account. This would seem to provide evidence of a direct contribution as required in *Lloyds Bank v Rosset* (1991), which would thereby establish an interest on behalf of Michael. His contributions do appear to be substantial in terms of meeting the mortgage requirements and it seems that the £80,000 mortgage that was initially required has reduced to some £20,000 outstanding now. Therefore, if one could argue that there is a joint contribution to the mortgage instalments then Michael will acquire some kind of interest in the home. There is the further possibility that this interest may have been enlarged by his efforts each weekend, renovating and designing the interior of the home.[2]

According to *Lloyds Bank v Rosset* (1991) the only way that this contribution would suffice would be if it were to be substantial in money or money's worth to the improvement of the property. In *Lloyds Bank* itself the wife's decorating and supervision of workmen was insufficient to give rise to an interest. In Michael's case, much would depend upon the extent of the renovations that he carried out. The interior design really would be superfluous. However, the renovation and the amount of impact that is made on the transformation of the property would determine whether this would give or enlarge any interest in the home. Following *Lloyds Bank v Rosset* (1991), caution must be exercised in trying to give an interest under this head. The cases of *Cooke v Head* (1972) and *Eves v Eves* (1975) illustrate just how substantial the work must be in order to qualify under this head. However, there is the possibility that if Michael does not acquire an interest under a trust by virtue of this work he may nevertheless enlarge his interest in the home by reference to the **Matrimonial Proceedings and Property Act 1970 s 37**. This section provides that where a husband or wife contributes in money or money's worth to the improvement of property in which, or in the proceeds of sale of which, either or both of them have the beneficial interest, the person who contributes shall, if the contribution is of a substantial nature and not subject to any agreement to the contrary, be treated as having acquired by virtue of his contribution a share or an enlarged share. The extent of such a share is the extent that the court considers just and equitable.

Here it could be argued that Michael has contributed to the improvement of the property. His work can be measured in money or money's worth; he has spent every weekend for a

---

2   It is easier to establish a beneficial entitlement if there has been a direct financial contribution to the ownership of the property and therefore this is what is considered first. In this case Michael would get a beneficial entitlement because of his contributions towards the mortgage. It is more doubtful whether his work on the house by itself would be enough to gain him a beneficial interest.

substantial period of time; and it does seem to be the sort of work that would normally be paid for if done by someone else. The question is, then, whether the work is of a substantial nature. Ordinary everyday do-it-yourself and common repairs to property should not suffice to enlarge Michael's interest. However, if the work has been substantial and has improved the house then he ought to be entitled to enlarge his share. The enlarged share must not be negated by any agreement by the spouses and the court has a discretion in deciding to what extent Michael's share will be increased.

In conclusion, therefore, the house is now valued at £150,000 with a mortgage outstanding of £20,000; this leaves equity of £130,000 in the house. The initial deposit of £20,000 by Sarah represents one-fifth of the original value of the home; the remaining four-fifths was contributed to by both parties in paying the mortgage and since their intention appears to have been that they should require a joint interest by so doing, the mortgage contributions will be split two-fifths to Michael, two-fifths to Sarah. This would give Michael a two-fifths share in the equity and Sarah three-fifths share in the equity. However, some adjustment may need to be made for the improvement effected by Michael's renovations and, on balance, it would seem that the couple would more or less be jointly entitled to any proceeds of sale.

In *Midland Bank v Cooke* (1995) it was stressed that it is important to establish an interest under a constructive trust by reference to the strict rules in *Gissing v Gissing* (1971) and *Lloyds Bank v Rosset* (1991). However, once the common intention to share can be shown by reference to those rules, as it can in this case, then, in quantifying the shares of the parties, the court can take into account the whole history of the relationship, including behaviour and contributions that would not suffice in themselves to create the interest in the first place. Thus, whilst Michael's renovations would not suffice as evidence of a common intention giving rise to a constructive trust, they can be referred to so as to determine the size of the shares the parties intended. This arguably reinforces the argument that the parties should have more or less equal shares here.[3]

# QUESTION 27

Arthur and Guinevere married 16 years ago, and they have three children, aged 12, 10 and 8 respectively. The matrimonial home, Camelot, was bought when they married, with a

---

3   Although this question is divided into four parts, the answer does not give the same consideration to all the parts. Far more discussion is spent on the issue of who owns the house. This is unsurprising. It is likely to be the most important issue for the couple themselves and it is the one where there is the most legislation and case law to apply. Sometimes, a student will be faced with a question which is divided into parts where the examiner sets out the marks available for each part. In this case, the student should allocate her time and words in answering the question proportionally according to the marks available.

deposit of £10,000 provided by Arthur's parents as a wedding present, and the remaining cost paid by mortgage. The house was registered in Arthur's name only. Guinevere worked briefly before the children were born, and has worked as a teacher since the youngest child started school. The mortgage instalments were paid from a joint bank account into which both Arthur and Guinevere paid their salaries. Two years ago, Guinevere used £15,000 she won in a competition to re-decorate and re-carpet the house.

The mortgage on the house was virtually paid off when Arthur decided to go into business on his own. He borrowed £50,000 from the Westland Bank and secured the loan on the home, without Guinevere's knowledge. The business failed; Arthur defaulted on the mortgage, and has left Guinevere.

The Westland Bank is seeking to evict Guinevere from Camelot, and she does not wish to leave.

Advise Guinevere on:

(a)  her property rights, if any, in Camelot;
(b)  whether the bank will be successful in evicting her.

## How to Answer this Question

(a)  Examination of property entitlement will be under normal rules of property law, not the **MCA 1973**.

❖   She has no legal entitlement, so must examine beneficial entitlement. Was there a common intention to share any detrimental acts by Guinevere?

❖   Look at deposit, contributions to the mortgage from the bank account, and the use of the competition prize.

❖   Consider the **Matrimonial Proceedings and Property Act 1970 s 37**.

(b)  The way of protecting her interest would be by relying on the **Land Registration Act (LRA) 1925 s 70(1)(g)**, to claim an overriding interest that binds the bank. However, it would then be necessary to consider the provisions of the **Trusts of Land and Appointment of Trustees Act 1996 s 14** whereby the bank could apply to sell the property.

## Applying the Law

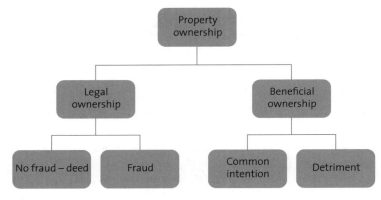

*Part a – Ownership of Camelot can be illustrated in terms of legal and beneficial ownership.*

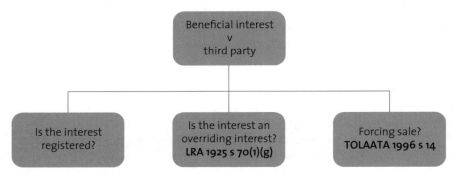

*Part B – The potential outcome of Bank v Guinevere.*

# ANSWER

(a)  Guinevere is seeking advice on her property rights, if any, in Camelot, the matrimonial home. Normally, on the breakdown of a marriage, a spouse would be better served by seeking a financial settlement under the wide powers of the **Matrimonial Causes Act 1973**. However, in this case, these powers could only resolve the financial situation between Arthur and Guinevere on divorce. Guinevere's most immediate problem concerns her possible eviction by the bank who are her husband's creditors. Her best chance of avoiding or postponing this is if she can show that she has an entitlement in property law to the home. This may then possibly be enforceable against the bank.

Any such interest must be determined according to strict rules of property law (*Pettitt v Pettitt* (1970)), with no room for the court to order what seems fair in the circumstances.

On the facts, it is clear that Guinevere has no legal interest in the property which is registered in Arthur's name only. The original conveyance will be conclusive unless it can be shown that there was fraud or mistake: *Goodman v Gallant* (1986). Consequently, there is no legal or beneficial entitlement evidenced in the conveyance. There does not appear to be any subsequent declaration of trust either, since that must be in writing (**Law of Property Act 1925 s 53(1)(b); Law of Property (Miscellaneous Provisions) Act 1989 s 2**). Therefore, any beneficial entitlement on Guinevere's part must be by way of implied, resulting or constructive trust, which does not need to comply with formalities.

Although technically there are legal differences between these three kinds of trust, the courts frequently make no attempt to distinguish (*Gissing v Gissing* (1971)), since the basic requirements of the trusts are the same. Such trusts require evidence of a common intention to share an interest in the property, together with detrimental acts by the party seeking the beneficial interest. The technical distinctions between the trusts arise in how such a common intention is established, or deemed to exist, by the courts.

Often a common intention is established by pointing to a direct contribution made by a party towards the acquisition of the home. This may be the provision of a deposit or part of a deposit, or by paying some of the mortgage. Such a contribution would tend to show an intention to share, unless it could be argued to be a loan, *Sekhon v Alissa* (1989). The amount of the share is usually in proportion to the parties' respective contributions (*Cowcher v Cowcher* (1972)), unless the contrary intention can be shown. In the present case, the initial deposit came from Arthur's parents as a wedding present to the couple. Wedding presents do not always belong to the couple jointly; it depends on the intention of the donor (*Kilner v Kilner* (1939)). Arthur's parents could arguably be said to be providing a gift for them both to share. In *McHardy & Sons v Warren* (1994) the Court of Appeal held, in a case such as Arthur's and Guinevere's, that where the husband's parents had provided a deposit as a wedding gift, there was a common intention to give the wife a beneficial interest. Somewhat surprisingly, the Court of Appeal held that this gave her a half-share with her husband, not just in the proportion of the home that the deposit represented, but in the whole home. This case would benefit Guinevere enormously, but has been subject to criticism since it would enable the wife to defeat a creditor's claim.

In addition to the deposit, it seems that the mortgage instalments have been paid from a joint bank account, into which both parties paid their salaries. Although there was a period during which Guinevere did not work, it can be argued that by their behaviour the parties have provided evidence of a joint enterprise. They both placed all their income into this account for their joint use and benefit, and neither has reserved any individual interest (*Chapman v Chapman* (1969)). This would reinforce the argument that they have equal joint interests.

Guinevere has made the further investment of her £3,000 competition prize to redecorate the house and buy new carpets. This would be an indirect contribution, and likely, following *Lloyds Bank v Rosset* (1991), to be inadequate since it is not substantial. Minor redecoration and the buying of household goods does not acquire or enlarge an interest at common law: *Pettitt v Pettitt* (1970). Neither will her contribution as wife and mother assist her: *Burns v Burns* (1984).[4]

The only other way in which Guinevere may increase her interest is by way of the **Matrimonial Proceedings and Property Act 1970 s 37**. This is available to spouses only and she must show that she has made a substantial contribution in money or money's worth to the improvement of the home. On the facts, although £3,000 is a lot of money, it will not have added much, if anything, to the value of the property, since it was used to pay for things that improve the quality of life for the occupier, rather than increase the value of the property. Only if the property had been very run-down or possibly derelict would she succeed.

It therefore seems likely that Guinevere would be able to establish a beneficial interest in the property, possibly in equal share with Arthur. Applying the principle in *Midland Bank v Cooke* (1995) the whole history of the relationship and the parties' conduct and contributions can be looked at to determine the size of shares intended. Thus, once Guinevere establishes an interest under a trust according to the strict rules in *Gissing v Gissing* (1971) and *Lloyds Bank v Rosset* (1991), she could argue that there was an intention that they should have equal shares. However, she should be advised that the courts will scrutinise carefully any such claim which would have the effect of depriving a third party creditor of his rights: *Midland Bank v Dobson* (1986).[5]

(b) It seems, that Guinevere has a beneficial interest in the home however, the Westland Bank have made a mortgage advance to Arthur which they now wish to recover. This depends on whether the bank are bound by Guinevere's interest. In the case of registered land, the bank take free of interests that are not registered, unless the interest is an overriding interest: **LRA 1925 s 70**. Guinevere's interest may be overriding because of her occupation of the home (**LRA s 70(1)(g)**), and will bind the bank unless they made enquiry which did not disclose her interest (*Williams & Glyn's Bank v Boland* (1981)). She and the children were clearly in occupation, which does not necessarily need to be continuous or exclusive: *Kingsnorth Finance v Tizard* (1986). Any bank lending to a man should make enquiries of the existence of a spouse and be alerted to the possibility of her having an interest.

---

4   The above cases illustrate that only rarely will work done or money given to improve the home environment lead to a beneficial interest.

5   See **Stack v Downton** (2007) and **Jones v Kernott** (2011) on how beneficial shares in property should be quantified. The latter determined that although an equal division would be the starting point, this could be rebutted depending on the facts.

Thus, it would seem that the bank are bound by her interest. It is then necessary to see if the bank could force a sale of the property. The bank have a charge on the property, but have not, as yet, declared Arthur bankrupt. The appropriate provision is the **Trusts of Land and Appointment of Trustees Act 1996 s 14** and the court will make such order as it feels is just and reasonable in the circumstances of the case. The court will look at the interests of the creditors, and the conduct of the spouse, Guinevere, in contributing to the situation. In the present case, the bank have behaved somewhat rashly by granting a mortgage to Arthur without seeking Guinevere's consent and Guinevere has not contributed to the bankruptcy situation. She clearly needs a roof over her head and those of the children, and does not appear to have any substantial resources that would enable her to rehouse herself. The children are still young and need a stable home and this is a genuine case of Guinevere having a real interest, not just a sham arrangement to defeat creditors. In the present case, Guinevere should be able to resist the order for sale, at least whilst the children are still young. However, the courts do not lightly entertain s 14 applications that will leave genuine creditors without recourse. Therefore, it is still possible that a court, depending on the value of the home, might order a sale, since Guinevere's half-share might be sufficient for her to rehouse herself.

In *Mortgage Corp v Shaire* (2000) the judge thought that **s 14** had altered the law in favour of the family vis-à-vis the creditor. It was stated that a distinction could be drawn between orders for sale in favour of a creditor in bankruptcy situations, where the creditor was likely to succeed, and orders for sale in favour of a bank or building society which has a charge over the property, and is protected in the long-term, where the family might have a greater chance. This greater flexibility may be necessary to enable the courts to comply with the **Human Rights Act 1998**. **Article 8** of the **European Convention** confers the right to respect for family and private life, and by automatically ordering a sale of the home against the wishes of a blameless spouse there may be a violation.

# QUESTION 28

Eric and Elsie were married 40 years ago, and lived in a house purchased by Eric with a deposit of £300, the remaining mortgage of £3,000 being paid by Eric over the following 25 years. The house is now valued at £140,000 and is registered in Eric's sole name. Elsie worked for the first eight years of the marriage, using her earnings to pay all the household expenses, which Eric could not otherwise have afforded. She did not work while the two children of the marriage were small, but has worked for the past 20 years. Elsie's earnings have been used by the couple for household expenses, to install central heating, and recently to add a conservatory to the back of the house.

Eric has just died, leaving all his property to Freda, his secret mistress. Advise Elsie on what her beneficial entitlement is, if any, to the matrimonial home, and how, if at all, her position may be improved.

## How to Answer this Question

The question involves a discussion of Elsie's property law entitlement to a share in the home. She will again need to rely on trust principles and/or the **Matrimonial Proceedings and Property Act 1970 s 37**.

The **Trusts of Land and Appointment of Trustees Act 1996 s 14** must be considered in case Freda applies for a sale.

Further attention should be paid to the **Inheritance (Provision for Family and Dependants Act) 1975** as it applies to applications by a spouse of the deceased.

## Applying the Law

*Elsie's entitlements can be understood as falling into the categories illustrated above.*

## ANSWER

In this case, since Eric has died, Elsie's entitlement in the matrimonial home will need to be determined by reference to the ordinary rules of property law. There is no power for the court to order what it considers just and equitable under the **Matrimonial Causes Act 1973**. Instead, Elsie's entitlement to the home or a share of it vis-à-vis her husband's mistress, Freda, will be determined strictly according to the property law entitlement of both women: *Pettitt v Pettitt* (1970). The legal interest in the property was registered in Eric's name only, and consequently would pass on his death according to his will. The original conveyance in Eric's name would be conclusive as to legal entitlement in the absence of fraud (*Goodman v Gallant* (1986)), and this would pass to Freda if Eric's will is valid. There is no documentary evidence of legal or beneficial entitlement for Elsie, either in the original conveyance or in any subsequent written document: **Law of Property Act 1925 s 53(1)(b); Law of Property (Miscellaneous Provisions) Act 1989 s 2**.

Consequently, Elsie will only be entitled to the property if she can establish an interest under an implied, resulting or constructive trust, since no formal requirements are necessary in such cases.

The basic requirements of these trusts are the same (*Gissing v Gissing* (1971)), and the courts tend to ignore the technical distinctions between them. There must be a common intention to share an interest in the property, and the party seeking the beneficial interest, Elsie, must show she acted to her detriment.

The usual method of sharing a common intention is to point to a direct contribution to the purchase and acquisition of the property. In the present case, Elsie did not pay the deposit, nor did she pay any mortgage instalments. However, for the first eight years of the marriage, her earnings paid for household expenses, thereby enabling Eric to pay the mortgage, which he otherwise could not have afforded. This is arguably sufficient to show a common intention (*Hazell v Hazell* (1972)), since, without her contribution, there was no way that Eric could have bought the house. However, Elsie only contributed for eight years initially, and then for the last 20 years of the marriage she paid household expenses. For the last 20 years, however, it appears that Eric could manage financially without her paying household expenses. Following *Lloyds Bank v Rosset* (1991), it is unlikely that the mere payment of household expenses amounts to a sufficiently substantial indirect contribution by Elsie. These could easily be discharged without a common intention that she should acquire or enlarge her share by so doing. There is no evidence of any express agreement by Eric and Elsie that her contributions would acquire her an interest (*Eves v Eves* (1975)), and so, consequently, the second period of contribution will be disregarded.

Elsie may also argue that she has contributed by installing central heating and a conservatory. *Lloyds Bank v Rosset* (1991) requires that such contributions should be substantial. In *Re Nicolson (Decd)* (1974), the installation of central heating was felt to be substantial, and a conservatory may make a substantial contribution to the improvement of the property. Thus, it should be possible to evidence the common intention to share by reference to Elsie's first eight years' contributions, the central heating and conservatory.

Clearly these show that Elsie acted to her detriment, and so she should have a beneficial entitlement to a share in the home. In assessing the size of the share, *Midland Bank v Cooke* (1995) suggests that the whole history of the relationship can be examined to determine what size share the parties intended. This may mean that other aspects of Elsie's behaviour which were insufficient to create an interest may, nevertheless, be referred to at this second stage to give her a larger share of the home, possibly as much as one half.

There is the further possibility of relying on the **Matrimonial Proceedings and Property Act 1970 s 37** to argue that the central heating and conservatory amount to a substantial contribution in money or money's worth to the improvement of the home. This would enlarge her original interest from her eight years' contributions.

Once Elsie establishes an interest in the home, this will bind Freda. Elsie is in actual occupation of the home and by virtue of the **LRA 1925 s 70(1)(g)** she has an overriding interest which would bind any subsequent purchaser. There will be no possibility of Freda arguing she was unaware of Elsie's existence, and since Freda is not a bona fide purchaser she will inherit the property subject to Elsie's interest.

Technically, they would both have interests under a trust for sale, and Freda might apply to the court for an order for sale under the **Trusts of Land and Appointment of Trustees Act 1996 s 14**. The court can make such order as it sees fit in the circumstances of the case. An examination of Elsie's interests and the purpose of the trust, which had been to provide a home for Elsie and Eric, will be made, and the court will need to consider whether to order a sale and divide the proceeds between the two women.

If Elsie considers that her share under property law is inadequate, she may consider an application to the court under the **Inheritance (Provision for Family and Dependants) Act 1975**. The wife of the deceased may apply and must show that her husband's will failed to provide reasonable financial provision for her. This is an objective determination, and does not depend upon what her husband Eric wished or thought reasonable. **Section 1(2)(a)** provides that the court must consider whether the financial provision made is reasonable in the circumstances, whether or not the provision is required for the spouse's maintenance. In this case, no provision has been made for Elsie and even though she may be working, and capable of supporting herself, it seems likely that no reasonable provision has been made.

The general view of the provisions of the Act is that they are designed to ensure that the spouse of the deceased is in a similar position on death as she would have been on divorce: *Re Besterman (Decd)* (1984).

**Section 3(1)** provides for a number of factors to be considered, including the resources of the applicant and other beneficiaries, the size and nature of the estate, and any other relevant matter, including the conduct of the applicant. Little is known of Freda's position and financial dependence on Eric, but Elsie appears to have been a devoted and supportive wife for 40 years, and entitled to some provision from Eric's estate. For a spouse, the length of the marriage as well as the age of the spouse and their contribution to the marriage should also be examined: **s 3(2)**. Elsie has for many years worked, and looked after the home and children, and this would ensure she receives the provision she deserves. This would mean that she could obtain an order giving her a larger share in the home, or even allowing her to remain there until her death (*Harrington v Gill* (1983)). Little is known about whether Eric had any other financial assets that could be used to provide periodical payments for Elsie, but at least she can use the Act to ensure that her position is improved.

# Domestic Violence and Occupation of the Home

## INTRODUCTION

When a relationship deteriorates, it will often be necessary to examine what protection from personal violence is available. There is also the issue of who should occupy the former home. These areas of law have, in the past, been criticised as a 'hotchpotch of enactments' per Lord Scarman in *Richards v Richards* (1984), and have undergone reform and rationalisation in the **Family Law Act 1996**. **Part IV** of the Act dealing with these matters came into force in 1997.

The **Family Law Act 1996** renames the rights of occupation that used to exist under the **Matrimonial Homes Act 1983** as matrimonial home rights, and these rights are defined in **s 30(2)**. A court order under **s 33** of the Act will be needed before a spouse can be excluded from the dwelling house. The significant change introduced is that these rights exist, not only in relation to dwelling houses that are the joint homes of the parties, but are extended to cover dwelling houses that the parties intended to be their joint homes, even though they may never have lived there together.

The **Family Law Act** replaces the various orders available under the different jurisdictions with the occupation order, but divides applicants into two categories. The entitled applicant applies under **s 33**, and the non-entitled applicant may apply under **ss 35, 36, 37** or **38**, depending on whether the respondent is entitled or not. The **Domestic Violence Crime and Victims Act 2004** has removed the **Family Law Act 1996 s 41**.

Non-molestation orders are reformed and dealt with in **s 42**, which depends on the concepts of 'associated person' and 'relevant child' to determine the availability of such orders. The definition of 'associated person' has been widened by the **Domestic Violence Crime and Victims Act 2004**. The ability of the courts to attach powers of arrest has also been rationalised and improved, and can be found in the **Family Law Act 1996 s 47**. Breaching a non-molestation order is now an arrestable offence.

This is an area where the **Human Rights Act 1998** implications will need to be monitored. Occupation orders interfere with a person's occupation of his home, and regard must be had to the **ECHR Art 1** relating to peaceful enjoyment of possessions, **Art 8** relating to respect for private and family life, and **Art 6** relating to a fair trial.

## EXAM QUESTIONS

Problem questions involve advising the victim or perpetrator of domestic violence and may be combined with divorce, maintenance or property issues. Essay questions would be evaluating the orders available under the **FLA 1996**.

# QUESTION 29

The sooner the range, scope and effect of these powers are rationalised into a coherent and comprehensive body of statute law, the better. Per Lord Scarman in *Richards v Richards* (1984).

Do you consider that the **Family Law Act 1996** provisions relating to domestic violence and occupation of the home address Lord Scarman's concerns and will result in improved protection for the vulnerable and those at risk?

## How to Answer this Question

❖    Look at fragmented jurisdiction in the past.

❖    Has the **FLA 1996** improved the situation?

❖    The different treatment of spouses and cohabitants.

❖    The **Domestic Violence Crime and Victims Act 2004**.

## Applying the Law

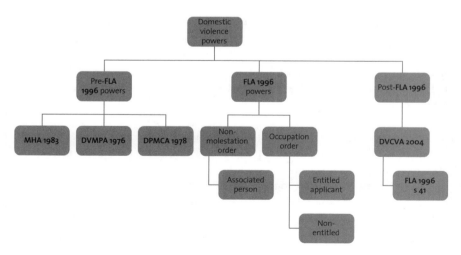

*This diagram shows how the different powers associated with domestic violence have evolved through legislation since Lord Scarman's comments.*

# ANSWER

The criticisms made by Lord Scarman were directed at law that had developed on a piecemeal basis, and consisted of a variety of enactments and inherent powers that varied from court to court. The 'hotchpotch of enactments' consisted of the **Matrimonial Homes Act 1983**, the **Domestic Violence and Matrimonial Proceedings Act 1976** and the **Domestic Proceedings and Magistrates' Courts Act 1978**. All these statutes contained various methods of seeking occupation of a home, and some gave a measure of protection from personal violence. However, the procedures varied from court to court, the principles to be applied also varied, and some measures were available only to spouses whereas others were available to cohabitants. Little wonder that this confusing and anomalous situation led the Law Commission in its report in 1992 on Domestic Violence and Occupation of the Family Home to recommend abolition of this variety of enactments and their replacement with a single, comprehensive, statutory formula that would apply to all courts. This would obviate the need to gamble on which court was likely to give the most favourable response, and would encourage a uniform and consistent approach by the courts to the issues of violence and occupation of the home. The Law Commission included a draft bill, and it is this bill that has provided the basis for the **Family Law Act 1996** provisions on domestic violence, which came into force in October 1997.

The previous law provided a number of options for spouses, and more limited avenues for cohabitants, but left others at risk to depend upon the inherent jurisdiction of the court. With the increasing incidence of cohabitation as a long-term way of life for many couples, that position could not be justified, and for those who were not in the standard heterosexual relationships, the law offered little in the way of protection from domestic violence. The Law Commission proposed a radical shake-up in the categories of applicant who would be able to use the new legislation, and the proposals have been accepted.[1]

As well as spouses and those who are living together as husband and wife, applications can be made by ex-spouses and ex-cohabitants. This recognises that, on the breakdown of such relationships, problems may occur and the threat of violence can continue long after a relationship has ended. Similarly, those who have been parties to an agreement to marry are qualified to make applications. These qualifications are recognised in the **Family Law Act** by the concept of 'associated persons', to be found in **s 62**. However, the concept of associated person is wider than the above categories, and includes those who live or have lived in the same household, provided this is not a landlord/tenant or employer/employee relationship. It also includes close relatives of a person or his/her spouse, whether by blood, marriage or adoption. This list includes mother, stepmother, grandmother,

---

1   Note how this question refers to the societal context within which changes to domestic violence legislation were enacted. This Is useful as providing a background against which their effectiveness can be examined.

daughter, granddaughter, aunt, sister, niece, father, stepfather, grandfather, son, grandson, uncle, brother and nephew. This recognises that such relationships can frequently give rise to issues of domestic violence and occupation of family homes. Those who are parents of the same child, or who have or had parental responsibility for the same child, are also associated persons, as are those who are parties to the same family proceedings, since these situations can often lead to tension and conflict.[2]

The Law Commission also proposed extending the categories to include those who have had a sexual relationship with each other. Many such relationships turn sour and expose a party to the threat of violence or molestation. This would have been a controversial extension of the law and could have caused difficulty in practice if the sexual nature of the relationship was disputed, or would have been embarrassing. The Act does not contain such a provision, and so, only those with a sexual relationship and who have lived together were initially associated persons. More recently, the **Domestic Violence Crime and Victims Act 2004** has extended the definition to include couples who have had an intimate relationship but have not actually lived together.

The Act follows the Law Commission's recommendations and does not limit relief to heterosexual cohabitants. Provided the couple lived together, it does not matter whether their relationship was homosexual, heterosexual or not sexual at all. This led to considerable criticism in some sections of the press, as indicating an undermining of marriage and an encouragement of cohabitation and homosexuality. The Government responded by pointing out that the Act does seek to promote marriage, and does, in some respects, give more favourable treatment to those who are married. However, there are those who argue that the Act did not go far enough, and that the concept of associated persons is an unnecessary limitation on those who can seek assistance.

The Act also introduces the concept of 'relevant child' in **s 62(2)**. This is a child who is living with a party to proceedings or might reasonably be expected to live with a party, any child in relation to which an application under an adoption order or the **Children Act 1989** is in question in the proceedings, and any other child whose interests the court considers relevant.

It may be that those persons falling outside the categories recognised in the **Family Law Act 1996** can be given some protection by the **Protection from Harassment Act 1997**, or by the seeking of an injunction under the inherent powers of the court.

Under the old law, applicants seeking personal protection faced different criteria in different courts. In the Magistrates' Court it was necessary to show actual violence or the

---

2    Although wide, the definition of associated person does not cover all individuals who might be affected by molestation. It does not, for instance, cover an ex-partner's new partner.

threat of it before an order could be made, whereas in the County Court relief was available to prevent molestation. This meant that spouses who had been the victims of harassment and pestering that stopped short of violence could get no assistance in the Magistrates' Court, yet their lives could still be made extremely unpleasant by such behaviour. The Law Commission recommended that the County Court approach be adopted in all courts, so that there would be no need to wait until the situation had escalated into violence before assistance could be sought.

The Act prefers the Law Commission approach, and provides for non-molestation orders in s 42. Such orders are available to protect an applicant who is an associated person and/or any relevant child. The application may be made in conjunction with other family proceedings or may be made on its own, or it is possible for the court to make an order without an application being made if it is hearing other family proceedings and considers the order should be made. This power for the court to make an order of its own accord is an advance on the old law, and is to be welcomed in that it gives the court the power to respond to damaging situations that arise as other proceedings unfold.

The court will consider all the circumstances of the case in determining whether to make an order, including the need to ensure the safety, well-being and health of the applicant and relevant child (s 42(5)). Thus, there is a change in emphasis away from the old law that concentrated on the nature of the respondent's violent conduct to the new consideration of the effect on the applicant and child. The term molestation is not defined in the Act but would include conduct other than violence. Consequently, harassment and pestering, violence and threats would all be restrained by the order, which can be made for a limited time or until further order (s 42(7)). Molestation was defined in *C v C (Non-Molestation Order)* (1998) as deliberate conduct involving a high degree of harassment, and did not cover an ex-wife giving embarrassing information about her ex-husband to the newspapers.[3]

It is possible for the court to accept an undertaking from respondents instead of making an occupation order or non-molestation order (s 46), but no power of arrest can be attached to an undertaking (s 46(2)). This means that a court cannot accept an undertaking from a respondent if it would otherwise have had the grounds for attaching a power of arrest to the non-molestation or occupation order. By virtue of s 47, if the court makes a non-molestation order and the respondent has used or threatened violence against the applicant or child, then a power of arrest must be attached, unless the court is satisfied that in all the circumstances the applicant and child will be adequately

---

3   The non-molestation order is a civil power aimed at protecting the victim, not at punishing the person responsible for the molestation. It makes sense therefore that the focus is on the impact on the victim rather than on the nature of the violent conduct.

protected without one. This makes it much more likely that a power of arrest will be attached than under the old law, and gives a greater measure of protection to applicants.

The Law Commission recommended that non-molestation orders should be capable of lasting for indefinite periods of time, and the Act provides that such an order may be made for a specific period or until a further order is made (s 42(7)).

Under the old law, a victim of domestic violence was often placed in the difficult position of having to instigate proceedings against a former loved one about whom there might still be mixed feelings. In addition, there was the extra fear that the commencement of proceedings might provoke further violence. In many cases, the police would be involved in attending incidents of violence, but, with the victim often unwilling to pursue a criminal complaint, little effective protection could be given. The Law Commission made the radical proposal of allowing the police to apply for civil protection on behalf of the victim of domestic violence. This could well encourage victims to seek police help, and stop them feeling responsible for commencing actions against the respondent. In s 60 provision is made for rules of court to be drawn up allowing certain prescribed persons or representatives to act and bring proceedings for the protection of victims of domestic violence.

In cases involving occupation of the home, the old law varied in the principles to be applied in determining applications and the powers available. The Family Law Act 1996 renames the rights of occupation in the Matrimonial Homes Act 1983 and calls them 'matrimonial home rights'. Such rights are still only given to spouses, and matrimonial home rights are defined in s 30(2) as the right not to be evicted or excluded from the home unless by court order, and the right if not in occupation to enter and occupy with a court order. They exist in relation to dwelling houses that are, or have been, or were intended to be, the joint home of the parties. The Act takes up the Law Commission's recommendation that such rights should exist in relation to a house that, whilst never actually the home of the parties, had been intended by them to be so. Matrimonial home rights exist if one spouse has an entitlement to occupy the dwelling house by virtue of a beneficial estate, contract or other enactment, and the other spouse has no such entitlement, or has an equitable right only.

Such rights are important in relation to occupation of the home because they will almost inevitably mean that an applicant for an occupation order, who is a spouse, qualifies as an entitled applicant within s 33 The Act draws a distinction between entitled applicants and non-entitled applicants for occupation orders, but simplifies the old law by creating a single occupation order. However, the criteria to be applied in deciding whether to make the order, whilst contained in one Act, vary according to the nature of the applicant and respondent. There is concern that time may be wasted with argument as to the exact nature of the applicant's status, before the appropriate criteria can be selected.

The Law Commission thought it appropriate to retain some distinction between those seeking occupation of a home in respect of which they had some rights, and those seeking to occupy a home in respect of which they had no such rights. Those who have an interest have traditionally always stood a better chance of achieving occupation than those who do not, and this will certainly continue under the Act. Applicants with a beneficial entitlement, or a contractual entitlement, or entitlement to occupy by virtue of any enactment, or matrimonial home rights, will be deemed 'entitled applicants' (s 33(1)). The court can make an order in respect of a dwelling house that is, or was, intended to be the home of the applicant and a person with whom the applicant is associated. This concept of associated person is widely defined in s 62 and does not limit the making of occupation orders to married couples or those who are cohabiting heterosexuals.

The order can contain a number of provisions (s 33(3)), including requiring the respondent to allow the applicant to enter and remain in the house or part of it, and restricting or terminating the respondent's right to occupy the house or part of it, and excluding the respondent from the area where the home is situated.

The factors in s 33(6) govern whether an order will be made and the type of regulatory order that will be granted. These factors require the court to consider all the circumstances of the case, including the housing needs and resources of the parties, the likely effect of any order or non-exercise of powers by the court on the health, safety or well-being of the parties and any relevant child and the conduct of the parties in relation to each other and otherwise.

In some cases the court has a choice of whether or not to make an occupation order, whereas in other cases, the 'significant harm' cases, the court is compelled to make an order. Under s 33(7), if it appears that the applicant or relevant child is likely to suffer significant harm attributable to the conduct of the respondent if the order is not made, then the court must make an order, unless the respondent or relevant child is likely to suffer equal or greater significant harm if the order is made. This requires the court to first consider whether there is the likelihood of significant harm, and then balance the harm of making an order with the harm of not making an order (*Dolan v Corby* (2011)). This means that the entitled applicant gets the benefit of a statutory presumption that in cases of risk of significant harm an order should usually be made.

Harm is defined in s 63 to mean ill-treatment or impairment of mental or physical health with the additional criteria of impairment of development for a child. Ill-treatment includes both physical and sexual abuse in relation to a child, and development is widely defined to include physical, emotional, intellectual, social or behavioural development. The concept of 'significant' is likely to mean considerable or important, if guidance in earlier cases on the meaning of such wording in other statutes is followed: *Humberside County Council v B* (1993).

Entitled applicants can thus seek an order against a wide range of respondents, provided the respondent is an associated person, and there is no maximum period for which an occupation order will be granted. This is to be contrasted with the position of the non-entitled applicant, where orders can last for a six-month initial period, which can then be renewed for an additional six-month period.

The non-entitled applicant can seek an order but only against a spouse, former spouse, cohabitants or former cohabitants. Thus, the category of respondent is more severely limited. If the respondent is entitled to occupy the house, and is a spouse or former spouse, application should be made under s 35, whereas if the respondent is entitled, but is a cohabitant or former cohabitant, application should be made under s 36.[4]

This would require the court to first consider the making of an occupation rights order, giving the right to occupy the home, and then to make a regulatory order excluding the other party. Under s 35, in making an occupation rights order, the court will take all the circumstances of the case into account, including the housing needs and resources of the parties and any relevant child; the financial resources of the parties; the likely effect on the health, safety and well-being of the parties and any relevant child of any order or no order being made; the conduct of the parties in relation to each other and otherwise; the length of time that has passed since the parties lived together; the length of time since the marriage was dissolved; and the existence of any proceedings between the parties under the **Children Act 1989** or in relation to ownership of property.

If the parties were not married but had cohabited, s 36 requires the court to consider the housing needs and resources of the parties; their financial resources; the likely effect on the health, safety and well-being of the parties and any relevant child of any order or no order being made; the conduct of the parties in relation to each other and otherwise; the nature of the relationship, specifically that they have not given the same level of commitment as a marriage; the length of time they have lived together as husband and wife; whether there are any children; the time that has passed since they lived together; and the existence of any proceedings between the parties under the **Children Act 1989** or in relation to ownership of property (s 36(6)).

Thus, it can be seen that the cohabiting nature of the relationship does not carry the same weight as a marriage would, and specific regard is had to the length and nature of the cohabiting relationship.

If an occupation order is made, then the court can make a regulatory order excluding the respondent from the home or restricting his occupation. The factors influencing the court

4   There is a tension between domestic violence powers and property rights and this is particularly marked when a non-entitled applicant is applying for an occupation order against someone who has an interest in the property.

in determining whether to make such an order are the housing needs and resources of the parties; their financial resources; the effect of any order or failure to make an order on the health, safety or well-being of the parties or relevant child; the conduct of the parties in relation to each other and otherwise; the likelihood of significant harm to the applicant or relevant child if no order is made; and the likelihood of significant harm to the respondent if an order is made. With non-entitled applicants, unlike the position with entitled applicants, there is no compulsion to make an order on the basis of a risk of significant harm. This puts cohabitants at a disadvantage compared to spouses, since spouses will usually be entitled applicants by virtue of their matrimonial home rights. However, the **Domestic Violence Crime and Victims Act 2004** arguably improved the position of cohabitants by removing **section 41**.

If neither the applicant nor the respondent is entitled to occupy, and this is only likely to be so in the rare cases of squatters and bare licensees, then orders can be sought under s 37 if the parties are spouses or former spouses, and s 38 if they are cohabitants or former cohabitants. The s 37 factors mirror those in s 35, and contain the statutory presumption in favour of making an order for a spouse if there is the risk of significant harm to the spouse or relevant child. **Section 38** contains the same factors as in s 36 but there is, again, no statutory presumption in favour of an order where there is the risk of significant harm to a non-entitled cohabitant.

In conclusion, the new law goes a long way to answering Lord Scarman's criticisms of the old law. To find the law relating to occupation orders and non-molestation orders in one statute is helpful, but the provisions are nonetheless complex, and will involve categorising applicants before entitlement can be examined according to the correct section of the statute. In addition, there are those who argue that the statute goes too far in offering protection to those beyond the traditional married relationship, whereas there will be others for whom the distinction between those who are married and those who are not cannot be justified.

## Common Pitfalls

This question is about domestic violence and the occupation of the home and therefore your answer needs to concentrate on occupation orders. As always with an essay question, do not just discuss domestic violence in general, but identify and discuss the issues specifically raised in the question.

## Aim Higher

Extra marks can be gained through critical analysis of the current law, especially if this is backed with clear illustrations from case law.

# QUESTION 30

Heidi and Ian, both aged 19, began to live together because Heidi was pregnant. When the baby was born, Ian suspected that he was not the baby's father as the baby's appearance was totally different from his and Heidi's. He said nothing about this at first, and behaved normally towards Heidi and the baby. The couple share a small one-bedroomed flat, and have had numerous arguments. Ian has a short temper and has frequently smashed household objects in his anger at Heidi's burnt cooking. One day the couple were out shopping when they met a friend who made a joke about the fact that the baby looked nothing like Ian. Ian exploded with rage and pushed the trolley full of groceries at Heidi, badly bruising her legs. He then pushed the pram over in his haste to leave the supermarket. Although the baby was unhurt, Heidi was too scared to go to their home, and has been staying with her mother. Ian, full of remorse, keeps telephoning to speak to Heidi, who will have nothing to do with him. These telephone calls are occurring with increasing frequency, and the last one included a comment by Ian that his family would not stand by and let Heidi make a fool of him.

Heidi wishes to return to her flat with the baby, but does not feel she would be safe there with Ian. Advise Heidi on her possible options.

Advise Heidi, on the assumption that:

(a)    she and Ian are married;
(b)    she and Ian are not married.

## How to Answer this Question

This question requires examination from the standpoint of Heidi and Ian being married, followed by an examination of the position if they are unmarried.

Both situations are now governed by the **Family Law Act 1996**. If the couple are married:

❖    consider matrimonial home rights under s 30;
❖    look at excluding Ian by obtaining an occupation order under s 33;
❖    examine the factors in s 33(6) and s 33(7);
❖    consider seeking a non-molestation order under s 42.

If the couple are not married:

❖    no matrimonial home rights;
❖    exclusion by way of occupation order under s 33 or, more likely, s 36;
❖    examine the factors in s 36 regarding occupation rights orders and regulatory orders;
❖    consider non-molestation order under s 42.

## Applying the Law

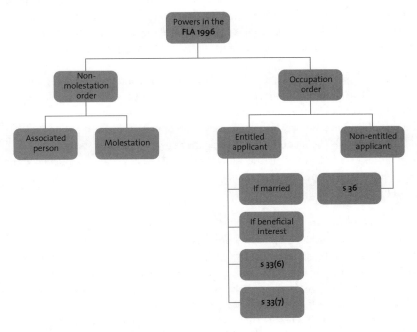

*How the **FLA 1996** applies in this situation is illustrated here.*

# ANSWER

(a) Heidi needs to obtain protection from domestic violence, and occupation of the flat that has functioned as a matrimonial home. If Heidi is married to Ian, she may have matrimonial home rights in relation to the flat, since it has been the matrimonial home (**Family Law Act 1996 s 30(7)**). It is not clear from the facts whether it is only Ian who is entitled to occupy the flat. If Ian is the sole tenant, then Heidi, as the non-entitled spouse, is given matrimonial home rights by **s 30**, which are defined in **s 30(2)** as the right not to be evicted or excluded from the home unless by court order, and the right, if not in occupation, to enter and occupy with a court order. If they are both joint tenants, then **s 30(9)** gives Heidi the same rights. Heidi can therefore return to the flat, but would rightly be concerned about the safety of this course of action. Consequently, she will need to see whether or not Ian can be excluded, and this will only be possible by way of a court order under **s 33**.[5]

5   The **FLA 1996** provides two orders – the non-molestation order which protects the beneficiary from molestation, and the occupation order which controls occupation of the family home. In answering a domestic violence question, the first step is to determine what the victim wants and therefore which is the more appropriate order. If the occupation order is the most suitable order, the question then is whether the victim is applying as an entitled or a non-entitled applicant.

Heidi is an entitled applicant under s 33; she is entitled to occupy the home because she has matrimonial home rights. The occupation order can require Ian to allow Heidi to enter and occupy the flat, and can prohibit Ian or restrict him from exercising his right to occupy the flat, or the area in which it is situated. Since the flat is so small, it is not feasible to expect Heidi to occupy part of the flat, with Ian occupying the rest.

The factors in s 33(6) govern whether an order will be made and the type of regulatory order that will be granted. These factors require the court to consider all the circumstances of the case, including the housing needs and resources of the parties; the likely effect of any order or non-exercise of powers by the court on the health, safety or well-being of the parties and any relevant child; and the conduct of the parties in relation to each other and otherwise. The baby is a relevant child within s 62(2) since it lives with either party, and this is regardless of whether the baby is Ian's child or not.

In some cases, the court has a choice of whether or not to make an occupation order, whereas in other cases, the 'significant harm' cases, the court is compelled to make an order. Under s 33(7), if it appears that the applicant or relevant child is likely to suffer significant harm attributable to the conduct of the respondent if the order is not made, then the court must make an order, unless the respondent or relevant child is likely to suffer equal or greater significant harm if the order is made. This requires the court to first consider whether there is the likelihood of significant harm, and then balance the harm of making an order with the harm of not making an order (*Dolan v Corby* (2011).[6]

Harm is defined in s 63 to mean ill-treatment or impairment of mental or physical health, with the additional criterion of impairment of development for a child. Ill-treatment includes both physical and sexual abuse in relation to a child, and development is widely defined to include physical, emotional, intellectual, social or behavioural development. The concept of 'significant' is likely to mean considerable or important, if guidance in earlier cases on the meaning of such wording in other statutes is followed: *Humberside County Council v B* (1993).

Ian has behaved very badly towards Heidi and the baby. Even though he may be upset and suspicious, this does not justify his explosive and violent temper. Throwing and breaking objects, just because his dinner is burnt, is excessive and the incident in the supermarket certainly gives cause for concern about the safety of both Heidi and her baby. The persistent telephone calls and possible threats would all strengthen Heidi's

---

6   If the court determines that the applicant or a relevant child is suffering or would be likely to suffer significant harm this creates a presumption in favour of the order. The court will then only not make an order if the respondent shows that (s)he would be at greater risk of harm if an order were to be made than the applicant or relevant child would be if an order were not to be made.

argument that she and the baby run the likely risk of significant harm if no order is made.

Little is known about the living conditions at Heidi's mother's home, but it is not good for the development of the child to be living in cramped conditions. Heidi would seem to have nowhere else to go, yet returning to the flat is not a realistic option whilst Ian remains there. Ian, on the other hand, has behaved in a reprehensible way towards Heidi and the baby and could well find alternative accommodation. His violence does not appear to be isolated and the facts seem to indicate the likelihood of significant harm. This would mean that the court must make an order unless Ian would be likely to suffer equal or greater significant harm if the order were made. The consequences of the order for Ian would be that he would need to find alternative living accommodation. There is no evidence to suggest that he would find this impossible, nor is there evidence to suggest that he would suffer any other kind of harm. Consequently, it seems that the court will make an order allowing Heidi to occupy the flat and excluding Ian from the flat. It may be that, given the nature of Ian's behaviour and the threats he has made, the court will go further and exclude him from the general area where the flat is situated. If an order is made, it can be for a specified period, or until an event takes place, or until a further court order. In this case it appears that the flat is rented, and the order may well be of greater duration than if the flat was owned by Ian.

If the court makes an occupation order in respect of the flat, it has power to make ancillary orders under s 40(1), to order either party to pay rent, mortgage, repairs or outgoings on the property. It does not seem appropriate here for an order to be made compensating Ian for the loss of his right to occupy. Whether any order is made depends on all the circumstances of the case, including the financial needs, resources and obligations of the parties (s 40(2)). On the facts, little is known about the resources of the parties and whether Heidi can pay anything towards the rent, or whether Ian should contribute. Clearly, an order could be made requiring Heidi to take care of the contents of the flat, and, since she has matrimonial home rights, any payment by her in respect of the rent will be treated as if made by Ian; the landlord will be bound to accept her payment (s 30(3)).

It would also be sensible for Heidi to apply for a non-molestation order under s 42. This order would prohibit the respondent from molesting the applicant if the applicant is an associated person with the respondent and/or any relevant child. As explained earlier, Heidi and Ian are associated persons by virtue of their marriage (s 62(3)), and the baby is a relevant child (s 62(2)). Such an application can be made with the application for the occupation order, or can be made regardless of whether or not an occupation order is sought (s 42(2)). Consequently, if Heidi remains at her mother's home and does not seek an order in relation to the flat, it would nonetheless be advisable to seek the non-molestation order.

The court will consider all the circumstances of the case including the need to ensure the safety, well-being and health of the applicant and relevant child (s 42(5)). Thus, there is a change in emphasis from the old law's concentration on the nature of the respondent's violent conduct, to the new consideration of the effect on the applicant and child. The term molestation is not defined in the Act but would include conduct other than violence. Ian's harassment, pestering, violence and threats would all be restrained by the order, which can be made for a limited time or until further order (s 42(7)). It is possible for the court to accept an undertaking from respondents instead of making an occupation order or non-molestation order (s 46) and it may be that sometimes, when a respondent is brought to court, he sees the error of his ways and is prepared to give such an undertaking rather than have an order made against him. No power of arrest can be attached to an undertaking (s 46(2)), and so a court cannot accept an undertaking from a respondent if it would otherwise have had the grounds for attaching a power of arrest to the non-molestation or occupation order. By virtue of s 47, if the court makes such an order and the respondent has used or threatened violence against the applicant or child, then a power of arrest must be attached, unless the court is satisfied that in all the circumstances the applicant and child will be adequately protected without one. This makes it much more likely that a power of arrest will be attached than under the old law, and the facts in the present case seem to indicate that a power of arrest is likely to be attached, given the violence and continuing threats.

It is unlikely that the facts of this case justify the draconian measure of applying for the orders *ex parte*, and it does not seem likely that the s 45 criteria will be met unless there is the threat of immediate harm to Heidi and the baby. This will mean that Ian will have notice of Heidi's applications, and be able to make his own representations as to why an order should not be made.

(b)  If Heidi and Ian are not married, then Heidi cannot have matrimonial home rights in relation to the flat, and she would only be entitled to occupy the flat if she too were a tenant. Even then, she would have no right to exclude a joint tenant: *Ainsbury v Millington* (1987). Consequently, Heidi would need to use the provisions of the **Family Law Act 1996** to seek an occupation order in relation to the flat, and a non-molestation order in relation to her and the baby. Heidi and Ian are still associated persons by virtue of being persons who are or who have been living together as husband and wife, and the baby is still a relevant child.

To apply for an occupation order, it would be necessary to see if Heidi and Ian are 'entitled' persons. Clearly, Ian as the tenant is an entitled respondent, but it is not clear whether Heidi is an entitled applicant. If she is also the tenant then she would be entitled within s 33(1) and the earlier discussion on the occupation order under s 33 would apply. However, if Heidi is not entitled to occupy the flat by virtue of a beneficial estate, interest or contract, or any enactment giving her the right to remain in occupation, then s 33 will not apply.

Instead, she will only be allowed to apply for an occupation order against a respondent who is or was a spouse or cohabitant. Ian falls into this category, and so the application will be made under s 36 since Ian and Heidi were cohabitants rather than spouses. The order, if granted, will not only allow her to occupy, but will expressly grant her the right to occupy, which she otherwise would not have.

In making an occupation rights order, the court will take all the circumstances of the case into account, including the housing needs and resources of the parties and any relevant child; the financial resources of the parties; the likely effect on the health, safety and well-being of the parties and relevant child of any order or no order being made; the conduct of the parties in relation to each other and otherwise; the nature of the relationship; the length of time they have lived together as husband and wife; whether there are any children; the time that has passed since they lived together; and the existence of any proceedings between the parties under the **Children Act 1989** or in relation to ownership of property.

In this case Heidi and Ian have cohabited, but as both are still only 19, this will not have been for a particularly lengthy period. They have a child, and Ian has been violent and threatening. Clearly, both Ian and Heidi need a home, and as Heidi is staying in what appears to be unsatisfactory living accommodation with her mother, it seems likely that the court would be prepared to grant her occupation rights in respect of the rented flat.[7]

In addition, the court can make a regulatory order in respect of the flat whereby Ian's occupation right will be restricted or suspended, or he may be required to leave the flat or area in which it is situated. The factors influencing the court in determining whether to make such an order are the housing needs and resources of the parties; their financial resources; the effect of any order or failure to make an order on the health, safety or well-being of the parties or relevant child; the conduct of the parties in relation to each other and otherwise; the likelihood of significant harm to the applicant or child if no order is made; and the likelihood of significant harm to the respondent if an order is made.

On the facts, the needs of Heidi and the baby would seem to take priority, as they will suffer significant harm if Ian is allowed to remain in the flat, whereas Ian will suffer the inconvenience of having to rehouse himself if an order is made. Consequently, an order is likely to be made, but the order is limited to six months' duration, and can only be extended once further in the case of cohabitants. Thus, this would provide some interim

7    There is no equivalent provision to s 33(7) in s 36 and therefore nothing that might potentially create a presumption in favour of an order.

protection for Heidi and the baby, but would not give a longer period of protection which she might have obtained had she been married.

The same provisions in **s 42** regarding non-molestation orders would apply to Heidi as a cohabitant in the same way as it did if Heidi were married to Ian. The two would still be associated persons by virtue of having lived together as husband and wife, and the baby would still be a relevant child. Thus, there is no distinction in relation to protection from molestation between spouses and cohabitants, but it can be seen that a cohabitant can be at a disadvantage when seeking occupation of the home.

### Common Pitfalls

In a problem question be sure that you identify which is the most appropriate order and why, and if you decide that an occupation order should be applied for, be clear whether the applicant is entitled or not and therefore under which section she or he will apply.

### Aim Higher

Extra marks can be gained through good understanding of the statute and case law, especially the different approaches adopted by the courts to the balance of harm test.

# QUESTION 31

Julie has been living with Darren for the past year in a house owned by Darren. Julie has just given birth to a baby boy, Billy, and she has a daughter, Gemma, by a previous partner, Rick. Rick was violent to Julie and Gemma and has written several threatening letters to Julie from jail. Rick is due to be released from jail presently.

(a)   What, if anything, can Julie do to try to protect herself and her family from Rick?
(b)   Julie has been told by her friend that as she is Darren's common law wife, there is no need for her to get married in order to be able to stay in the home. Is this correct?

## How to Answer this Question

(a)   Consider non-molestation orders under the **Family Law Act 1996 s 42**:
  ❖   possibility of power of arrest;
  ❖   *ex parte* application?
(b)   Explain concept of matrimonial home rights that exist for spouses but not cohabitants:
  ❖   look at occupation orders for entitled and non-entitled applicants.
Note that this question does not just concern domestic violence, but also property law.

## Applying the Law

Part a – domestic violence powers under the FLA 1996.

Part b – property rights for married and non-married couples.

## ANSWER

(a) In order to determine whether Julie can apply for a non-molestation order under **s 42** against Rick, it is necessary to consider whether Julie and Rick are associated persons within the definition in the **Family Law Act 1996 s 62**. Persons are associated if they are or have been married. There is no evidence of such a relationship here.

They will also be associated if they are or were cohabitants, that is, lived together in the same household as husband and wife. This may have been the case here, or the couple may merely have lived in the same household, and be associated by virtue of this. Rick and Julie are not relatives, but they are the parents of the same child, and this would suffice to make them associated within the **Family Law Act 1996 s 62(3)(f)**.

Gemma is clearly a relevant child within s 62(2) as she is a child living with a party to the proceedings, as is Billy, even though he is not Rick's child. Consequently, Julie can seek a non-molestation order in respect of herself and both of her children. However, Darren cannot be protected by an order applied for by Julie, and would need to make his own application. He could face difficulty in doing this because there is no evidence that he and Rick are associated persons. They have never lived in the same household, and the only other possibility is that they both have or had parental responsibility in relation to the same child. If Julie and Rick were married then Rick would have had parental responsibility for Gemma, but if they were not married then only Julie would have parental responsibility for Gemma. There is no indication that Darren has parental responsibility for Gemma, and so no non-molestation order can be made under the Act in relation to Darren.[8]

Julie can seek a non-molestation order against Rick as a freestanding application; she does not need to be taking any other family proceedings. The court has a discretion whether or not to make the order and will look at all the circumstances of the case, including the need to secure the health, safety and well-being of the applicant and the two relevant children. There is no requirement that the respondent has to have been violent; the order can be widely drafted to afford protection not just from violence but from pestering and harassment, and can specifically forbid letters and other attempts at communication. Clearly, Rick's violent past and present vindictive campaign would indicate a need for a non-molestation order to be made in order to safeguard Julie and the children.

The order can be for a limited time or until further order (s 42(7)). It is possible for the court to accept an undertaking from respondents instead of making an occupation order or non-molestation order (s 46), but no power of arrest can be attached to an undertaking (s 46(2)). Consequently, a court cannot accept an undertaking from a respondent if it would otherwise have had the grounds for attaching a power of arrest to the non-molestation or occupation order. By virtue of s 47, if the court makes a non-molestation order and the respondent has used or threatened violence against the applicant or child, then a power of arrest must be attached unless the court is satisfied that in all the circumstances the applicant and child will be adequately protected without one. This makes it much more likely that a power of arrest will be attached than under the old law, and it seems that the facts in the present case indicate that a power of arrest is likely to be attached, given the past violence perpetrated by Rick and his continuing threats.

Since Rick is still in jail and unable to actually harm Julie or the children until his release, it seems unlikely that an *ex parte* order will be necessary. If, however, Rick's release were imminent, and Julie needed immediate protection, an *ex parte* order could be obtained if

---

8    As Darren's situation illustrates, although the definition of associated person is broad, it will not cover every individual who might be affected by domestic violence.

it would be just and convenient to do so (s 45). It would be necessary to stress the threat of harm to Julie if the order were not made immediately, although a full hearing would be ordered later, at which point Rick could make representations.

(b) Darren is the sole legal and beneficial owner of the home in which he, Julie and the children live. As such, Julie, as a cohabitant, has no right to remain without Darren's permission unless she obtains a court order. If Julie were to marry Darren she would acquire matrimonial home rights under the Family Law Act 1996 s 30. These are defined in s 30(2) as the right not to be evicted or excluded from the home unless by court order, and the right, if not in occupation, to enter and occupy with a court order. These rights exist in relation to any dwelling house that is or was intended to be the joint home of the parties. This means that Darren could not evict her unless he obtained a court order permitting him to do that, and it also means that Julie would be an entitled applicant in any proceedings she might bring to have Darren excluded from the home.

A person with matrimonial home rights can also pay rent or mortgage or other household outgoings, and this has the same effect as if made by the other spouse. This gives a measure of protection, in that she can continue to pay rent or mortgage payments, and if she does so and the mortgagee brings proceedings against her spouse, she can apply to be made a party to those proceedings. There is also protection, in that occupation by a spouse with matrimonial home rights is treated for the purpose of the Rent Acts and Housing Acts as occupation by the other spouse. Matrimonial home rights are also registrable as a notice on the register for registered land and as a Class F land charge for unregistered land, thus giving a measure of protection against subsequent purchasers of the home.

If the relationship between Julie and Darren were to deteriorate then it may be necessary for Julie to seek to occupy the home with the children and to have Darren excluded. If Julie were to marry Darren, then, even though the house is solely owned by him, she would be an entitled applicant by virtue of her matrimonial home rights (s 33(1)). The court would have jurisdiction to make an order in respect of the house since it is, or has been, or was intended to be, the home of Julie and Darren, with whom she is associated by virtue of marriage (s 62(3)(a)). The court can enforce Julie's right of occupation and can restrict or suspend Darren's rights and require him to leave the house or part of the house or area in which the house is situated. These regulatory orders are then considered in the light of the circumstances of the case, including the housing needs and resources of the parties; their financial resources; the likely effect of any order or failure to make an order on the health, safety or well-being of the parties or relevant child; and the conduct of the parties in relation to each other and otherwise. The court can then exercise its discretion over whether to make an order.

If, however, under s 33(7) it appears that the applicant or relevant child is likely to suffer significant harm attributable to the conduct of the respondent if the order is not made, then the court must make an order, unless the respondent or relevant child is likely to suffer equal or greater significant harm if the order is made. This requires the court to, first, consider whether there is the likelihood of significant harm, and then balance the harm of making an order with the harm of not making an order. In *B v B* (1999), a woman left her violent husband and his child, taking her baby daughter with her. She applied for an occupation order, and the case was a significant harm case under **s 33(7)**. However, the balance of harm test meant that the husband and his child were permitted to remain in the home, as the husband's child would suffer more harm if the order were made than the wife and six-month-old baby would if no order were made.

Harm is defined in **s 63** to mean ill-treatment or impairment of mental or physical health with the additional criteria of impairment of development for a child. Ill-treatment includes both physical and sexual abuse in relation to a child, and development is widely defined to include physical, emotional, intellectual, social or behavioural development. The concept of 'significant' is likely to mean considerable or important, if guidance in earlier cases on the meaning of such wording in other statutes is followed: *Humberside County Council v B* (1993). Thus, depending on what Darren does and its effect on Julie and the children, the court may be forced to make an occupation order.

If an order is made, it can be for a specified period, or until an event takes place, or until further court order. It remains to be seen whether the new Act will result in courts departing from their previous view that excluding spouses with property interests should only be a short-term measure.

If Julie does not marry Darren, and merely continues to live with him, her status as a so-called 'common law wife' does not put her in the same position as an actual spouse. As already indicated, she has no matrimonial home rights, and since she has no other interest or rights in the house, she is not an entitled applicant under **s 33**. She and Darren are, or have been, cohabitants living together as man and wife (**s 62(3)(b)**). Any application by Julie to occupy the home and have Darren excluded would fall to be determined under the **Family Law Act 1996 s 36**. This would require the court to first consider the making of an occupation rights order, giving Julie the right to occupy the home, and then to make a regulatory order excluding Darren.

In making an occupation rights order, the court will take all the circumstances of the case into account, including the housing needs and resources of the parties and any relevant child; the financial resources of the parties; the likely effect on the health, safety and well-being of the parties and relevant child of any order or no order being made; the conduct of the parties in relation to each other and otherwise; the nature of the relationship, the length of time they have lived together as husband and wife; whether there are any children; the time that has passed since they lived together; and the existence of any proceedings between the parties under the **Children Act 1989** or in relation to ownership of property (**s 36(6)**).

Thus, it can be seen that the cohabiting nature of the relationship does not carry the same weight as a marriage would, and specific regard is had to the length and nature of the cohabiting relationship.

If an occupation order is made, then the court can make a regulatory order excluding Darren from the home or restricting his occupation. The factors influencing the court in determining whether to make such an order are the housing needs and resources of the parties; their financial resources; the effect of any order or failure to make an order on the health, safety or well-being of the parties or relevant child; the conduct of the parties in relation to each other and otherwise; the likelihood of significant harm to the applicant or child if no order is made; and the likelihood of significant harm to the respondent if an order is made. With non-entitled cohabitants, unlike the position with entitled applicants, there is no compulsion to make an order on the basis of a risk of significant harm. This puts cohabitants at a disadvantage over spouses who will usually be entitled applicants by virtue of their matrimonial home rights.

If occupation orders are made for non-entitled cohabitants under s 36, they can only last for an initial period of six months with the possibility of a further six month extension on one occasion only. This contrasts with the position of an entitled applicant who may well be given an order of unlimited duration.

Thus it can be seen that whilst there is little difference in treatment between spouses and cohabitants for non-molestation orders, the spouse gets more favourable treatment in relation to occupation of the home than those who do not marry.

# QUESTION 32

Amy married Ben two years ago after her marriage to Charles had ended in divorce. She did not obtain any substantial financial settlement as Charles was a penniless destitute. After their marriage, Amy and Ben lived together in the matrimonial home which Ben had bought in his name ten years ago. Amy's two children, Diana and Edward, aged eight and six respectively, also lived with the couple.

As time has gone on, Amy has become increasingly bad-tempered with Ben and the children, although she has never actually been violent. She has joined a very extreme religious cult and, since Ben disapproves of it, she has become increasingly critical of his 'heathen influence' on the children. Amy has frequently criticised Ben in front of the children, becoming hysterical if he denies any of her suggestions. On one occasion, Ben slapped Amy whilst she was hysterical. Ben is very fond of the children, who view him as their father, since they have had little or no contact with their birth father, Charles, since they were babies.

Five weeks ago, Amy told Ben during the course of a heated argument that she was no longer prepared to allow him to corrupt her children and, against Ben's wishes, she left, taking the children with her. They are all now staying with Amy's parents, Fred and Gertie, in their cramped council flat.

Amy has since confronted Ben, saying that their relationship is over, but that she will never divorce him for religious reasons. She told him to leave the matrimonial home so that she could return with the children, and she is adamant that he cannot remain.

Ben is very unhappy and does not want to leave his home. He still loves Amy and believes that it is the influence of the cult that is causing her to behave like this. Amy has threatened court action, and Ben seeks advice as to what Amy might achieve by this.

▶ Advise Ben on his legal position under the **Family Law Act 1996**.

## How to Answer this Question

❖   The position under the Family Law Act 1996
❖   Amy has matrimonial home rights under s 30
❖   She can only exclude Ben by obtaining an occupation order under s 33
❖   Examine the factors in s 33(6) and s 33(7)
❖   Are there any grounds for seeking a non-molestation order under s 42?

This is slightly different from the usual domestic violence question in that the student is advising the defendant.

## Applying the Law

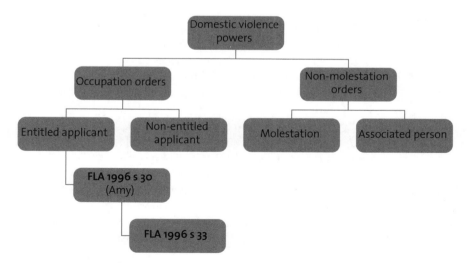

*The application of domestic violence powers in this answer is illustrated here.*

# ANSWER

The **Family Law Act 1996 Part IV** has made wide-ranging changes to the mechanisms by which occupation of the home and issues of domestic violence will be resolved. Whilst many of the principles of the pre-Family Law Act law are retained, many of the problems identified in the law have been addressed, and the simplification of the law into one enactment is a significant improvement.[9]

In this case, Ben is the legal owner of the dwelling house, and since Amy has no legal or beneficial interest, she is given matrimonial home rights under **s 30**. These are defined in **s 30(2)** to mean the right not to be excluded or evicted from the dwelling house by the other spouse except by court order under **s 33**, and the right to enter and occupy the home with leave from the court, if not in occupation. Amy is not occupying the home at present, but the dwelling house was at one stage the matrimonial home, and so **s 30** applies. Consequently, the issue of whether Amy can return and exclude Ben from the home will need to be resolved by the court under its powers in **s 33** to make occupation orders.

Amy is an entitled applicant by virtue of her matrimonial home rights in respect of the dwelling house (**s 33**). Ben would also be an entitled applicant if he were to apply for an occupation order excluding Amy as he has the beneficial estate or interest in the home. The court can have jurisdiction to make a **s 33** occupation order if the dwelling house is, has been or was intended to be the home of the applicant and another person with whom the applicant is associated. The concept of associated person is defined in **s 62(3)**. Ben and Amy are clearly associated persons on the basis of their marriage. The court can, therefore, make an order regulating the occupation of the home. These orders can allow a person to remain in occupation, or to enter and occupy the home or part of it. It is also possible to prohibit the respondent from exercising his right to occupy, and require him to leave the home, or part of it, or the area in which it is situated.

Whether an order will be made in Amy and Ben's case and the type of any order depends on the application of the factors in **s 33(6)**. These require the court to take into account all the circumstances of the case, including the housing needs and resources of the parties and any relevant child, the financial resources of the parties, the likely effect of any order or non-exercise of powers by the court on the health, safety or well-being of the parties and any relevant child, and the conduct of the parties in relation to each other and otherwise. The court can exercise its powers to make or refuse an order in such cases. In some cases the court has no choice, and is compelled to make an order. These are the so-called 'significant harm cases'. The court is required to make an order under **s 33(7)** if it appears that the applicant or relevant child is likely to suffer significant harm attributable

---

9   In an exam with limited time, a general introduction like this is not necessary and in a coursework answer with a limited amount of words, this general introduction could also be sensibly reduced.

to the conduct of the respondent if the order is not made, unless the respondent or relevant child is likely to suffer equal or greater significant harm if the order is made. This requires the court to balance the harm done by making the order with that of not making the order to the respective parties and the relevant children.[10] The concept of relevant child is explained in s 62(2). Both Diana and Edward are relevant children since they live with Amy, even though they are not Ben's natural children.

To see whether the court is compelled to make an order or whether it has a choice, it will be necessary to examine the concept of significant harm as it applies to Amy, Ben and the children. Harm is defined in the **Family Law Act 1996 s 63** to mean ill-treatment or impairment of mental or physical health for an adult or child and the additional criterion of impairment of development for a child. Ill-treatment is not confined to physical ill-treatment and can include sexual abuse in relation to a child. Development means physical, intellectual, emotional, social or behavioural development. In the present case, it would be necessary to consider whether the impact of an order or lack of one would affect the parties or children in a way that can constitute significant, that is, considerable and important, harm. Ben's isolated act of violence, whilst not to be condoned, is unlikely to be repeated and, therefore, it seems likely that Amy would be unable to show that the risk from not making the order would be the likelihood of significant harm to her or the children. Clearly the living conditions for her and the children are far from desirable, but there is little to suggest that excluding Ben would achieve anything other than to cause him inconvenience and difficulty. Amy cannot demonstrate a threat to her health, and so the court will not be compelled to make an order. Instead it will look at the factors in s 33(6) to see whether or not to make an order.

Both parties need homes, Amy needs adequate accommodation for her and the children, and this need is not really being met by the cramped conditions at her parents. Ben also needs somewhere to live, and if evicted he would not, as a single person, be a priority for local authority housing, although he may have more flexibility if he has income to pay rent in the short term. If the children were to live with Ben, this would increase his claim to remain in the home, but the presence of the children with Amy strengthens her claim to be able to enter and occupy. There is little evidence of detriment to Amy's health or that of the children if an order were not made, and although Ben has been violent once, his conduct has otherwise been good. Amy, on the other hand, has behaved in an extremely provocative manner and has contributed significantly to her own misfortunes. It may be that the court would be reluctant to exclude Ben without evidence that this is really essential. If an order were to be made, it can be for a specified time, or until an event takes place or until a further court order (s 33(10)). It remains to be seen whether

. . . . . . . . . . . . . . . . . . . . . . . . . . . . . . . . . . . . . . . . . . . . . . . . . . . . . . . . . . . . . . . . . . . . . . . . . . . . . . . . . . . . . . . . . .

10  Under **s 33(7)** if the applicant or a relevant child is suffering or is likely to suffer significant harm, then there is a presumption in favour of an order being made; the respondent must convince the court that (s)he would suffer greater harm were an order to be made than the applicant would suffer were the order not to be made.

the court will vary its practice under the old law of viewing exclusion of the spouse with the property interests as a short-term measure.

If an occupation order is made in relation to the dwelling house, either to let Amy occupy, or to exclude Ben or Amy, then the court has power to make ancillary orders under s 40(1) to order either party to pay the rent, mortgage, repairs or other outgoings on the property; or to pay the non-occupying party compensation for the loss of their right to occupy; or to make orders in respect of the furniture. The test as to whether such an order should be made is to consider all the circumstances of the case including the financial needs, resources and obligations of the parties (s 40(2)). There is no evidence regarding these matters in the present case, but if Amy has no resources it will not be possible to order her to make any such payments, although she can be required to take good care of the furniture.

It may also be possible for either Ben or Amy to apply to the court for a non-molestation order (s 42). This prohibits the respondent from molesting a person who is associated with the respondent or who is a relevant child. As explained earlier, Amy and Ben are associated within s 62, and the children are relevant children. The order can be made on application in any family proceedings or as a freestanding application, or can be made by the court of its own motion.This means that the application can be made by the parties as an adjunct to the application for an occupation order, or the order can be made regardless of the fact that no application was made, if the court considers it necessary. Family proceedings are defined in s 63, and include applications under the **Family Law Act 1996 Part IV**.

In deciding whether to make an order the court would take into account all the circumstances of the case, including the need to ensure the safety, well-being and health of the applicant or relevant child. The term molestation is not defined in the Act, but would include conduct which is not necessarily violent, such as harassment and pestering, as in the old law. Ben has behaved violently on one occasion, but it was the result of prolonged provocation by Amy, and was limited. Amy, on the other hand, has behaved in a way that could be argued to amount to harassment. It would be difficult to justify a non-molestation order being made here, but if one were to be made, it could be made in general terms, or be more specific and prohibit certain behaviour (s 42(6)). The order may last for a limited period of time, or until a further order (s 42(7)).

This is not a case of extreme urgency where it would be just and convenient to grant an *ex parte* order (s 45(1)), and so Ben should receive notice of any application that Amy wishes to make, and must be prepared to marshal his arguments as to why an occupation order or non-molestation order should not be made. Since Ben has used or threatened violence against the applicant, Amy, there is the risk that the court could attach a power of arrest to any order it makes (s 47(3)). However, the second requirement – that there is a risk of significant harm to the applicant or relevant child if the power of arrest is not immediately attached – is extremely unlikely to be satisfied in Ben's case. It may be that Ben could avoid an order being made by giving an undertaking not to be violent again, under s 46, although undertakings are only possible in cases where there are no grounds to attach a power of arrest (s 46(3)).

In conclusion, Amy's arguments and claims against Ben seem somewhat flimsy and may not justify the making of an occupation order in her favour. If any order were to be made, given the circumstances, it is likely to be short term, to avoid the overcrowding until Amy can be re-housed. A non-molestation order does not seem necessary.

# Parental Responsibility and Private Law Disputes Relating to Children

**7**

## INTRODUCTION

The **Children Act 1989** revolutionised the way in which disputes concerning the upbringing of children should be handled by the courts. It also helped shift the emphasis away from parental rights and towards the concept of parental responsibility. The Act further introduced the statutory non-interventionist policy (**Children Act 1989 s 1(4)**) and recognised the need to avoid delay (**Children Act 1989 s 1(2)**).

## CONTENTS OF PARENTAL RESPONSIBILITY

Parental responsibility is defined as the rights and responsibilities that a parent has in relation to a child. Although there is no list of what this includes, students should know what sorts of decisions are included within parental responsibility. Often exam questions will focus on whether a carer with parental responsibility can take a decision without the agreement of other carers with parental responsibility, and students should be aware that for most decisions there is no duty to consult, let alone obtain agreement. The statutory exceptions to this change of surname and removal from the jurisdiction are dealt with in **s 13**. The rights of the carer without parental responsibility are set out in **s 3(5)**. Another issue is how parental responsibility can be reconciled with the rights and increasing autonomy of the older child (*Gillick v West Norfolk and Wisbech AHA* (1986)).

## ACQUISITION OF PARENTAL RESPONSIBILITY

### The Child's Mother

The child's mother automatically has parental responsibility whether the child's parents are married or not. If the parents are married it is under **s 2(1)** of the **Children Act 1989** and if the parents are unmarried it is under **s 2(2)** of the **Children Act 1989**. The law considers the child's mother to be the woman who has given birth to the child.

### The Child's Father

Whether the child's father has parental responsibility automatically depends on whether the child's parents are married. A husband is presumed to be the father of any children born to his wife during the marriage and under **s 2(1)** of the **Children Act 1989** he automatically has parental responsibility for these children.

In contrast, the unmarried father will only get parental responsibility if he has signed a parental responsibility order with the mother (**Children Act 1989 s 4(1)(b)**), or if he has been granted it by the court (**Children Act 1989 s 4(1)(c)**), or following the introduction of the **Adoption and Children Act 2002** if he has been registered or re-registered as the child's father.

# The Parental Responsibility of Step-parents and Others

As for step-parents, they can gain parental responsibility by adopting the child, through a residence order or through a parental responsibility agreement (with both the child's birth parents agreeing), or through a court order to award parental responsibility. If the child was conceived after 6/4/2009, the lesbian partner of the birth mother may be the legal parent (**Human Fertilisation and Embryology Act 2008**).

Other non-parents can gain parental responsibility through a residence order (**Children Act 1989 s 8**), through adoption, or through a special guardianship order. Finally, the local authority will have parental responsibility for the child following an emergency protection order (**s 44(4)(c)**) or following a care order (**s 33(3)(a)**).

Often more than one person will hold parental responsibility for the child; however, with the exception of adoption, a person will not lose parental responsibility just because another person has gained it.

# THE PRINCIPLES OF THE CHILDREN ACT 1989

The main principle of the **Children Act 1989** is that the child's welfare is paramount (**s 1(1)**). This principle must be applied by the court in any question relating to the child's upbringing. If the court is deciding whether to make a **s 8** order, it will be guided by the checklist in **s 1(3)** to decide what is in the child's welfare (**s 1(4)**). Often exam questions will involve applying this checklist and identifying the factors that are relevant. In doing this, students should pay proper attention to previous case law.

**Section 1** also states that delay is harmful to the welfare of the child and that an order should only be made if it produces a benefit for the child.

# SECTION 8 ORDERS

Disputes about children often relate to whether a **s 8** order should be made. The **s 8** orders are:

❖ Residence orders – this determines where the child lives. In recent years a leading issue has been the use of shared residence (*Re K (Shared Residence Order)* [2008] EWCA Civ s 26, *N A (Joint Residence: Parental Responsibility)* [2008] EWCA Civ 867, *T v T* [2010]).
❖ Contact orders – this order requires the person with whom the child lives to allow the holder of a contact order to have contact with the child. Case law on contact

orders often relates to contact and domestic violence and contact and implacable hostility (*S (A Child)* (2010)).

❖ Specific issue order – under this order a parent can be required to exercise their parental responsibility in a particular way.

❖ Prohibited steps order – under this order a parent can be prohibited from exercising their parental responsibility in a particular way.

In answering a problem question on **s 8** orders, it is first necessary to determine whether the applicant has a right to apply for that **s 8** order (**Children Act 1989 s 10(4), s 10(5)**) or whether the leave of the court is required (**Children Act s 10(9), s 10(10)**).

# QUESTION 33

Rupert and Sally married ten years ago and have three children, William, aged eight, and twins, Polly and Molly, aged five. William has excelled at school and has been offered a scholarship at a private boarding school that specialises in the education of gifted children. Rupert is delighted, as he went to boarding school himself, but Sally is unhappy about William going away to school at such a young age, and is opposed to private education for political reasons. Polly has recently been diagnosed as having a rare form of leukaemia, and her best chance of survival is to receive a bone marrow transplant. The family have all been tested, and Molly is the closest match. The operation to donate bone marrow carries a slight risk to Molly, but the doctors are confident that it could be successful. Rupert is keen that the transplant goes ahead, but Sally has religious objections to such surgery.

▶ **Advise Rupert as to what he can do, given that he and Sally disagree on what should be done for the children.**

## How to Answer this Question

Begin by explaining parental responsibility, and who has it in relation to these children. Also consider what each parent can do to fulfil this responsibility.

Then outline the various **s 8** orders available, and whether application may be made as of right or with leave. The general policy of non-intervention and the delay factor should be mentioned.

In relation to children's schooling:

❖ the welfare principle;
❖ the **s 1(3)** checklist and relevant discussion of the factors.

In relation to the medical treatment:

❖ the welfare principle;
❖ the **s 1(3)** checklist and the difficulty of non-therapeutic medical care.

## Applying the Law

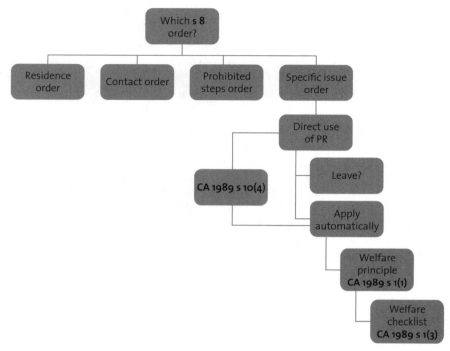

This diagram shows how the **Children Act 1989 s 8** relates to parental responsibility and the welfare principle in this scenario.

# ANSWER

Rupert is the father of the three children concerned, and since he is married to their mother, Sally, he has parental responsibility for his children (**Children Act 1989 s 2(1)**). Sally, as their mother, also has parental responsibility, which is defined in the **Children Act 1989 s 3(1)** as 'all the rights, duties, powers and responsibilities and authority which by law a parent of a child has in relation to the child and its property'. This concept emphasises the obligations of both Rupert and Sally to care for and to nurture their child, providing it with a stable and loving background in which it can mature to a responsible adult. Parents do not own children, and it is clear from the **Children Act 1989** that the paramount consideration will always be the welfare of the child in issues concerning her upbringing: **s 1(1)**. Thus it is immaterial what the parents want; unless their wishes accord with the child's interests, their wishes will be disregarded in any court order.

In normal everyday situations, both parents exercise parental responsibility, and each can do so independently of the other: s 2(7) The old parental veto that existed before the **Children Act 1989** has gone, and consequently either Rupert or Sally, or both, can act to discharge their parental responsibility and make decisions in relation to the child. However, in the present case, it is unlikely that William could be sent away to school, or the twins operated on, just on Rupert's instructions.

There is obviously an enormous difference of opinion between Rupert and Sally as to what should happen to their children. There is no evidence that the couple will be divorcing, or taking any other family proceedings, so both have the option of making an application for one or more of the orders in the **Children Act 1989 s 8** the relevant orders being the prohibited steps order and the specific issue order. A specific issue order is the mechanism whereby a party can raise a particular issue and seek the court's ruling and guidance on the matter. A prohibited steps order prohibits the taking of 'a step which might be taken by a parent in meeting his parental responsibility'. It would seem that if Sally were to apply she would want to prohibit William being sent to school or the transplant from Molly to Polly; whereas Rupert would want to enable these steps to be taken and might seek a specific issue order. Regardless of who makes the application, the principles to be applied by the court are the same.[1]

As parents, both Rupert and Sally can apply as of right for such orders: **Children Act 1989 s 10(4)** In dealing with such an application, the court must take into account the non-interventionist policy in s 1(5) This requires the court to refrain from making an order unless making an order is better than not making one. This emphasises the commitment of the Act to encouraging agreement and conciliation rather than acrimonious litigation. Unfortunately, Rupert and Sally are too far apart to reach agreement, and as these issues are of enormous importance, it would seem likely that the court's intervention is justified.

Once the court becomes involved in a s 8 application, it must lay down a timetable to ensure that the proceedings continue as quickly as possible: s 11 Delay is regarded as 'likely to prejudice the welfare of the child' (s 1(2)), and so these proceedings will need to be determined as a matter of urgency given the need for medical treatment in the case of the twins and for William to progress with his education.

---

1   Note that a specific issue order and a prohibited steps order should not be used where a contact or residence order would be effective. In any problem involving s 8 orders, it is a good idea to adopt the approach taken here:
(1) Identify which is the most suitable s 8 order and explain why.
(2) Can the applicant apply for that s 8 order or does (s)he need leave and if leave is needed, would it be granted?
(3) Applying the principles of the **Children Act 1989** and in particular the welfare principle as interpreted by the welfare checklist, would the order be made.

In determining the **s 8** application, the court must consider the statutory checklist in **s 1(3)** of the Act. The child's welfare is, as ever, the paramount consideration in matters concerning its upbringing (**s 1(1)**), and therefore the guiding principle will be to serve the child's best interests, not necessarily those of the parents.

The controversy concerning William's schooling needs to be resolved and the starting point will be to consider William's wishes. The facts do not disclose whether he is keen to go away to school, or whether he would rather remain at home and go to a local school. As a gifted child, it may be that William has a greater understanding and maturity than the average eight-year-old, and so his wishes would be considered. However, it is unlikely that he will have reached the point whereby his opinion would be decisive. This has generally been accorded to teenagers (*Stewart v Stewart* (1973)), as they are likely to appreciate the long-term consequences of their decisions. In *Marsh v Marsh* (1977) the views of an eight-year-old girl were not decisive, but William is more articulate than most eight-year-olds. If he has been pressurised or 'coerced' by either parent, then his views may be disregarded: *Re S (Infants)* (1967).[2]

The physical, emotional and educational needs of the child must also be considered. Eight years old is very young to go away to school, but many English schoolchildren are sent away to boarding school at that age, or even younger. Little is known of William's character other than that he is educationally gifted. If he is an independent and confident child, he may be able to make the transition to boarding school very smoothly, but if he is more nervous he may find separation traumatic. More also needs to be known about his schooling; is he so gifted that he cannot benefit from ordinary schooling available locally? The courts place great store on the importance of education (*May v May* (1986)), and this may indicate which proposal is in William's best interests. Certainly his mother's political views are irrelevant as to what kind of education would most benefit this particular child. By being sent away to school, he will lose everyday contact with his sisters, but would still be able to see them during holidays and possibly weekends.

The effect on William of being sent away to school has already been considered and, looking at his age, sex, background and relevant characteristics, would require a consideration of the family expectations for William. If he has grown up in a family atmosphere where it was generally accepted that children would go away to school, then it is more likely that the court would agree with the boarding school option. If, however, the notion of sending a child away to school was alien to this family, then it may be too traumatic and difficult for William to adjust to. Rupert himself went away to school, but Sally is opposed to the idea, and much would depend on the kind of child William is.

....................................................................................................................

2    Be aware that applying the welfare principle and welfare checklist can be a delicate and uncertain exercise and you may struggle to reach a conclusion as to whether an order is in the child's welfare.

Looking at the issues regarding the medical treatment for the twins, it will be necessary to consider both Molly and Polly separately. Polly is seriously ill and it is part of the obligations of a parent to ensure that their child is properly cared for. Consent to medical treatment is needed, unless in an emergency, and so Polly's transfusion will need to be agreed, or ordered. Clearly, the transfusion is therapeutic in relation to Polly; without it she may die, with it she has a good chance of living. It is not clear whether Sally's objections are to Polly receiving the transplant, or to Molly being the donor, or to both. If there is disagreement over Polly's treatment, then again the court must be satisfied that making an order is better than not making one (s 1(5)) – the non-interventionist policy. Given the opposing views of the parents, it does seem that some intervention by the court will be necessary.

The welfare of Polly will be the paramount consideration (s 1(1)), and the court will need to consider whether it is in her best interests to have the treatment proposed in line with the s 1(3) guidelines. The child, at five, is probably too young to realise the implications of her decision, and so, although her wishes might be considered, they would probably not carry much weight. If there was evidence that she had been coerced by either parent, then the views would be disregarded: Re S (Infants) (1967). The physical, emotional and educational needs of the child would also be considered, and it is obvious that Polly is very sick and needs treatment. Whilst the courts might be sympathetic towards a parent whose child had undergone extensive painful treatment for a terminal condition when that parent wanted to choose for the child to die with dignity, the courts will usually order treatment if the child has a good chance of leading a life of some quality afterwards: Re B (1981). Polly does have a good chance with a transplant, and so treatment is likely to be ordered, even though Sally has religious objections. The courts will always put the physical need of the child above the religious or spiritual belief of the parent: Jane v Jane (1983). If nothing is done for Polly she will die, and the court will act to ensure that she receives treatment.

Nevertheless, in Re T (A Minor) (1996), the court upheld a mother's refusal to subject her child to a liver transplant. Without the transplant the child would die and there was a reasonable chance that with the transplant the child might live. However, the procedure was risky, involved extensive surgery and would have needed the wholehearted commitment of the mother in helping her child through the very painful procedure. The Court of Appeal felt that since the parents clearly loved their child, and were doing what they thought best, it would not be in the child's best interests to order major invasive surgery, which would require major commitment on the part of the mother to a procedure she firmly believed was not in her child's best interests. The court stressed that this was an unusual case, and did not abandon the usual presumption in favour of courses of action that would prolong life. In the present case there are distinguishing features, in that a bone marrow transplant, whilst a major procedure, may not be as extensive as a liver transplant. Also, in Re T neither parent felt strongly that the procedure should be carried out. If Rupert is close to his daughter and prepared to support her through her treatment, then the court will usually order the transplant.

The next issue is whether the transplant should come from Molly. Obviously, the operation is not strictly therapeutic in relation to Molly. She is healthy and does not need medical treatment. However, if no transplant takes place, her twin sister may die. Again, the parents' opposing views mean the court's intervention is justified, and the welfare of the child, Molly, must be the paramount consideration (s 1(1)). She is very young for her wishes to be accorded much weight, but, if it has been explained to her that she can help her sister but that she will need an operation, her attitude could be useful. If she is very unwilling, it will be harder to order the transplant than if she is keen to help her sister. Clearly, there is a slight risk to Molly, as there is in all medical and surgical procedures. But this risk of harm would have to be offset by the possible harm to her if her sister dies. For twins, the trauma of the death of one twin is very great, and it may be that emotionally Molly would benefit from trying to assist Polly. The court has a difficult balancing exercise, but if the statistical chances of complications are fewer, then the transplant will probably be ordered. It does not place Molly under any continuing disability since the bone marrow deficiency will be made up quickly.[3]

In *Re R* (1993), the court suggested that applications concerning medical treatment for children should always be made to a High Court judge. Before the **Children Act 1989**, such applications were usually by way of invoking the inherent jurisdiction of the High Court to make the child a ward of court. In *Re O (A Minor) (Medical Treatment)* (1993), this use of wardship was approved of, but in *Re R* (1993) the court suggested that a s 8 order was nevertheless the appropriate way to proceed. In *Re CT* (1993) it was stated that wardship was a residual jurisdiction that should only rarely be used when the s 8 orders were inadequate. Thus, it would be appropriate for all the issues regarding William, Polly and Molly to be resolved using the **Children Act 1989 s 8**, and not wardship. In *Re T (A Minor)* (1996) wardship was used as the applicant for the order for the transplant was not one of the parents.

# QUESTION 34

Samantha, aged 14, lived with her parents, Janet and John, and her younger brother, Martin, aged nine, in the family home. For some time, Samantha has been arguing with John, primarily about her attitude to school and her relationship with her boyfriend, Zak, aged 17. Last month, after yet another argument with her parents, Samantha left home and went to stay with Zak at Zak's mother's home. Zak's mother is rarely at home and has no objection to Samantha staying there, but Janet and John want their daughter to come home.

Samantha has refused to return, and has threatened her parents that she will 'divorce' them, as she has read of similar cases in the newspapers. She also tells them she is going to the family planning clinic to obtain the contraceptive pill.

▶ **Advise Janet and John as to whether Samantha can do this.**

........................................................................................................

3    Notice how in this scenario there is more than one child whose welfare needs to be considered.

## How to Answer this Question

❖ The concept of parental responsibility, how it may be exercised and by whom, must be considered.

❖ The difficulty of conflict between parent and child should be explored.

❖ The role of s 8 orders and the problem of leave for a child's application is then considered, with an account of the non-interventionist policy and approach to delay.

❖ First consider the welfare principle and the s 1(3) checklist as it applies to this girl.

❖ Rule out the use of wardship.

## Applying the Law

This diagram shows how parental responsibility in this scenario can be understood in relation to *sections 3 and 8* of the *Children Act 1989*, and the effect of key cases on this relationship.

# ANSWER

Janet and John are Samantha's parents and as such one or both of them will have parental responsibility for Samantha. Parental responsibility is defined in the **Children Act 1989 s 3(1)** as 'all the rights, duties, powers and responsibilities and authority which by law a parent of a child has in relation to the child and its property'. This concept is based on an obligation to nurture and care for a child, and replaces the somewhat possessory concept of parental rights, whereby some parents viewed their children as possessions to be controlled. There is, consequently, no automatic right for Janet and John to insist that their teenage daughter does as they say. Parental responsibility is borne by the natural mother of the child, and by the father if he was married to the mother at the time of the child's birth or conception: s 2(1). Janet definitely has parental responsibility, and John may also have it automatically if he is married to Janet.

There is clearly a conflict here between the views of Janet and John as to what is best for their daughter, and Samantha's own views. As Samantha is a 14-year-old teenager, she can no longer be physically controlled in the way that a young child can, and parents have to accept that as their child grows older they will do less controlling and more advising: *Gillick v W Norfolk and Wisbech Area Health Authority* (1985).[4] In this case, there is genuine concern on the part of the parents about the suitability of their daughter's living arrangements and her relationship with Zak. This relationship would seem to be sexual, or about to become so, given Samantha's comments about contraception, and it is a criminal offence to have sexual intercourse with a girl under 16, even if she is a willing participant. Janet and John are also concerned about Samantha's education which they have a duty to ensure she receives: the **Education Act 1944**. They could attempt to remove Samantha from Zak's home, but can only use reasonable force; if excessive force is used then there may be an assault (*R v Smith* (1985)). Ultimately, this might provoke Samantha into seeking assistance from the courts.

There is no automatic right for a child to apply for an order under the **Children Act 1989. Section 10(8)** of the Act specifies that a child will need leave from the court to apply for one of the range of orders in **s 8**, and leave will only be granted if the court is satisfied that the child has sufficient understanding to make the proposed application. Samantha may wish to apply for a residence order which would determine where she should live, a prohibited steps order to stop her parents removing her from Zak's home, and the issue of contraception could be raised as a specific issue order if still in dispute (**Children Act 1989 s 8**).

The court will look at Samantha's age, maturity and understanding before granting leave. A degree of conflict between teenagers and their parents is inevitable, and the courts have made it clear that the **Children Act 1989** is not to be used by any disgruntled

---

4    A child is '*Gillick* competent' to take decisions for themselves over things that are part of parental responsibility when the child is of sufficient understanding and maturity. It is judged on the individual child and whilst some will be *Gillick* competent at 14, others will not be.

teenager (*Re C (A Minor) (Leave to seek s 8 order)* (1994)). It should only be used where there is a genuine breakdown in the relationship between parent and child, and where there is such deep disharmony and mistrust that the court's intervention is necessary: *Re AD (A Minor)* (1993). Such applications are viewed as being serious and sensitive enough to warrant consideration by the High Court, and so Samantha's case, regardless of where it was commenced, would be determined by the High Court.

In *Re C (Residence: Child's Application for Leave)* (1995) the court held that in deciding whether to give leave for a child to make a a s 8 application, the child's interests are important, but are not the paramount consideration. The s 10 principles that apply when other people apply for leave do not apply to children where the consideration is whether the child has sufficient understanding. The court can also take into account the likelihood of the application succeeding. Here, the conflict is between Samantha and her parents, but the court cautioned in *Re C* about the detrimental effect of allowing a child to be a party to proceedings between arguing parents, where the child might hear evidence that could cause upset.[5]

Samantha is 14, and 14-year-old girls would normally have sufficient maturity to realise the long-term consequences of applying to live apart from their parents. The facts disclose that Samantha has not been doing well at school, but there is nothing to suggest that she is of below average intelligence. Her emotional maturity would need to be examined, but she seems to be exercising some degree of responsibility in seeking contraceptives, and it is likely that she is of sufficient maturity and understanding to be given leave to apply for a s 8 order. A 14-year-old's wishes were respected in a case involving education (*Re P (A Minor) (Education: Child's Wishes)* (1992)), and unless Samantha comes across in court as a petulant and stubborn child, it is likely she will be given leave to apply for a s 8 order.

In dealing with applications for s 8 orders, the court is required to take into account a number of important factors. The first of these is the non-interventionist policy (s 1(5)), which requires the court to consider whether making an order is better than not making any order. This is in line with the philosophy of the **Children Act 1989** which is to encourage consensus, with the court's involvement seen as a last resort. It would seem that Samantha's relationship with her parents has probably deteriorated beyond the point where they are able to reach agreement; they seem to be opposed to each other, and so in a contested s 8 application the court's involvement seems inevitable.

---

5    Note that the test for leave to apply for a **s 8** order is different if it is a child who is applying.

Once the court becomes involved, it must have regard to the fact that 'delay in determining the question is likely to prejudice the welfare of the child': s 1(2). It will therefore be necessary to ensure that the dispute over Samantha's upbringing is resolved as quickly as possible, and to ensure that this happens the court will draw up a timetable for the proceedings ( s 11).

In a disputed s 8 application, the court must also have regard to the statutory checklist in s 1(3). The **Children Act 1989 s 1(1)** makes the child's welfare the paramount consideration, and therefore this dispute will be resolved in the way in which Samantha's welfare is best served. The checklist in s 1(3) lists a number of factors that should be considered, and these will be examined in turn.

First, the ascertainable wishes and feelings of the child concerned (in the light of her age and understanding) will be examined. As explained earlier, a mature 14-year-old will usually be able to express her wishes sensibly, and will be able to make decisions in her long-term interest: *Stewart v Stewart* (1973). However, the cases where greatest credence has been given to the wishes of the child have involved a child having to choose between two suitable parents or family members. In the instant case, Samantha is choosing to live away from her parents at Zak's house. It is not clear whether she has a positive relationship with Zak's mother, and it may be argued that it is not in Samantha's long-term interests to effectively live with her 17-year-old boyfriend whilst she is still only 14. If it appears that pressure has been put on her by Zak, then her views may be discounted ( *Re S (Infants)* (1967)) if they are not in her long-term interests.

It will then be necessary to examine Samantha's physical, emotional and educational needs. She is still 14 years old, and has a need for a certain level of care and guidance. Zak's mother does not seem keen to play an active part in Samantha's upbringing, and she has a rather relaxed attitude that might not be in Samantha's best interests. The sexual nature of Samantha's relationship with Zak is something again that the court may be unwilling to condone positively by ordering that she, in effect, lives with him. Janet and John could also argue that they are able to provide a stable and caring home, and that Samantha has just been rebelling against their authority and trying to get her own way. By leaving to live with Zak, Samantha's relationship with her brother might suffer, and the courts take the view that siblings can offer each other support: *C v C* (1988). There is also genuine concern that Samantha's schooling will suffer if she lives with Zak since Zak's mother does not seem concerned to ensure Samantha goes to school. Education is viewed as important ( *May v May* (1986)) and the court will be unlikely to make a residence order if there will be a detrimental effect on Samantha's education.

The court will also look at the likely effect on Samantha of any change in her circumstances. It is considered undesirable to uproot children, since disrupting the status quo is often detrimental to the child's welfare: *J v C* (1970). However, Samantha has only been at Zak's for one month; it can hardly be said to be disruptive to return her to her parents. It would seem that her parents ought to be able to provide greater stability of care than Zak's mother, who does not seem very concerned for Samantha's welfare.

Looking at Samantha's age, sex, background and any characteristics of hers which the court considers relevant, it would seem that 14-year-old girls often have difficulty with their parents, yet are still in need of parental guidance. The next consideration is the harm that Samantha has suffered, or is at risk of suffering. There is no suggestion that Samantha has been harmed or abused by her parents, and this is to be contrasted with the evidence of the under-age intercourse she is having with Zak that a residence order would facilitate and condone.

The capacity of Samantha's parents and of any other relevant person to meet her needs would also be an important factor in determining where Samantha should live. Janet and John have discharged their parental responsibility towards Samantha in the past, and there is no evidence of any undesirable conduct or failings on their part. However, Samantha cannot be allowed to fend for herself; yet the consequences of allowing her to live at Zak's home would appear to be exactly that. Zak's mother is unconcerned about Samantha's welfare, and seems unlikely to make the positive contribution of alternative care in other cases. Zak is only 17, and it seems unlikely that he could promote Samantha's welfare.

Therefore, despite her wishes to live with Zak, the illegal nature of the sexual relationship and the apparent lack of concern for her welfare exhibited by Zak's mother mean it is extremely unlikely that Samantha would be able to obtain a residence order permitting her to live there.

However, the issue of contraception is likely to be resolved in Samantha's favour. In *Gillick*, the House of Lords recognised that whilst the law prohibited sexual intercourse with girls under 16, many such girls did engage in unlawful intercourse. A girl of sufficient maturity to have a sexual relationship and to seek contraceptive advice and services ought to be able to protect herself against pregnancy. It would not be in Samantha's best interests to prevent her from using contraception, as this would only lead to an unwanted pregnancy, which is hardly in the interests of the welfare of a girl of 14. This would give a competent child the right to consent to medical treatment against her parents' wishes; however, it seems that the *Gillick* decision has its limitations, and a *Gillick* competent child cannot refuse medical treatment that his or her parents consent to: *Re M (Medical Treatment: Consent)* (1999).

There is no point in trying to use the inherent jurisdiction of the High Court to make Samantha a ward of court. In *Re CT* (1993), it was stressed that wardship is exceptional and should only be used where the s 8 orders do not adequately cover the problem being experienced in relation to the child. The only possible justification for Samantha being warded would be if her parents wanted to prevent her association with Zak. It would have to be shown that this was an extremely undesirable relationship, which could not be dealt with by making a **s 8** order. If Samantha were to become a ward of court, then the court would have responsibility for her welfare and could deal not only with where she lived, but also provide continuous control and supervision to prevent undesirable relationships. Samantha's welfare would be the only consideration, but this is an extreme measure to take.

## Common Pitfalls

Many questions on private law and children will be based on applications for **s 8** orders. Identify which order best meets the applicant's needs and then decide whether they can apply of right or whether they need leave. In any application the child's welfare will be paramount and this will be assessed using the welfare checklist. Do not list or discuss every factor in the checklist but identify those which are most pertinent and apply them critically using case law to show how these issues are viewed by the courts.

## Aim Higher

Extra marks will be given for good critical understanding of how the child's welfare has been interpreted and also for a critical understanding of the limitations and difficulties of this as a test.

# QUESTION 35

Nina and Rob lived together for five years, during which time their children, Tara, now aged five, and John, now aged two, were born. Nina and Rob's relationship began to deteriorate last year, and they agreed to separate. Nina moved out of the home she shared with Rob, taking the two children to live in a house in the next village. Rob was a frequent visitor to see Nina and the children, and the relationship was amicable until Nina formed a relationship with Brad, a handsome young labourer. Rob was very jealous, and one night, after drinking heavily, he went to Nina's house and stabbed Brad to death. He was tried for murder, but convicted of manslaughter and sentenced to seven years' imprisonment.

Whilst Rob was on remand, Nina allowed Tara to visit her father on three occasions, but not John, who was only a baby. Nina wants nothing more to do with Rob, and does not want him to have anything to do with the children. Rob has written to her, demanding his 'parental rights'. She has also received a letter from Rob's mother, Jean, asking to see the children.

▶ Advise Nina on whether Rob can apply for a parental responsibility order, Rob's entitlement, if any, to see the children, on what steps Rob's mother could take to see the children, and how these issues would be resolved.

## How to Answer this Question

This question involves an unmarried couple and a dispute over the children of the relationship.

❖ Parental responsibility should be explained, together with who may exercise it and how.
❖ Parental responsibility orders (PRO).
❖ Then the role of the s 8 orders should be considered, including the parents' right to apply without leave and the general non-interventionist policy and need to avoid delay.
❖ Then the children's welfare must be considered in the light of the s 1(3) checklist, and contact with the father and grandmother must be explored.

## Applying the Law

This diagram illustrates how the **Children's Act 1989** applies in Nina's situation.

# ANSWER

Rob is the natural father of the two children, Tara and John, but since he did not marry the children's mother, Nina, he may not have parental responsibility for the children. English law has chosen not to give unmarried fathers automatic parental responsibility and, whilst the **Adoption and Children Act 2002** has amended the **Children Act 1989 s 4**, the unmarried father still does not get automatic parental responsibility. There are currently three ways in which an unmarried father might acquire parental responsibility. The first is if he is registered as the child's father on their birth certificate. The other two ways in which an unmarried father can acquire parental responsibility are through an agreement with the mother or through a court order. Given that Nina and Rob were living together when the children were born, it is possible that he was named on the birth certificate.

Parental responsibility is defined in the **Children Act 1989 s 3(1)** as 'all the rights, duties, powers and responsibilities and authority which by law a parent of a child has in relation to the child and its property'. Thus the emphasis of the Act is on the obligations of parenthood, and the prime feature is that in questions of the child's upbringing, their welfare is of paramount importance: **s 1(1)**. In this case, it would be wrong, therefore, to talk of Rob's right to see his children; rather, the emphasis is on what is in the best interests of the children.

If Rob was not named on the birth certificate then he will have to get parental responsibility through an order or through an agreement. It is extremely unlikely that Nina would consent to Rob having parental responsibility in the present circumstances, and so he would need to apply to the court. This would be a question of the child's upbringing, and therefore the child's welfare is the paramount consideration, not the feelings of Nina or Rob (*Re G (A Minor) (Parental Responsibility Order)* (1994)). The usual attitude of the court is to grant parental responsibility to fathers who have demonstrated an attachment and commitment to their children (*Re E (Parental Responsibility)* (1995)). Whilst Nina's feelings about Rob are understandable, he did have a relationship with his children, and if he shows remorse and is unlikely to be violent again, then it may be possible for him to obtain the order. In *Re T (A Minor) (Parental Responsibility: Contact)* (1993), parental responsibility was refused to a father who had been guilty of serious violence to the mother and cruelty to the child. In the present case, Rob has not been violent to Nina or the children, nor has he ill-treated the children.[6]

In *Re P (Parental Responsibility)* (1998), it was suggested that the correct test should be to examine the level of commitment and attachment the father has demonstrated to the children and his reasons for seeking the order. In the present case Rob has shown attachment and commitment and does not appear to be seeking the order so that he can interfere unnecessarily in the children's lives, as was the case in *Re P (Parental Responsibility)* (1998). It may be in the child's best interests to know that his or her father had sufficient commitment to seek the order: *Re M (Contact)* (1998).

The effect of an order is to give the father a say in the upbringing of his children, but it would not allow him to 'interfere in matters within the day-to-day management of the child's life': *Re P (A Minor) (Parental Responsibility Order)* (1994). In *Re S (A Minor) (Parental Responsibility)* (1995) it was held that a father who has had involvement in the upbringing of his children and is committed to their welfare can have parental responsibility, but that this does not automatically mean he will have contact with the children if the mother opposes this. Then the court will consider whether to make a contact order.

----

6    Even if Rob is awarded PR, this does not mean he would be given other orders, for example, a contact order.

Rob, as the natural father of the children, can apply, as of right, for one of the **s 8** orders: **s 10(4)**. These orders are residence orders, determining where the child should live; contact orders, determining whether and how frequently a child should see a particular person; prohibited steps orders, which forbid the taking of a measure; and specific issue orders, which resolve a particular dispute over the upbringing of the child. It is obviously not appropriate for Rob to seek a residence order, as he is not in a position to care for his children at present. However, he might seek a contact order which, if granted, would allow Tara and/or John to visit their father.[7]

When considering whether to grant an order, the court must bear in mind the non-interventionist policy: **s 1(5)**. This requires the court to make orders only where to do so is better than making no order at all. If no order is made in the present case, it is extremely unlikely that any agreement will be reached amicably between the parties. The circumstances of the breakdown in the relationship and subsequent homicide have ensured animosity and bitterness which are not conducive to the co-operation sought by the Act. There would obviously need to be a court-imposed settlement to this problem.

Clearly, any delay in resolving the problem would be prejudicial to the children's welfare, and the court is required to bear this in mind (**s 1(2)**), and draw up a timetable for the future conduct of the case to ensure that delay is kept to a minimum (**s 11**). This issue of contact between the children and their father concerns their upbringing and the **s 1(3)** checklist must be considered by the courts in making any contested **s 8** order. The paramount principle is that of the child's welfare (**s 1(1)**) but, in deciding how best to promote it, the court must have regard to the factors in **s 1(3)**. These include the ascertainable wishes and feelings of the child concerned (in the light of his age and understanding); his physical, emotional and educational needs; the likely effect on him of any change in circumstances; his age, sex, background and other relevant characteristics; any harm he has suffered or is at risk of suffering; how capable his parents and any other relevant person are of meeting his needs; and the range of powers available to the court under the Act.

Here, Nina will clearly have the children living with her, and the court needs to consider the issue of contact only. Both children are very young, and it is unlikely that John, aged two, can articulate any wishes, and he probably has no recollection of his father. Tara is aged five and will almost definitely remember her father, and may want to see him, since she will find it difficult to understand the enormity of what he did. However, Tara is considerably younger than the age at which the court tends to view the child's wishes as decisive; this is normally around the teenage years (*Stewart v Stewart* (1973)). She will have little awareness of the long-term consequences of her decisions, and so her views

----

7    A contact order could also be for indirect contact, for example that Rob is able to write to the children, or telephone them.

would be treated with caution. If she expressed a vehement opposition to visiting her father, the court would discount this if it were felt to be the result of pressure from Nina: *Re S (Infants)* (1967).

By examining the physical, emotional and educational needs of the children, the court usually recognises the desirability of maintaining or establishing contact with a natural parent: *Re H (Minors) (Access)* (1992). Rob is the natural parent of the two children concerned, and in normal circumstances contact would be inevitable. However, there is the difficulty caused by the crime he has committed. The courts are reluctant to expose children to persons of extreme depravity or criminality: *Scott v Scott* (1986). Rob has not been violent to the children, and has otherwise been a good father. It is arguable that the child's need for contact, especially Tara who had an established relationship with her father, outweighs any moral judgement on the behaviour of Rob. This is easier to sustain if Rob exhibits genuine remorse and regret for what has occurred. If, however, he is unrepentant, the court might be concerned that the children will receive wrong messages about crime from their father, thereby doing them moral harm.

This issue of harm and the risk of it would count against Rob if there was any moral danger to the children through contact, or any risk that they would be exposed to physical danger. Much will depend, therefore, on the attitude Rob has exhibited towards his crime, and possibly to Nina. It might not be in the children's interests to have contact with their father if he is threatening and aggressive towards their mother. It seems likely that if a contact order is made, it will be made in respect of both children. Although John has no recollection of his father, it would be divisive to treat these siblings differently, as they have to live as a single family unit (*S v S* (1988)), and both ultimately have the same need to maintain blood relationships. This contact could be by way of visits to prison, letters, phone calls, etc. The court can specify the steps that Nina has to take to ensure contact is maintained, such as requiring her to read out Rob's letters to the children (*Re O (Contact: Imposition of Conditions)* (1995)). If, however, Nina is deeply opposed to the idea of contact, and it can be shown that this causes her great distress, then the child's interest in seeing its natural parent may have to give way to its interests in maintaining a happy and healthy caring parent. Consequently, if contact is genuinely damaging to Nina's mental or physical health, then no order will be made: *Re B (A Minor) (Access)* (1992). However, Nina must comply with any order that the court makes, or else she faces being sent to prison for contempt: *A v N (Committal: Refusal of Contact)* (1997).

Regardless of the issue of contact with Rob, Nina must also deal with the issue of contact with Jean, Rob's mother and the children's grandmother. Jean is not entitled to apply for a s 8 order as of right; instead she must seek leave from the court (**s 10(2)**). In granting leave, the court will consider the factors in **s 10(2)**, namely the type of order being sought, the relationship between the applicant and child, and the risk of the application disrupting the child's life, thereby causing harm. Here, Jean would be seeking a contact order which would enable her to have a relationship with her son's children. Rob and

Nina were never married, and so Rob has no parental responsibility which would enable him to arrange contact. Whether leave would be granted would depend on the kind of relationship Jean had with the children previously. If she had formed an integral part of their lives, playing the role of grandmother, it is likely that she would be given leave. She would be seeking to reinforce an existing relationship and would not be seeking merely to interfere and disrupt.

If leave is granted, then the usual principles of non-intervention (s 1(5)), delay (s 1(2)), and welfare being paramount (s 1(1)) apply. The statutory checklist in s 1(3) would require the court to consider the children's wishes, but, as mentioned earlier, this will not carry much weight. The desirability of maintaining relationships with close blood relatives is an established principle, and it is difficult to see that it would be in the best interests of the children to be deprived of the love and affection of a grandmother because of the actions of their father. This assumes that Jean has played a part in their lives, and does not seek to disrupt or upset the children. There does not seem to be risk of harm, and Jean's ability to care and cope with the children might determine the kind of contact permitted. This could be by way of telephone calls, letters, visits or possibly even staying visits to their grandmothers. Only if such contact could be demonstrated to be damaging to Nina's health, given the exceptional circumstances of the case, would contact be denied: *Re B (A Minor) (Access)* (1992).

# QUESTION 36

Oliver and Penny lived together for eight years, during which time two children, Abigail, aged six, and Beatrice, aged four, were born. There is a very strong bond between Oliver and the two children as he works from home and has spent a great deal of time with them. Penny has been a successful journalist, travelling all over the world to cover assignments. She has recently met and fallen in love with Jimmy, an out-of-work hippy, who has an ambition to hitchhike throughout the world. Penny has announced to Oliver that she might go to join Jimmy and she would then be taking the girls with her. She has also said that whilst Abigail is Oliver's daughter, Beatrice is the result of an affair she had with another journalist, Neil.

Oliver is distraught at the prospect of losing the girls, both of whom he loves very much. He does not believe Penny's story about Beatrice, but, even if it is true, he says it does not change the way he feels about Beatrice.

▶ **Advise Oliver.**

## How to Answer this Question

❖ Parental responsibility for both girls must be considered, who has it and how it may be exercised.

❖ It will be necessary to consider Beatrice's status as Oliver's child.

❖ Then consider whether Oliver needs leave to apply for a s 8 order.

❖    Explain the range of **s 8** orders, the general non-interventionist policy and need to avoid delay.
❖    Then look at the welfare of the children in the light of the **s 1(3)** checklist, and the difficulty faced if they are taken abroad.

## Applying the Law

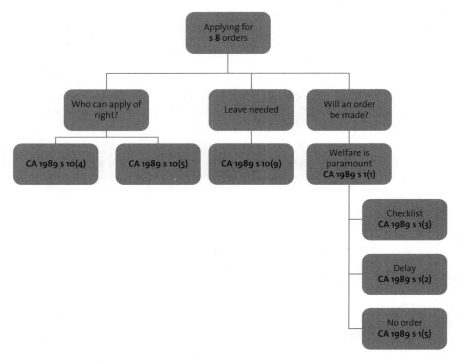

*This diagram shows the application of **Children's Act 1989 ss 10** and **8** in this scenario on issues of welfare and Oliver's access to his children.*

# ANSWER

Oliver's position regarding the two children, Abigail and Beatrice, is somewhat complicated as he is not married to their mother, Penny, and there is a possible dispute over Beatrice's paternity. Penny has parental responsibility for both girls (**Children Act 1989 s 2(1)**), and this is defined in the **Children Act 1989 s 3(1)**, as 'all the rights, duties, powers and responsibilities and authority which by law a parent of a child has in relation to the child and its property'. As a result Penny can choose where her daughters should live, and she is under no legal obligation to involve Oliver in these decisions. If Oliver wishes to be involved in the future upbringing of the two girls, he will need to apply for a court order under the **Children Act 1989 s 8**.

A natural father of a child can apply for a s 8 order as of right, and so Oliver can definitely make an application in relation to Abigail. The position regarding Beatrice is more complex. If she is Oliver's child then he has the right to apply for a s 8 order (**Children Act 1989 s 10(4)**), but if she is not his child then his right to apply must be based on the fact that Beatrice has lived with him for at least three years (**s 10(5)**). This permits an application for a residence or contact order, but not for a prohibited steps order or a specific issue order, where leave would be required. **Section 10(9)** provides the criteria to be applied in deciding whether to grant leave. In the present case, Oliver has a close relationship with Beatrice and she is not likely to be harmed by any disruption, and therefore he would probably be given leave to make his s 8 application. Leave will usually be granted to those with a genuine interest in this child's welfare, and would be refused to those who were merely seeking to meddle and interfere.

As well as the issues relating specifically to a s 8 order, it may be desirable to deal with the issue of Beatrice's paternity. As Oliver and Penny were never married, there is no assistance from the presumption of legitimacy. Consequently, Beatrice's paternity will need to be settled by way of blood tests or DNA genetic testing. These can be ordered by the court (**Family Law Reform Act (FLRA) 1969 s 20(1)**), and if Penny refuses to comply without good reason then adverse inferences can be drawn (**FLRA 1969 s 23(1)**). In the present case, it seems likely that testing would be ordered, as it is usually in the child's best interests to know who his or her father is: *S v S* (1972).

In determining Oliver's application for a s 8 order, it must be borne in mind that the welfare of the child is the paramount consideration in issues concerning its upbringing: **Children Act 1989 s 1(1)**. Thus, the court will consider what is in Abigail's and Beatrice's best interests, not necessarily what the parties want. There are a number of orders available under s 8, namely a residence order, determining where the children should live; a contact order, dealing with the arrangements for contact and visits; a prohibited steps order, which can be used to prohibit the taking of a particular step; and a specific issue order, which can be used to seek the court's assistance on a particular issue. The last two orders should not be sought if the matter could be dealt with by way of a residence or contact order (**Children Act 1989 s 9(5)**), and so Oliver would be best advised to seek a residence or contact order initially. Any unresolved issues could then be dealt with by way of a prohibited steps or specific issue order.

In dealing with an application for a s 8 order, the court must have regard to the non-interventionist policy in s 1(5) of the Act. This provides that the court should not make an order unless the making of an order is better than not making one. The policy of the Act is to encourage consensus and agreement wherever possible, but unfortunately Oliver and Penny seem unlikely to agree where the children should live, and so a court order may be necessary.

Having become involved, the court must recognise that delay will often prejudice the welfare of the children (**s 1(2)**) and, with this in mind, a timetable for the future conduct of proceedings must be set (**s 11**). The welfare of the children is the paramount consideration (**s 1(1)**), and the statutory checklist in the **Children Act s 1(3)** provides a list of factors to be considered.

The first factor is the ascertainable wishes of the child in the light of their age and understanding. Both Abigail and Beatrice are quite young, and are well below the age where their opinions would be viewed as decisive: this is usually around the teenage years (*Stewart v Stewart* (1973)), where the child is able to appreciate the long-term consequences of their decisions. Most children aged six and four will wish to have contact with both parents, but may be unable to grasp the implications of a choice of residence. If the girls have been coached or pressurised, then their views will be disregarded: *Re S (Infants)* (1967).

The court will then consider the physical, educational and emotional needs of the children. Here the children are both young girls, and traditionally there has been a preference for keeping young girls with their mother: *Re W (A Minor)* (1983). In *Plant v Plant* (1982), it was stressed that usually there are obvious advantages in leaving young children in the care of their mother, unless she is incapable or unsuitable. This would in the past have favoured Penny but, in *Re H (A Minor)* (1980), it was emphasised that times had changed and that many fathers were as capable as mothers of looking after small children. Ultimately, it is a question of the welfare of the children, and there are obvious advantages to young girls being with their mothers, especially through puberty. However, in the present case, the mother has been frequently absent, and the girls have been cared for predominantly by their father. There is nothing to suggest that he has been unable to minister to their needs, and so it should not necessarily be assumed that the girls will go to their mother.

It is obviously necessary to provide the children with a caring, stable upbringing, and Oliver would be able to do this. Penny, on the other hand, has had a busy career and is proposing to join her new boyfriend, hitchhiking around the world. This lack of a stable home base and the possible educational disadvantages may well count against Penny; *May v May* (1986) shows the importance attached to a good education.

The court will try to ensure that Abigail and Beatrice remain together, as siblings derive considerable support from one another: *Adams v Adams* (1984). The likely effect of change must also be considered, as the tendency is to preserve the status quo and avoid unnecessary disruption: *J v C* (1970). The girls have been used to their home and being looked after by Oliver, whilst Penny was away working. To uproot them from this, remove Abigail from school, and subject them to the peripatetic existence that Penny has in mind, would arguably be detrimental to their welfare. Oliver is able to provide greater continuity of care and, in *Riley v Riley* (1986), the court expressed a preference for the children living with a parent who could provide continuity of care in one place as opposed to the parent who was constantly on the move.

The age, sex and background and any other relevant characteristics of the children are considered, together with the risk of harm to the children. There is no suggestion that Jimmy is an unsavoury character or would harm the girls, but the travel plans of Penny and Jimmy seem unconventional and possibly hazardous for such small children.

Lastly, the capabilities of the parents and any other relevant person of meeting the child's needs must be considered. There is often an advantage if a parent can show that they have an established and suitable relationship with a parent substitute, as the child's interests are often better served in a two-adult household. Here, Jimmy and Penny's relationship is very new, and Jimmy is an unconventional person who does not seem to fit the stereotype of the replacement father. Oliver has no partner that we are told of, but he has been a loving and caring parent to the girls and has a good chance of obtaining a residence order.

However, if the court grants a residence order in favour of Oliver, then he must also be given parental responsibility to enable him properly to care for the girls: s 12(1). The parental responsibility of Penny will not end just because a residence order has been made in favour of Oliver. Penny should still continue to play an important part in her daughters' lives, and it is likely that she would be given generous contact with the girls. In *Re H (Minors) (Access)* (1992), the court stressed that it would usually be in the child's best interests for contact to be maintained with natural parents.

In the unlikely event of Penny being granted the residence order, then again it is probable that Oliver would be granted generous contact with the girls. A person in whose favour the residence order is granted cannot remove a child from the jurisdiction for more than one month without the written consent of everyone with parental responsibility or leave of the court: s 13(1). Therefore, Oliver could not remove the children if he had a residence order, but it would seem that Penny could if she had the order, as no one other than she would have parental responsibility for the children. It would therefore be necessary to seek a prohibited steps order under s 8 if Oliver wished to prevent Penny subsequently taking the children overseas. The courts would, however, usually allow the children to accompany an emigrating parent who has a residence order in their favour: *Chamberlain v de la Mare* (1982). However, Penny is not remarrying, nor is her way of life overseas going to be settled or stable and so the court might feel that the disruption of contact with Oliver is not in the children's interests, given that they are so fond of him: *Re K (A Minor)* (1992).[8]

---

8    If a residence order were in force, then **Children Act 1989 s 13** would apply with the effect that the girls could not be taken outside the jurisdiction for more than a month without the approval of both parents with parental responsibility.

To conclude, it would seem that Oliver should seek a residence order to enable the two girls to live with him, and this, in the circumstances, should be forthcoming. In the course of this application, it may be that Beatrice's paternity will be resolved. In any event, Oliver should be allowed generous contact and should seek to prohibit the taking of the children overseas, by way of a prohibited steps order.

# QUESTION 37

Mike and Laura are getting divorced, but they are having difficulty making arrangements for their two children, Kate, aged 13, and Julia, aged six. Laura has set up home with Ian in his small house, which she admits will be cramped if both girls join her. Kate does not like Ian and is refusing to join her mother, complaining that Ian is bossy and makes her life a misery. Kate has a good relationship with Mike and wishes to stay with him. Mike is remaining in the former matrimonial home, having managed to raise enough cash by way of a mortgage to buy out Laura's share. Laura is unhappy with Kate being with Mike; she feels Kate is too young to make a decision and has been swayed by Mike's promises of a puppy if she stays with him.

Mike has agreed that Julia can live with Laura, as she is disabled and he would find it difficult to give her the care she needs. However, he is anxious to be able to see her each weekend and during the week if he can. Laura is opposed to this, claiming that it would be disruptive and she is keen that Julia looks on Ian as her new father. Mike has heard rumours that Laura is encouraging Julia to use Ian's surname instead of his.

▶ Advise Mike.

## How to Answer this Question

❖ Introduction should explain parental responsibility and the procedure for filing arrangements for children on divorce. Then consider the non-interventionist policy and need to avoid delay.

❖ Continue by outlining the various s 8 orders available to deal with these problems, namely where the child should live, the issue of contact and change of surname.

❖ Take each issue in turn and look at the child's welfare in the light of the s 1(3) checklist.

❖ Where Kate should live will be affected by her wishes as well as the parties' respective abilities to care for her.

❖ Contact with Julia is usually viewed as desirable; explain why.

❖ Then deal with the special provisions on change of surname.

## Applying the Law

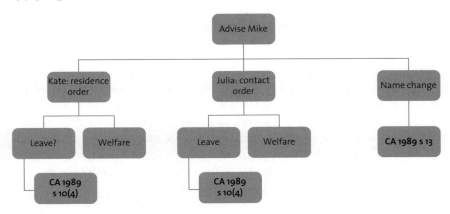

*The key parts of the Children Act 1989 at work in this scenario are sections 13 and 10 – the flowchart above shows how these are applied in relation to Mike's contact with Julia and the welfare aspects of both the contact and disabled access to Kate's residence.*

# ANSWER

Since Mike and Laura were married, they both have parental responsibility for their children: **Children Act 1989** s 2(1). This is defined in s 3(1) as 'all the rights, duties, powers and responsibilities and authority which by law a parent of a child has in relation to the child and its property'. Both Mike and Laura will continue to have parental responsibility after divorce, as the **Children Act 1989** emphasises the continuity of parental care, and the emphasis is also on the obligation of the parent to meet the needs of the child, rather than the outdated concept of parental rights. Consequently, the important and paramount issue here is the welfare of the children (s 1(1)) rather than the wishes of the parties.

There are three issues that need to be resolved, namely, where Kate should live; the extent of Mike's contact with Julia; and the use of a different surname for Julia. The **Children Act 1989** tries to encourage consensus between the parents where possible, and the non-interventionist approach is enshrined in the Act: s 1(5). On divorce, the parties are required to file a statement of arrangements for the children, detailing the measures that have been agreed and the areas of disagreement. If the parties have reached agreement there will be no need for the court to intervene, but if, as here, there are unresolved issues then the court will need to make the decision as to what is best for the children.

The court has jurisdiction on divorce to make one or more of the s 8 orders, namely a residence order; a contact order; a prohibited steps order; and a specific issue order. The first issue concerns where Kate should live and this should be dealt with by way of a residence order. Mike would be able to apply for a residence order as of right as he is her father ( **Children Act 1989 s 10(4)**. Delay is usually prejudicial to the welfare of the child ( s 1(2) and therefore it is necessary for the court to draw up a timetable for the conduct of the case ( s 1) in order to minimise delay.

In determining where Kate should live, the court will have regard to the  s 1(3)checklist, bearing in mind that Kate's welfare is the paramount consideration:  s 1(1) The factors in  s 1(3)include the ascertainable wishes and feelings of the child (in the light of their age and understanding); the physical, emotional and educational needs of the child; the likely effect of any change in circumstances; the child's age, sex, background and other relevant characteristics; any harm which she has suffered or is at risk of suffering; and how capable the parents and any other relevant person are of meeting the child's needs.

Kate's parents cannot agree where she should live and Kate herself has exhibited a preference for staying with her father, Mike. Kate is aged 13, an age where her wishes are likely to be given weight by the courts: *Stewart v Stewart* (1973) Assuming Kate is reasonably intelligent and articulate, she is likely, at 13, to appreciate the long-term consequences of her decision. She has a good rapport with her father, but does not have a good relationship with Ian. There seems to be genuine difficulty, given Ian's forceful behaviour, and it may be argued that the attitude displayed by Ian and Laura in relation to Kate's sister, Julia, illustrates a somewhat heavy-handed attempt to replace Mike in the children's affections. This could be upsetting for Kate. Laura's view that Kate is too young to decide would probably not be shared by the court, and in  *Marsh v Marsh* (1977) a child of 12 was able to state her preference.[9]

The only concern might be that Mike's promise of a puppy might be viewed as a bribe or pressure ( *Re S (Infants)* (1967)), but given Kate's age and prior good relationship with her father, it is unlikely that this influenced her decision. Kate's physical, emotional and educational needs must be considered, and it is usual for teenage girls to live with their mother, who are often better equipped to deal with the problems of puberty: *Re W (A Minor)* (1983) On the other hand, in  *Re H (A Minor)* (1980) this view was not given great weight by the Court of Appeal, who recognised that in many cases a father may be in a position to provide better care for a particular child than its mother. Kate has a better rapport with her father, and her relationship with her mother may be very strained if forced to live there. Both Mike and Laura can provide Kate with a home, although Mike's position is more comfortable than Laura's cramped house. Whilst material advantages get little weight ( *Stephenson v Stephenson* (1985)), it does seem that the situation for Kate would be better if she lived with her father. The usual position of keeping siblings together for the mutual support they give each other ( *Adams v Adams* (1984) might not apply so strongly here, given the large age gap between the children, and the fact that

......................................................................................................

9    Applying the welfare checklist can be a delicate balancing exercise. Previous case law will give you some idea of how courts have interpreted and weighed the various factors in the past.

Julia is disabled may mean that the needs of the individual girls should be considered separately ( *B-T v B-T* (1990)).

At present, Kate has been staying with her father, and the court will consider the effect of changing this. There is generally a reluctance to disturb the established status quo ( *J v C* (1970) but, in the instant case, it would be difficult to argue that Kate's presence with Mike is so established that it cannot be varied ( *Allington v Allington* (1985), especially since Laura has maintained contact. However, the desirability of a stable upbringing is very important, and working fathers often experience difficulty when faced with bringing up a child. The courts have frequently preferred the continuous care of the mother:  *Re K* (1988) However, in such cases, the children have been very young, whereas here Kate is 13 and would be at school for most of the time that Mike was at work, and would presumably be happy with after-school activities and care until her father returned home.

There is no suggestion that Kate would be at risk of harm with either parent, and they both seem to have been loving and capable parents. Nevertheless, Kate has a better relationship with her father, and her antagonism towards Ian may be difficult to overcome. It would seem, therefore, that Kate's welfare would best be served by making a residence order in favour of Mike, with generous contact between Kate and Laura and Julia. Laura's parental responsibility for Kate would continue, despite the residence order.

The situation concerning Julia raises two controversial issues, that of contact and change of surname. The parties are agreed that Julia should reside with Laura, and consequently there will be no need for a residence order, based on the non-interventionist policy in s 1(5) However, the degree of contact is not agreed and so the court will need to consider making a contact order under  s 8 Mike, as a parent, can apply as of right ( s 10(4) and the problem will be resolved by the use of the  s 1(3)checklist to ascertain what is best for Julia since her welfare is paramount ( s 1(1).

Julia is only six years old, and the nature and extent of her disability are unknown. Not a lot of weight would be attached to her wishes, as given her age she is unlikely to have the understanding of the long-term implications of a decision:  *Stewart v Stewart* (1973) However, it is generally recognised that it is in the interests of her emotional needs to have contact with her natural parent:  *Re H (Minors) (Access)* (1992) Mike has been a good father to Julia and contact would only be denied if it were damaging to Julia. The court would not be sympathetic to Laura's desire to replace Mike with Ian as Julia's father; this is generally viewed as being confusing and upsetting for a child. Julia has had a relationship with Mike for the past six years, and it would be in her interests for this to be maintained. Contact by telephone or letter may be difficult, and it seems likely that Mike will be allowed to visit Julia. Whether it will be practicable for him to take her out or have her stay with him will depend on the extent of her disability. It is desirable for there to be generous contact between parent and child but it may be necessary to restrict Mike's contact with Julia to certain periods. This provides a degree of certainty for Laura and Ian, who are trying to build a family life together, without being interrupted at unpredictable times by Mike wishing to see Julia. It would also enable Julia to be better prepared, and so some kind of formalised contact may be ordered.

A contact order, like a residence order, does not usually extend beyond the child's sixteenth birthday. However, in exceptional circumstances, it may do so (**Children Act 1989 s 9(6)**) and, if Julia's disability is profound, then a longer order may be necessary.

The problem of Julia's surname has caused Mike some concern since Laura seems to want Julia to adopt Ian's surname. It is not possible to change a child's surname without permission from all those with parental responsibility or with leave from the court: s 13(1). It is unlikely that the court would order a change of surname, as it usually is in the child's interests to preserve this link with her father: *W v A* (1981). The change would only be permitted if the child had actually been using the changed name for a long time: *R v R* (1982).[10]

If there is no residence order in force in relation to Julia, then Mike could apply for a prohibited steps order to prohibit the use of the new surname, or raise as a specific issue order the question of what name Julia should be known by. As indicated earlier, the court tends to preserve the child's name, and in *Re PC (Change of Surname)* (1997) the court stressed that one parent with parental responsibility cannot change a child's surname without the consent of the other parent with parental responsibility.

# QUESTION 38

'Neither parent should be encouraged or permitted to think that the more intransigent, the more unreasonable, the more obdurate and the more unco-operative they are, the more likely they are to get their own way.' *Re O (Contact: Imposition of Conditions)* (1995) 2 FLR 124 at pp 129–130.

▶ Discuss how successfully English Courts have dealt with the difficulty of the obstructive parent.

## How to Answer this Question

❖ The problem of the obstructive parent – denial of contact, refusal to follow court order, alienation of the child.

❖ Contempt of court – an inappropriate remedy?

❖ Variation of the order – rewarding bad behaviour?

❖ Shared residence order as a solution – the development of its use by the courts, why it is without problems.

---

10  **Section 13** of the **CA 1989** means that Laura would not be able to change Julia's surname without Mike's agreement. If Mike were to refuse, Laura would have to apply for a specific issue order and seek the courts' consent to a name change.

❖    Children and Adoption Act 2006: contact activity directions (**Children Act 1989 s 11A**), monitoring contact (**Children Act 1989 s 11H**), warning notices (**Children Act 1989 s 11I**), enforcement orders (**Children Act 1989 s 11J**), compensation for financial loss (**Children Act 1989 s 11O**).

## Applying the Law

This diagram outlines the main issues that have been decisive in the courts' dealings with obstructive parents.

# ANSWER

Private law child cases often take place against a background of family tensions and separations. It is perhaps unsurprising therefore that one of the main difficulties faced by the courts is that of the hostile and obstructive parent. Section 8 orders are supposed to be based on the child's welfare (**Children Act 1989 s 1(1)**); nevertheless, the hostility of the resident parent to an order can sometimes be a factor. If a parent is very disturbed by the making of an order, this could affect their ability to care for the child and may be an argument against making the order. A parent may deliberately or subconsciously transmit their hostility to the child. If a child, especially an older child, is very reluctant to see the parent, the court may find it very difficult to order him or her to do so.[11]

11    This question is about hostility and the making of **section 8** orders. It should focus on that rather than just discussing **s 8** orders in general.

Despite this, courts are clear that they will not allow the hostility of one parent to restrict the contract of another. This means that in some cases, s 8 orders will be made despite the hostility of a parent; nevertheless, it does not mean that these orders will always be followed and this raises another issue: that of the enforcement of s 8 orders. One option is to charge the obstructive parent with contempt of court with the possibility of that parent being imprisoned. This is rarely used. Imprisoning the parent with care, whilst undoubtedly hard towards them, also punishes the child, who not only has their home life severely disrupted, but who will also often feel responsible for that punishment. Another possibility is to vary the order to try and find something that the obstructive parent might find acceptable. For example, a parent may obstruct direct, unsupervised contact, but may be happy to promote indirect or supervised contact. The difficulty with this is that the child's welfare is being subverted to pander to the obstructive parent. If the court decided that direct contact was in the welfare of the child, this is what should be promoted, not the compromise of indirect contact. Furthermore, this option in a way rewards the obstructive parent for their behaviour.

Another option is to vary the order, but this time to replace direct contact with shared residence. The idea here is to prevent one parent losing contact with the child because of the hostility of the other parent and to prevent the child being alienated against that parent. Although courts used to be reluctant to order shared residence, more recently they have seen them as a way of promoting cooperation between the parents and of preventing a hostile parent from obstructing contact (A v A (Shared Residence) (2004) ). Alternatively, the court may transfer residence from the parent who is obstructing the contact to the other parent (V v V (Contact: Implacable Hostility) (2004) ). The advantage of this approach is that it does potentially allow the child to maintain and develop a relationship with both parents. However, it cannot be an answer in every case. There may be situations where due to the distance that the parents live from each other, sharing or transferring residence is not an option because of the disruption that it will involve to the child. There may also be times where a parent desperately wants direct contact with a child but is not able or willing to have residence for the child and there may be situations where it is in the child's welfare to have contact with a parent, but not to live with that parent.

In recent years, fathers' rights groups have promoted the idea that mothers frequently obstruct contact and that the courts are ill equipped or unwilling to deal with it. It is perhaps unsurprising therefore that the law in this area has recently been developed by the **Children and Adoption Act 2006** , which has introduced some measures into the **Children Act 1989** to promote and enforce contact. The new measures are aimed at checking that contract is followed through monitoring (**Children Act 1989 s 11H** ) and then in the case of non-compliance issuing warning notices (**Children Act 1989 s 11I** ) and then enforcement measures (**Children Act 1989 s 11O** ). The difficulty with these measures is that they are unlikely to please anyone. Parents denied access will likely prefer a more robust approach whilst others will regret the punitive approach adopted by the Act and the fact that this reform has been based on the assumption that objection to contact and refusal to follow court orders are always motivated purely by hostility and never by the child's welfare.

# QUESTION 39

Victoria and Albert are married and are both aged 45; they have three children, Edward, aged 14, Alice, aged ten, and Eugenie, aged two. The couple have recently separated, after Eugenie made certain remarks that Victoria construed as being allegations of sexual abuse against Albert. Albert has vigorously denied that anything improper occurred between himself and Eugenie, and states that Victoria was just looking for an excuse to leave him. Victoria has since moved into a large house owned by Alexandra, her lesbian lover, taking the children with her. Victoria wants the children to live with her, and does not want them to see Albert, whereas Albert is unhappy about the children being with Victoria and Alexandra.

▶ Advise Victoria on what approach the court would take concerning the children, if she were to divorce Albert.

## How to Answer this Question

❖ Begin by explaining the procedure for determining what should happen to the children on divorce and the availability ofs 8 orders if there is a dispute.

❖ Briefly outline parental responsibility, the non-interventionist policy and need to avoid delay.

❖ Determine the residence order by looking at what is in the child's welfare by reference to thes 1(3) checklist. The important issue is the effect of Victoria's lesbianism on her ability to care for her children.

❖ Then examine the problem the allegation of child abuse causes in relation to contact between the children and their father.

## Applying the Law

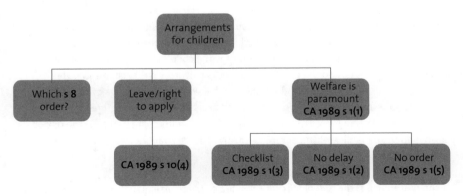

The application of the Children Act 1989 in relation to the arrangements for the children is shown in this diagram.

# ANSWER

If Victoria were to divorce Albert, then she would need to file a statement of arrangements for the children, indicating what areas of agreement there are. If there are unresolved areas, then it is possible for her to apply for one or more of the orders in the Children Act 1989 s 8 (s 10(1)) at the same time as taking these family proceedings. Nevertheless, it is possible to make a free-standing application for a s 8 order without seeking any other relief from the courts (s 10(2)), and this would be the sensible step to take if she is unsure about divorce.

Section 8 provides for four types of order, namely, a residence order, a contact order, a prohibited steps order, and a specific issue order. The first two orders seem relevant here, and it is not possible to obtain a prohibited steps order or specific issue order if a residence or contact order is more appropriate: s 9(4). As parents, both Victoria and Albert can apply for a s 8 order as of right: s 10(4).

Since Victoria and Albert were married at the time of the births of their children, they both have parental responsibility for the children: s 2(1). This is defined in s 3(1) as 'all the rights, duties, powers and responsibilities and authority which by law a parent of a child has in relation to the child and its property'. The emphasis is on the parental obligation to care for the children, and this parental responsibility continues, even after divorce or the making of a s 8 order.

The court will only intervene if absolutely necessary, and there is a non-interventionist policy (s 1(5)) of only making a s 8 order if this would be better than not making one. Since Victoria and Albert are implacably opposed to each other's proposals, an order will be necessary. To avoid delay, which is viewed as prejudicial to the welfare of the child (s 1(2)) once an application has been made for a s 8 order, the court will lay down a timetable for the future stages of the case: s 11.

A residence order determines where and with whom a child should live, whereas a contact order enables contact between a child and another person; in this case, a parent. The prime and paramount importance is the child's welfare (s 1(1)), not the wishes of the parents, and the court will apply the statutory checklist in s 1(3). This contains various factors, namely, the ascertainable wishes and feelings of the child; its emotional, physical and educational needs; the likely effect of any change in circumstances; the age, sex, background and other relevant characteristics; the risk of harm; and the capability of the parents and any other relevant person to meet the child's needs.

In the present case, the two older children will be able to articulate their views, whereas Eugenie, at two, will have little or no understanding of what is happening. Edward, at 14, is of the age at which a great deal of weight would be attached to his views. He is likely to be '*Gillick* competent' in the sense that he has the intelligence and maturity to make decisions with an awareness of the long-term consequences: *Stewart v Stewart* (1973). Alice is ten and, whilst her views will be considered, the weight accorded them will depend on her intelligence and maturity. In *Marsh v Marsh* (1977) the views of a 12-year-old and a nine-year-old were adhered to, and so Alice's views may well be taken into account. On the facts, nothing is mentioned as to the views of either child but, given the sensitive nature of Victoria's relationship with Alexandra, the ability of the children to accept this and not be unduly embarrassed by it will be important.

Looking at the physical, emotional and education needs of the children, together with their age, sex, background and other relevant characteristics, there are arguments both for and against Victoria. Eugenie is a young child, and there is a tendency to view young children as being better cared for by their mother: *Greer v Greer* (1974). Likewise, for older girls it might be argued that the problems of puberty are best dealt with by the mother: *Re W (A Minor)* (1983). Whereas for older boys, there is a somewhat weaker argument that they would be better served by being with their father, who can provide a role model for them in their adolescence: *W v W and C* (1968). However, these are now recognised as being generalisations, rather than presumptions, by the Court of Appeal in *Re H (A Minor)* (1990). The crucial question will be to look at the child's needs and see which parent can best meet those needs. There would need to be pressing arguments that Victoria's ability to provide care for her children should be overridden, and the main argument of Albert will be that Victoria's lesbianism prevents her from adequately caring for the children. In the past, this might have prevented the children from living with their mother, but now this is not necessarily so. However, if Albert was prepared to offer the children a home, then the court would look at the nature of the relationship. In *C v C (A Minor)* (1991), the court stressed that lesbianism was not an automatic disqualification of a mother from looking after her children. It is, however, an unusual background, but a sensitive, loving lesbian relationship can often be a more satisfactory environment for a child than a less sensitive or loving heterosexual relationship.

There have been cases where mothers such as Victoria have been given residence orders, since they were in a better position to provide continuity of care for their children (*Re K* (1988)), whereas the father who had to work could not. The living conditions of both Albert and Victoria seem adequate, and the court is not overly concerned by material advantage: *Stephenson v Stephenson* (1985). However, it is usually desirable to keep brothers and sisters together (*Adams v Adams* (1984)) because of the mutual support they derive from each other. The two older children in the present case are reasonably close in age and their interests could better be served by being together.

The possible effect of change is unlikely to be influential here, as the current living arrangements are recently arrived at (*Allington v Allington* (1985)), so there is really no status quo to disrupt. It would be necessary to consider whether there is any risk of harm from Albert. There are the allegations supposedly made by Eugenie, which have been strongly denied. Allegations of child abuse are very easily made, and a chance remark by a child can easily be misconstrued. There does not seem to be any evidence to support Victoria's allegation, and it might be difficult to convince the court that Albert was a risk to the children. Even if there had been sexual abuse, there is no absolute rule prohibiting contact between a child and the abusing parent (*H v H* (1989) ); much will depend on the circumstances of the case. Without wanting to trivialise sexual abuse of children, if the assault were not of the most serious nature and there was no lasting harm and genuine regret by the abuser, then the child may suffer more from a cessation of contact with the parent. Supervised contact may be in the child's best interests.

Looking at the ability of the parents to meet the children's needs, it seems that Victoria is more able to provide the day-to-day care that is usually desirable, and if Alexandra is a caring partner, this will improve her case, and consequently she may well obtain a residence order. It is nevertheless considered to be in a child's best interests to maintain contact with its father (*Re B (Minor) (Access)* (1984) ), and there would need to be pressing reasons for terminating such contact. There is no evidence that Albert has harmed Alice or Edward and the evidence of harm to Eugenie is not strong. Consequently, there is likely to be a contact order enabling the children to see their father, unless they do not wish to do so. Even then, the court would be mindful of the possibility that they had been pressurised by Victoria.

# Children and the Local Authority

## INTRODUCTION

Under the Children Act 1989, the local authority has duties to promote the welfare of children in their area. This may involve providing services for children in need or applying for compulsory court orders to protect these children from harm.

## SERVICES FOR CHILDREN IN NEED

The no-order principle (Children Act 1989 s 1(5)) and the idea that children are generally best raised by their parents means that the starting point for any social services involvement with a child in need is to provide services to the child and his/her family. The definition of children in need is set out in the Children Act 1989 s 17 and services for the child can include voluntary accommodation (s 20), day care, advice and guidance, and help finding a suspected abuser an alternative residence.

## INVESTIGATION OF CHILD ABUSE

The local authority has a duty to investigate child abuse or neglect. Under s 47 it has a duty to investigate if it has reasonable cause to suspect that a child is suffering or is likely to suffer significant harm. This is the provision that will be used to justify an investigation following a referral from a member of the public. Under s 37 there is a duty to investigate whether to apply for a court order if asked to do so by the court.

## THE CHILD PROTECTION ORDERS

Whilst the Children Act 1989 states that it is better to work in partnership, there will be times when the local authority will have to apply for compulsory child protection orders. You need to be able to identify what is the most appropriate order and whether the grounds for that order are met.

## THE SHORT-TERM ORDERS

There are three short-term orders in the Children Act 1989: the child assessment order (s 43), the emergency protection order (s 44) and the police protection order (s 46).

❖ The child assessment order – this order does not give the local authority parental responsibility and does not usually involve the child being removed. It can be made where there is reasonable cause to *suspect* that a child is suffering or is likely to suffer significant harm. The child's parents will have notice of an application for a child assessment order.

❖ The emergency protection order – this order will give the local authority parental responsibility and will often lead to the child being removed from the family home. There are two grounds under which the local authority can apply: either that there is reasonable cause to *believe* that the child is suffering or is likely to suffer significant harm, or that an investigation is being unreasonably obstructed. There are two procedures for applying – one which involves the parents having notice of the application and the other which is made *ex parte*. The **Children Act 1989 s 44A** means that the suspected abuser may be removed from the family home rather than the child.

❖ Police protection order – unlike the other orders this does not require the agreement of the court and can be made where there is reasonable cause to believe that the child is suffering or is likely to suffer significant harm.

## THE LONG-TERM ORDERS

There are two long-term orders – the care order and the supervision order, both of which require the threshold criteria in the **Children Act s 31** to be satisfied.

❖ The supervision order – this provides for a supervising officer to be appointed to befriend the child and family and promote the child's welfare within the family.

❖ The care order – the local authority gains parental responsibility for the child.

In order for a care order or a supervision order to be made, the court must be satisfied that the child is suffering or is likely to suffer significant harm due to lack of parental care or being beyond parental control (*Re B (Minors) (Sexual abuse: Standard of Proof)* (2008)).

## QUESTION 40

Harry and Isobel have two children, Jessica, aged 12, and Jack, aged 14. The local authority has received letters from the children's school, expressing concern over the well-being of the children. Jack is an unruly child and does not respond to discipline at school. He frequently does not attend school, and is making poor progress in his studies. The school is also concerned at reports that Jack spends time in the local shopping centre in the company of much older youths who have reputations for shoplifting and mugging.

Jessica has previously appeared to be a happy child but over the past few months she has become increasingly withdrawn and has occasionally been found weeping in the classroom. She refuses to talk to anyone about what is bothering her and will not undress for PE classes in front of anyone. Matters came to a head when Jessica fled in tears from a biology class on human reproduction. The school is concerned that Jessica may be suffering from sexual abuse.

The local authority's social worker has visited Harry and Isobel, who do not seem overly concerned, saying that 'boys will be boys, and Jessica's just moody'. Advise the local authority on the options open to it in respect of Jessica and Jack.

## How to Answer this Question

This question involves a consideration of the compulsory powers of the local authority to safeguard the well-being of the two children of the family. Both Harry and Isobel have parental responsibility, but there are concerns about their ability to properly discharge it. Mention the duty to investigate under s 47, and then consider each child separately.

In relation to Jack, the possible options are an education supervision order (s 36) or a care order (s 31). The basis for each order must be explored, as must the threshold criteria of likelihood of suffering significant harm. The child's welfare is paramount and the s 1(3) checklist should be discussed. The possibility of a supervision order should be considered.

Jessica's problem appears more serious, and needs to be investigated. The possibility of obtaining a child assessment order (CAO) (s 43) or, if necessary, an emergency protection order (EPO) (s 44), should be explored, together with the statutory basis for making such orders. Once Jessica's true situation has been assessed, then the option of a care order (s 31) should be explored.

## Applying the Law

The relationship between the compulsory powers of the local authority and their legal duty to investigate is illustrated here.

# ANSWER ----------------------------------------------------

Since Harry and Isobel are married both have parental responsibility for Jessica and Jack. Clearly, concerns are expressed in the instant case as to whether Harry and Isobel are properly fulfilling their parental responsibility. Just as the Children Act 1989 imposes duties on parents, it also imposes duties on the local authority. The Children Act 1989 s 47 requires the local authority to investigate cases where there is reasonable cause to suspect that the child or children concerned are suffering or are likely to suffer significant harm. The Act requires the local authority to act, wherever possible, in partnership with the parents of the children. Encouraging co-operation between parents and local authority and maintaining, wherever possible, the care of the child within the family are the guiding philosophies of the Act. It would appear that Harry and Isobel are unconcerned about the problems that their children may be experiencing, which possibly suggests that working with the family by providing support would be ineffective and instead a more coercive approach might be necessary.

In relation to Jack, he is not attending school and is associating with undesirable persons. The local authority has two real options open to it. It may apply for an education supervision order under s 36 of the Act or, if the case warrants it, it may apply for a care order under s 31 of the Act. (The wardship option which may have been available in the past is no longer available to local authorities since the passing of the Children Act 1989) Any application made under the Children Act 1989 will have the child's welfare as the paramount consideration ( s 1(1) and the court will be reluctant to intervene unless it can be shown that the making of an order is better than leaving things as they are ( s 1(5). An education supervision order is made on application, usually to the Family Proceedings Court, where the local education authority acts in consultation with the social services. The Children Act 1989 s 36 requires children of compulsory school age to attend school or else an education supervision order may be made. Jack is of compulsory school age and it does seem that he is not being properly educated according to his needs, age and ability, given the amount of time during which he is absent from school. Section 36(5) creates a presumption that a pupil at a school who is not attending regularly is not being properly educated. Thus, it would seem that it would be possible to show to the court that Jack is not being properly educated. If the court was satisfied of this, it could appoint a supervising officer to ensure that the child attends school. This supervising officer takes responsibility for guiding and assisting both the child, Jack, and his parents, Harry and Isobel, in understanding the importance of education and laying down certain guidelines to ensure that Jack does attend school.

The order will usually last for one year but it can be extended or conversely it can be discharged on application by the child, Jack, or his parents or, if all is going well, by the education authority. If, however, the supervision order does not succeed in getting Jack to attend school (and it may be that his undesirable associates play a part in this) then the local authority may need to consider the more drastic step of seeking a care order. A care order is available under the Children Act 1989 s 31 and is only available once the local authority has carried out preliminary investigations to see if any action is necessary to safeguard or promote Jack's welfare: s 47(1) Ordinarily, the local authority must consult both Jack and his parents but, if the case is an urgent one or consultation may prejudice Jack's welfare, the local authority may act without consultation. In any application for a care order, both Jack and his parents must have notice and be made respondents to the application. Since Jack is a child it is usually necessary to appoint a children's guardian to act to safeguard his interests. The children's guardian will talk with Jack and try to ascertain Jack's feelings and wishes in regard to the present position. As a 14-year-old child he is obviously entitled to be consulted and clearly his co-operation will be essential for the smooth running of any future plans concerning him. The statutory grounds for a care order are found in the **Children Act 1989 s 31**

The Family Proceedings Court must be satisfied that the child is suffering or is likely to suffer significant harm. This does not require proof on the balance of probabilities that there will be harm in the future; it is enough to show a real, significant likelihood of harm ( *Newham London Borough Council v AG* (1993) *Re B (Minors) (Sexual abuse: Standard of proof)* (2008). Harm includes ill-treatment or impairment of health and development. In the present case it does not appear that Jack is being ill-treated at home, but his lack of attendance at school, his association with somewhat undesirable individuals, and his parents' apparent unconcern at this, do seem to indicate that maybe his health and development are being impaired. The second criterion under s 31 is that the harm or likelihood of harm is attributable to the care being given to the child or likely to be given to him if the order is not made, not being what it would be reasonable to expect a parent to give him, or secondly, the child being beyond parental control. This is an objective standard based on what a reasonable parent could or could not do: *Lancashire County Council v A* (2000) In *Re O (A Minor) (Care Order)* (1992) the persistent truancy of a child was deemed suitable for a care order to be made and this would be the case here. Since neither Harry nor Isobel is able to control Jack to ensure that he attends school, or they do not particularly concern themselves over his attendance, this would show that it is not reasonable for them to behave in that way concerning the education of their 14-year-old son. Again, as with any **Children Act 1989** order, the child's welfare is the paramount consideration ( s 1(1) and, in order to determine what would be in Jack's best interest, the s 1(3) checklist would be examined.[1]

The first consideration in the checklist would be the wishes of the child, given his age and understanding. Jack is 14 years old and definitely at the age where the court would consider his wishes. However, this does not mean that he would be able to dictate to the court what he wished to do. Definitely, his disinclination to attend school would not result in the court deeming any care order unnecessary. In fact, his inability to behave maturely in respect of

---

1    There is a two stage process to deciding whether a care order or a supervision order would be made. The first stage is to determine whether the threshold criteria in the **Children Act 1989 s 31** are satisfied. If the threshold criteria are not satisfied, a care order or a supervision order can be made. If the threshold criteria are satisfied, the next stage is to see whether the general principles of the **Children Act 1989** support the making of a care order or supervision order.

his education may indicate that his wishes will not carry a great deal of weight. The second criterion on the checklist is the child's physical, emotional and education needs. Clearly Jack is in need of some guidance, and the fact that he is not attending school and is associating with somewhat dubious characters indicates that he is a child who seems to be drifting through life. The apparent unconcern of his parents seems to indicate that something must be done for Jack. However, whether this would necessarily require him to leave his home and be taken into the care of the local authority is another matter. The court may decide that a less draconian measure would be more suitable. Jack will have been consulted by his children's guardian as to his wishes and his views about remaining with his parents or leaving home to enter local authority care. If Jack wishes to remain at home it may be that the shock of being threatened with removal will be enough to make him mend his ways. If the court is of the view that Jack and his parents may be able to correct the defects with a little assistance from other persons, then maybe the education supervision order discussed earlier, or a supervision order, will be more appropriate. The supervision order under the s 31 criteria requires the threshold of harm in s 31 to be satisfied. However, the effect of a supervision order is very different. A supervision order does not vest parental responsibility in the local authority; instead, a supervising officer, either a local authority officer or a probation officer, is appointed to assist and befriend and advise the child and his parents (s 35(1)). The supervising officer will do what is necessary to ensure that the child is guided and that his welfare is promoted. Usually a supervision order lasts for one year but it can be extended up to three years by one application; to continue beyond the three-year period another application would be necessary. The supervising officer will try to give directions to Jack: telling him to attend school; possibly also requiring him to participate in certain activities; and imposing obligations with the consent of Harry and Isobel to help them deal with Jack and promote his welfare. In *Oxfordshire County Council v L* (1998) a supervision order was considered appropriate for six children. This was because the parents wanted to meet their obligations to their children, and with help from the local authority they were likely to be able to do so.[2]

The position regarding Jessica is somewhat more complex. The incidents at school give considerable cause for concern over Jessica's health and well-being. Nevertheless, it is not clear that there is any actual abuse and the local authority should proceed with caution in this very delicate area. As with Jack, a case conference should be held in which the child's welfare and situation should be discussed. On the other hand there is the concern that consultation with the parents and with Jessica may increase Jessica's unease and could be detrimental by causing delay. Consequently, the local authority needs to act to get to the bottom of the problem and to find out exactly what it is that is concerning

---

2   Although the discussion here suggests that a care order would lead to Jack being removed and contrasts it with the supervision order where the child stays in the parents' care, it is possible for a care order to be made but the child to be placed with the parents. The advantage of a care order where the child is placed with the parents over the supervision order is that in a care order the local authority would have parental responsibility for the child and therefore would be better able to control the parents' use of their parental responsibility.

Jessica and how, if at all, she has been abused. One option would be to apply to the court for a child assessment order. Such an order is available to the local authority and will enable it to find out exactly what is going on in relation to the child. However, full notice must be given by the local authority to both the child and the child's parents and, at the hearing, the court must be satisfied that the local authority has reasonable cause to suspect that Jessica is suffering or is likely to suffer significant harm; that an assessment of Jessica's health and development is required in order to establish whether or not she is suffering harm; and that it is unlikely that an assessment will be made or made satisfactorily without a child assessment order.[3]

In this case the school report of Jessica's behaviour does give rise to concern that Jessica has suffered some kind of harm. Her responses do not seem to be those of the average 12-year-old in such a situation. Whereas most 12-year-olds go through periods of modesty whilst changing, and also possibly show concern over learning the facts of life, Jessica's reaction appears extreme. It is also combined with a significant change in personality, all of which gives cause for concern. There is no need to show on the balance of probabilities that Jessica is likely to suffer significant harm, just that there is a real likelihood. Harry's and Isobel's response is somewhat dismissive and it does not seem likely that the local authority will be able to assess Jessica without a child assessment order. Such an order, if made, will only last for seven days and it does not affect Harry and Isobel's parental responsibility. The local authority has no parental responsibility during the lifetime of this order; the order merely requires Harry and Isobel to produce Jessica so that she can be assessed. This may mean that Jessica continues to live at home although it is possible for her to be assessed as an in-patient in hospital. If Jessica is to remain in hospital, then contact will usually be allowed under s 43 between Jessica and her parents. There is the possibility that a child of sufficient age and understanding may refuse to consent to the assessment. Clearly, Jessica is a disturbed and upset child, but hopefully, with proper explanation and reassurance, she will be happy to comply with the order. If the local authority is frustrated in its enforcement of the child assessment order or if concern exists that more immediate protection is required for Jessica, then an emergency protection order under s 44 of the Act may be sought. The basis of such an application is, first, that the local authority may apply if it has reasonable cause to believe that Jessica is likely to suffer significant harm if either she is not removed to accommodation provided by the local authority or she does not then remain in the place where she is being accommodated. A further option open to the local authority is to apply under s 44(1)(b), on the basis that enquiries are being made with respect to the child and that those enquiries are being frustrated by access to Jessica being unreasonably

---

3    The fact that the parents would have to be given notice of an application for a CAO might mean that an EPO would be preferred. With an EPO it is possible to apply either with or without notice. However, the grounds for applying for an EPO are tougher than those for applying for a CAO. With an EPO either the investigation has to have been unreasonably obstructed or there has to be reasonable cause to believe that the child is suffering or is likely to suffer significant harm.

refused by the parents, and the applicant will also need to show that they have reasonable cause to believe that access to the child is required as a matter of urgency.

The emergency protection order is a very draconian measure; it gives the local authority parental responsibility for the duration of the order ( s 44(4) and the local authority can take such action as is reasonable to safeguard or promote Jessica's welfare. The court will authorise the child's removal to local authority accommodation or it will order that the child remains in any hospital or other place where the child is being accommodated prior to the order being made. The court will consider whether contact should be allowed between Jessica and her parents and also whatever medical and psychiatric assessment is necessary. Usually the child will have contact with her parents but if it is considered that this would be detrimental to her welfare then contact can be refused and this refusal cannot be challenged. An emergency protection order lasts for eight days ( s 45(1), although it can be extended once more for a further seven days ( s 45(6) if the court has cause to believe that, if it is not extended, Jessica will suffer significant harm. The emergency protection order can be challenged by the child and her parents and anyone else having parental responsibility for her, after 72 hours have expired. However, a challenge is not possible if the parties were given notice of the hearing and were present at it ( s 45(11). Since the emergency protection order is a very dramatic step to take, the court will consider long and hard whether it is in the child's best interest for such an order to be made.

Under the **Children Act 1989 s 44A** it is possible for the court to make an exclusion requirement in respect of Harry if this would mean that Jessica would no longer suffer significant harm or be at risk of it. This would exclude Harry from the home as part of an interim care order or emergency protection order, provided that Isobel was able to care for Jessica and consented to the making of the order. This would mean that Jessica could remain at home if Harry were not there. As well as ordering this, the court can accept an undertaking from Harry that he would leave until matters were finally sorted out.

Clearly, in this case there are concerns as to what is troubling Jessica and it would seem that the parents' attitude is somewhat ambivalent, given the concerns expressed by the local authority. Whether this is sufficiently significant to give rise to the need for an emergency protection order is debatable. Concern has frequently been expressed at the hasty removal of children from their parents' care by local authorities; therefore it may be that the local authority would be best served by making an application for a child assessment order in the instant case, since the evidence of abuse is not sufficiently overwhelming to justify the application for the emergency protection order. An emergency protection order should only be sought if the child assessment order is being thwarted by Harry and Isobel, Jessica's parents. If either the child assessment order or the emergency protection order produces evidence that Jessica is in fact being abused, then the local authority will need to consider more long-term measures. The appropriate measure to take would be the care order under  s 31of the Act. The local authority may apply for a care order if it can establish the threshold criteria in  s 31 The local authority must first satisfy the court that Jessica is suffering or is likely to suffer significant harm and, secondly, that the harm or likelihood of harm is attributable to the care being given to Jessica or likely to be given to her if the order is not made, not being what it would be reasonable to expect a parent to give her; or that the child is beyond parental control. The evidence of Jessica's distress at school and her change in personality, coupled with the findings of the investigation, either under the child assessment order or emergency protection order, may substantiate the claim that Jessica is suffering significant harm. Harm under the Act means ill-treatment or impairment of health and development. Ill-treatment includes sexual abuse as well as physical and mental ill-treatment. If Jessica has indeed been sexually abused by either or both of her parents, then the criterion of harm will be satisfied and clearly, if nothing is done, Jessica will continue to suffer this significant harm. It is also necessary to show that the harm is because of the care being given to the child by her parents. If the parents are responsible for the abuse or are failing to act to protect Jessica from it, then their actions are not those of the reasonable parent and the s 31 criteria will be established. Jessica's welfare under s 1(1) of the Act is the crucial consideration and is paramount throughout. In cases of serious sexual abuse it will be necessary to remove the child from the family environment so as to ensure that the abuse does not continue. The s 1(3) checklist must be applied and Jessica's wishes must be ascertained. If she is being abused she will obviously have confused feelings about her parents and whether she wishes to remain with them or be removed into local authority care. This is not a case where the court can stand back and do nothing. The non-interventionist policy enshrined in s 1(5) of the Act will have to be put to one side as something needs to be done to ensure that Jessica's well-being is safeguarded.

Any care order that is made will last until Jessica is 18 unless it is discharged earlier either on application by the child, by her parents or by the local authority. Even though a care order is made, the local authority should consider the question of contact, especially in relation to the parents of the child. Usually contact will be allowed even though a parent may have abused the child. It will usually always be possible for the other innocent parent to see the child. Even the abuser may have limited supervised access to the child since it is often in the child's best interest for the relationship to be given the opportunity to be repaired. However, it is crucial to try to ensure that any abuse is not repeated. If Jessica is taken into care by the local authority, the local authority has a duty under s 22 of the Act to promote the child's welfare and to consider Jessica's wishes and those of her parents at all stages. The parental responsibility of Harry and Isobel does not end on the making of the care order and the local authority will still try to keep them involved in the upbringing of their child where this is still in the child's best interest. The local authority will consult Jessica to see how she wishes her future to unfold and it will also consult her parents if possible. In making any decisions about the child, s 22(5) of the Act requires the local authority to take into account the wishes and feelings of the child and her parents, and also to take into account the child's religion, racial origin and cultural background.

In conclusion, therefore, it can be seen that in relation to Jack the appropriate measures for the local authority are an education supervision order and, failing that, a care order or possibly a supervision order under s 31 of the Act. In relation to Jessica, however, more stringent measures may be needed. First, an investigation by way of a child assessment order will be required or, in an emergency, an emergency protection order. If either of these measures discloses that Jessica is being abused then it will be necessary to make a care order under s 31 of the Act. In relation to both children any application must have their welfare as the paramount consideration, and consequently it will only be when the full facts are known about Jessica and Jack that the appropriate order can be sought.

## Common Pitfalls

If you are advising the local authority be clear what measures are available on the facts and also what measures are likely to be the most effective and appropriate. An answer which vaguely and generally discusses all the long-term and short-term orders is unlikely to do well. It is far better to decide based on the facts which is the most appropriate order and explain why.

## Aim Higher

Good answers will show an awareness of the difficulties of this area of child law and will be sensitive to how the law has developed and may yet develop.

# QUESTION 41

Molly has three illegitimate children by different men, and has struggled to bring them up. Two years ago, Molly had a mental breakdown and was admitted into hospital. The two eldest children, both boys, were accommodated by the local authority with temporary foster parents, whilst the youngest child, a girl, was looked after by Molly's mother, Connie. When Molly was released from hospital, she demanded the return of her children, but was unable to cope with them, and severely neglected them. Again, the local authority and Connie stepped in to look after the children, at Molly's request, which they have done to date. Molly has recently begun to live with Frank, who has a criminal record of violence and sexual offences. Molly has indicated to the local authority that as soon as she feels up to it, she wants the children to live with her and Frank. Both the local authority and Connie are concerned about this, as Molly does not have a good record as a mother, and Frank's criminal record raises serious questions about his suitability as a substitute parent.

▶  Advise the local authority.

## How to Answer this Question

Begin by explaining the concept of parental responsibility and the local authority's obligation to provide assistance to Molly and the children as being a family in need: ss 17–20. This is a voluntary arrangement and does not give the local authority parental responsibility or any compulsory powers over the children.

This would only be possible on an application for a care order (s 31), and the threshold criteria of likelihood of significant harm must be established. The child's welfare is paramount and it may be that having examined the s 1(3) checklist, the court is satisfied that there is sufficient risk to justify the making of an order.

The possibility of speedy intervention by way of an emergency protection order (s 44) should be examined, and so should the possibility of the grandmother applying for a residence order under s 8.

## Applying the Law

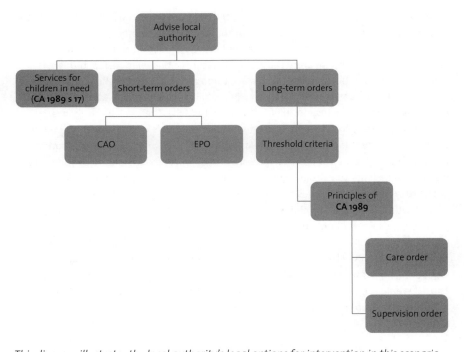

*This diagram illustrates the local authority's legal options for intervention in this scenario.*

# ANSWER

In this case the local authority requires advice on what steps, if any, it should take in relation to Molly's three children. It seems that Molly is the only person with parental responsibility over her children:Children Act 1989 s 2(2) . This parental responsibility places an obligation on Molly to promote her children's welfare and to provide for their everyday needs. In the case of a person such as Molly, where a parent experiences difficulty in coping with the demands that their children impose, the local authority has a statutory duty under theChildren Act 1989 s 17 to assist parents and children in need. This general duty to children in need requires the local authority to safeguard and promote the welfare of children within their area who are in need, and, so far as is possible, to promote the upbringing of children by their families by providing a range and level of services to assist with those children's needs:s 17(1) . To supplement this duty the local authority is also under an obligation to provide accommodation to children in need, where the person who has been caring for the children is prevented, whether permanently or not and for whatever reason, from providing the children with suitable accommodation or care:Children Act 1989 s 20 .

In this Molly's mental breakdown has prevented her from providing her children with the care that they require and so it is quite clear that the local authority has voluntarily entered into a relationship with Molly, whereby it has provided accommodation for the children. The essential nature of this relationship, though, is a voluntary one; a relationship has taken place through the consent of the parent, Molly. The local authority acquires no parental responsibility in the present situation and, instead, all the parental responsibility remains with Molly. The local authority has, by virtue ofs 22 , a duty to safeguard and promote the children's welfare and it is required to take into account the wishes and feelings of the children and the children's parents unders 22(4) . This requires the local authority, when making decisions, to consider those wishes and feelings and also the child's religious, racial and cultural background. In this case, little is known of the ages of the children and, as such, not much can be said about the impact of the children's views on how the local authority will proceed. However, the local authority has a duty to promote contact between the child and her parent and it is quite clear that until any compulsory powers are exercised, Molly has the right to contact with her children and she has the right to remove her children whenever she wishes without having to comply with any formal notice requirements. Thus, it would seem that Molly has the absolute right to remove her children from local authority care even though the local authority may be unhappy with her future living arrangements.[4]

4   A care order would be a useful order for the local authority because it would give them parental responsibility meaning they could direct how Molly exercised her parental responsibility.

The only option available to the local authority in relation to the two children in its care is to take care proceedings under the **Children Act 1989 s 31** . In relation to the child who is living with Molly's mother, Connie, the local authority again has the option of care proceedings. There is, however, the additional possibility that Connie, as a grandparent and someone with whom the child has had her home for a period of time, may apply for a residence order in relation to the child under the **Children Act 1989 s 8** . This residence order would enable the child to remain with her grandmother rather than return to her mother and her mother's new partner. There is the further possibility that Connie could apply for a residence order in relation to her other two grandchildren and each of these options will now be discussed in turn.

This application must be made to the Family Proceedings Court and the court must be satisfied, first, that the child is suffering or is likely to suffer significant harm. The two boys are at present suffering no harm but there is the likelihood that they may suffer significant harm if they return to their mother's care. Harm is defined in the Act as meaning ill-treatment which can include sexual, physical and mental ill-treatment and impairment of health and development. It does seem that if the children return to Molly, Frank's criminal record may pose a risk to them. Also, Molly's mental illness and her previous history indicate that the children's health and development may be impaired. It was held in *Newham London Borough Council v AG* (1993) that there is no need to prove the threshold criteria on the balance of probabilities; the court will be satisfied if there is a real significant likelihood of the child suffering harm. It is submitted that in the present case, given the seriousness of Frank's criminal record, this will be made out.

The second part of the statutory criteria is that the harm or likelihood of harm is attributable to the care being given to the child or likely to be given to him if the order is not made, not being what it would be reasonable to expect a parent to give him, or the child being beyond parental control. There is no evidence that the two elder children are beyond parental control, but the evidence does point to the level of care that the children might receive as not being at the level that it is reasonable to expect. If the statutory criteria are established, as in any **Children Act** order, the court must consider the child's welfare as its paramount consideration § 1(1) ), and in determining what is in the child's welfare the court will look at the **s 1(3)** checklist factors. The first of these factors is the ascertainable wishes of the children in the light of their age and understanding. As previously indicated, little is known of the age of these children, and if they are very young then the likelihood is that their wishes will not be given much weight. If the children are approaching teenage years then the court will give great credence to their wishes and to their fears about their future. If, as seems likely, the children are happy with the present arrangements and are concerned about returning to their mother, the court will be reluctant to allow this to occur. Clearly, the children's educational and physical and mental needs are being met in local authority care and there is serious doubt as to whether their mother would be able to meet such a need. There is also considerable benefit derived from keeping siblings together and it is not clear that Molly will be able to cope with both children. It is likely that both children have also had contact with their sister whilst she has been with their grandmother. Looking at the range of powers available to the court, the court is probably going to be mindful of the fact that a care order does give a certain degree of control over the children's well-being, whereas making no order at all would place the children at risk. This is not a case where the non-interventionist policy in s 1(5) would hold true.[5]

Care proceedings are usually taken after full notice is given to all the parties. This would require a children's guardian to be appointed in relation to the children and it would also require Molly to be given notice as a parent. This could alert Molly as to the steps the local authority is planning to take and may result in her demanding the immediate removal of the children from local authority accommodation. In the event of this occurring, the local authority may decide to apply for an emergency protection order under s 44 of the Act. An emergency protection order may be applied for on the basis in s 44(1)(a) that there is reasonable cause to believe that the child is likely to suffer significant harm if he does not remain in the place where he is presently being accommodated. This order is a somewhat draconian measure and it can authorise the child to remain in the place where he is presently being accommodated immediately prior to the order (s 44(4)(b)). This order gives the local authority parental responsibility for the children for its duration (s 44(4)(c)). However, the order only lasts for eight days (s 45(1)) although it can be extended once for a further seven days if there is reasonable cause to believe that, if the order is not extended, the children are likely to suffer significant harm.

If an emergency protection order is made, the court will give directions as to whether Molly is to be allowed contact with the children. There is little in the facts to require contact to be forbidden as Molly has not physically ill-treated the children. However, it is quite clear that contact with Frank should be prohibited. The emergency protection order can be challenged by the children or by Molly, the parent, under s 45(8), but this cannot be challenged until 72 hours have elapsed, and there will be no possibility of challenge if Molly was given notice of the hearing and was present at it (s 45(11)). This emergency protection order would give the local authority breathing space before a care order can be made. The care order under s 31 would probably need to be an interim order until the full facts can be put to the courts. If a care order is made, the local authority acquires parental responsibility for the children. Molly does not lose her parental responsibility but she will not be able to exercise it in a way that is inconsistent with the local authority's parental responsibility. By having a care order in relation to the children, the local authority can decide where the children should reside. This may be in local authority care or with foster parents or it may be that the local authority will arrange for the children to live with members of their family, either Connie, their grandmother, or maybe even Molly,

---

5   Applying for a care order or a supervision order is a two stage process. First the threshold criteria must be satisfied, and then, if they are satisfied, the court will consider whether the principles of the **Children Act 1989** support the making of an order.

provided she agrees not to reside with Frank. The care order will remain in force until the children are 18 unless it is discharged earlier either on application by the parent or by the child or local authority (s 39(1)) or, possibly, on the making of a residence order, for example, in favour of Connie, the grandmother. If a care order is made, contact is usually presumed to be in the child's best interest and, clearly, contact with Molly would not necessarily damage the children in any way. It is usually advantageous for children to maintain the relationship they have with their parents. However, it is not desirable for the children to develop any relationship with Frank and this is likely to be prohibited.

Turning to the child who is in the care of Connie, her grandmother, again the local authority could take care proceedings and seek an emergency protection order as indicated previously. However, there is the additional possibility that Connie, the grandmother, could seek a residence order under the **Children Act 1989 s 8**. A residence order would settle the child's arrangements in so far as it would determine where the child should live and it would give Connie parental responsibility. This would not terminate Molly's parental responsibility but, nevertheless, it would enable the child to remain with her grandparent. The difficulty here is that Connie, as a grandparent, will need leave in order to obtain a s 8 order. In deciding whether to give leave to Connie, the court will consider the nature of her application and her connection with the child. Clearly, she has a very close connection with the child and it does not seem that there would be any risk of her application disrupting the child's life. It is also quite clear that Connie's application would have the support of the local authority, in that the local authority has no desire for the child to return to her parent. However, this application would contradict the wishes and feelings of Molly, the child's parent, but, as in any application, the court would probably allow leave since there is a genuine concern on the part of the applicant for the welfare of the child.

If an application is made for a residence order under s 8, the paramount consideration is the welfare of the child under s 1(1). In determining what was in the child's best interests, the court would have regard to the factors in the checklist (s 1(3)). The ascertainable wishes and feelings of the child, given their age and understanding, would be considered by the court. However, as before, little is known of the age of the child and therefore little can be said about the weight that would be attached to her views. Her educational, emotional and other needs have been satisfactorily met by her grandmother over the past few years and it seems likely that the grandmother would be in a better position to meet those needs than the mother and her new partner. Indeed the mother has a poor history in relation to mothering skills, albeit not through her own fault, and it does not seem that the living conditions with Molly and Frank would be conducive to the child's best interest.

Although the court does like to keep brothers and sisters together because of the mutual support that they derive from one another (*Adams v Adams* (1984)), the children in this case have been used to living apart and therefore the mother's claim that she could accommodate them all together would have little weight. She has been unable to sustain in the past the obligation to care for all of her children together and it seems quite clear that the status quo would be disturbed if the child were removed from her grandmother's care to be given to her mother. Although generally there is an advantage in care being provided by a parent, the parent's conduct in the past has not been such to inspire confidence. The parent's new partner does seem to pose a risk to the future well-being of the children in that he has a violent record and a record that involves sexual offences. In *Scott v Scott* (1986) , the mother's partner had a history of violence and indecency and that offset any advantages that living with a mother would normally involve.

In conclusion therefore, it would seem that this child's best interests might well be served by her remaining with her grandmother. In deciding whether to make as 8 order, the court will have in mind the need to avoid delay (s 1(2) ) and the need to avoid unnecessary intervention (s 1(5) ). However, this is clearly a case where to allow the child to return to her mother may well wreak havoc with the child's welfare. Therefore the court will clearly have to consider whether to make as 8 order in relation to the grandmother or whether to grant a care order in relation to the local authority. It seems clear that the local authority and grandmother are united in their concern about the well-being of the child and it seems possible that either course of action could be employed for the welfare of the youngest daughter. However, in an emergency it may be necessary to couple either the care order or thes 8 residence order with an emergency protection order. It is important to note that only the local authority can apply for the emergency protection order. Connie, as a grandparent, would have no *locus standi* to make such an application if her daughter were to demand the return of the child.

# QUESTION 42

Sharon, aged 17, has one daughter, Jade, aged two, but has no idea who Jade's father is. The health visitor has contacted the local authority to express her concern about Jade. Sharon had failed to keep a number of appointments at the clinic, and when she had finally brought Jade, the child had a number of bruises. Jade is a boisterous and unruly child, and Sharon admits to finding her hard to handle.

When the health visitor asked Sharon about Jade's bruises, Sharon stormed out, telling the health visitor to mind her own business.

▶ Advise the local authority on what steps, if any, it should take.

## How to Answer this Question

Again, this question requires an understanding of the relationship between the local authority's duty to assist families in need and the compulsory powers that may be exercisable after a court order for a child at risk. Sharon has parental responsibility for Jade and the local authority has a duty to investigate cases where it is suspected the child is suffering harm (s 47 ). Co-operation with the parent is desirable. Then explore the duty to assist andss 17–20 under which Sharon could voluntarily seek local authority assistance in relation to Jade. If Sharon is unco-operative, then a child assessment order may be sought ( s 43 ), and, in extreme cases, an emergency protection order ( s 44 ). Both these options must be explored in detail. If there is a risk to Jade, then a care or supervision order should be sought ( s 31 ).

## Applying the Law

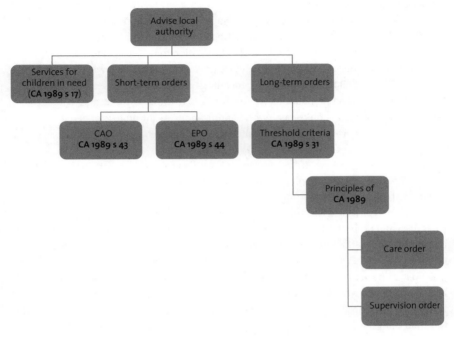

*This diagram illustrates the local authority's legal options for intervention in this scenario.*

# ANSWER

Sharon is the one person who has parental responsibility for Jade (Children Act 1989 s 2(2) ). Parental responsibility is defined as 'all the rights, duties, powers and responsibilities and authority which by law a parent of a child has in relation to the child and its property': Children Act 1989 s 3(1) . This stresses that Sharon has the obligation to care for her child, and to promote the child's welfare.

The health visitor's concern over Jade's welfare must be sensitively handled by the local authority; whilst they must obviously act swiftly to employ their statutory powers for a child at risk, they must also ensure that careful consideration is given as to whether any intervention is necessary.[6]

6 If possible the local authority should try and work in partnership with the child's parent(s) and should prefer using services for children in need over coercive measures.

It is quite common for small children to have bruises without there being any abuse, and parents who are stressed or under pressure may overreact to questions. The local authority needs to determine whether Sharon is managing her parental responsibility without the need for interference, whether some action is required either to assist Sharon and Jade on a voluntary basis, or whether to protect Jade using compulsory orders from the court. The **Children Act 1989 s 47** requires the local authority to investigate cases where there is reasonable cause to suspect that the child is suffering, or is likely to suffer, significant harm. The concern of an experienced health visitor should not usually be ignored, and do indicate that some kind of investigation may be called for. Initially, it would seem that the local authority should try to work in partnership with Sharon. The philosophy of the **Children Act 1989** is to encourage co-operation between parents and the local authority, and to maintain, wherever possible, the care of the child within the family. A social worker should speak with Sharon, and relevant professionals, such as doctors and health visitors, can be consulted to obtain their views on the family.

It will be possible to gauge Sharon and Jade's position after talking with Sharon, and possibly holding a case conference. If, as seems likely, Sharon is experiencing difficulty coping with the demands of bringing up a two year old child, then the local authority may be able to provide assistance. There is a general duty on a local authority to safeguard and promote the welfare of a child in need, and to do this by promoting Jade's upbringing within the family by providing services to help meet the child's needs: **Children Act 1989 s 17(1)**. Jade will qualify as a child in need if she is unlikely to achieve, or maintain, or have the opportunity of achieving or maintaining, a reasonable standard of health and development (s 17(10)) unless the local authority provides services to facilitate this. Health includes both mental and physical health (s 17(11)), and development includes the child's physical, intellectual, emotional, social or behavioural development.

Little is known about Sharon's socio-economic background, but it is likely that as a young single parent she is socially disadvantaged and not economically well-off. Her living conditions may be such that Jade is frustrated and bored, and might well qualify as a child in need. The local authority, in partnership with Sharon, could provide a range of services, including such things as nursery provision, clubs, etc to provide Jade with stimulation, and Sharon with some relief from the pressures of continuous child care.

The local authority could offer to accommodate Jade voluntarily under s 20 if Sharon is prevented (whether or not permanently and/or for whatever reason) from providing Jade with suitable accommodation or care. This can only take place if Sharon requests the local authority to assist her, and could be used to provide short-term care for Jade whilst Sharon sorts out other aspects of her life. Since this arrangement would be entirely voluntary, Sharon could remove Jade from the local authority's care at any time without having to comply with any formal requirements: s 20(8). Before the local authority provides accommodation for such a child, it must ascertain the wishes of the child (s 20(6)) but, as Jade is only two, this will not be possible. Whilst Jade is being accommodated by the local authority, it has a duty to safeguard and promote her welfare (s 22(3)) and to consult Sharon and take into account Sharon's wishes and the religious, racial, cultural and linguistic characteristics of the child (s 22(5)). Sharon would be encouraged to keep close contact with Jade and to remain involved with her, so that when Sharon's position has stabilised, she and her child can be reunited. The local authority does not acquire parental responsibility for a child voluntarily accommodated with it, and these measures are useful to help a family through difficult times.

It may be that, if Sharon persists in being evasive and abusive when asked about Jade, the local authority will need to satisfy itself that Jade is not suffering harm due to abuse or neglect. One option here would seem to be an application to the Family Proceedings Court for a child assessment order: **Children Act 1989 s 43**. This is the usual means of discovering what is happening to the child in circumstances where parental co-operation has not been forthcoming. The local authority must give notice of its application to Sharon, and the court will only grant an order if the applicant has reasonable cause to suspect that the child is suffering, or is likely to suffer, significant harm. Jade's bruising and Sharon's reluctance to take her to the clinic, and her aggressive reaction to the health visitor, might suffice to establish this. In addition, it is necessary to show that an assessment of the child is necessary to establish whether she is suffering, or is likely to suffer, significant harm, and that it is unlikely that any satisfactory assessment will be made without a child assessment order. Sharon's unco-operative stance makes it likely that the grounds for an order have been established. However, as with all orders under the **Children Act 1989**, the child's welfare is the paramount consideration (s 1), and the court will wish to ensure that there is as little delay as possible (s 1(2)), once it determines that making an order is better than not making an order (s 1(5)).

An assessment order lasts for a maximum of seven days, and Sharon will be ordered to ensure that Jade turns up at the appropriate time and place for assessment. Jade would normally remain at home, unless the order specifies that she remain in another place, for example, a hospital (s 43(9)). The local authority does not acquire parental responsibility.

If Sharon refused to comply with the child assessment order, or the local authority formed the view that Jade was in immediate danger, then an application could be made for an emergency protection order. This is a more serious measure, and should only be taken in cases where there is a clear, pressing need to protect a child at risk. The basis for granting an order under s 44 to the local authority is that there is reasonable cause to believe that the child is likely to suffer significant harm if she remains where she is and is not removed to local authority accommodation. The alternative is to show that enquiries are being made in respect of the child, and that those enquiries are being frustrated by Sharon unreasonably refusing access to Jade. There is then the need to show that access to the child is required as a matter of urgency. The emergency protection order lasts for eight days, although it may be extended for a further seven days: s 45(6) The order can authorise the removal of Jade from her home, and gives the local authority parental responsibility for the limited time the order is in force. The court will decide whether Sharon should have contact with Jade during this time, and the order can only be challenged by Sharon, or Jade ( s 45(8), once it has been in force for 72 hours, provided they had no notice of the original hearing ( s 45(11).[7]

If, after examining Jade, the local authority is still concerned about her well-being, then there are two further options available: the care order or supervision order ( s 31). The option of wardship is no longer available for local authorities. The local authority must apply to the Family Proceedings Court, or County Court and High Court in complex cases, making Sharon, the parent, and Jade, the child, respondents in the case.

The basis for a care or supervision order may be found in  s 31 and the court must be satisfied that the child is suffering, or is likely to suffer, significant harm, and this is attributable to the care being given to the child not being what it would be reasonable to expect a parent to give him, or the child is beyond parental control. There would be a need to establish significant harm which means ill-treatment, physical, sexual or mental abuse, or impairment of health and development. This must go beyond an occasional bruise, and it must be shown that the care being provided by Sharon falls short of what care can reasonably be expected.

---

7    The emergency protection order is a more serious order than the child assessment order. The EPO gives the local authority parental responsibility whereas the CAO does not and can lead to the child being removed. It is not surprising therefore that the grounds for obtaining the EPO are more serious than the grounds for obtaining the CAO – belief of abuse in the case of the EPO rather than suspicion in the case of the CAO.

# Adotion

## INTRODUCTION

Adoption involves the severing of the legal relationship between a child and his or her natural parents and the establishing of a new relationship with the adoptive parents ( *Webster v Norfolk County Council* (2009**)**. The law on adoption is set out in the **Adoption and Children Act 2002( ACA)**. This Act has extended the definition of who is able to adopt to include unmarried couples ( **Adoption and Children Act 2002 ss 50, 114(4)** and has made the welfare of the child paramount, whilst under the **Adoption Act 1976**it was only the court's first consideration. Adoption procedure has also been amended.

Under the new Act, adoption can either be an agency adoption, where the child is placed by the adoption agency, or a non-agency adoption, where the child does not have to be placed by an adoption agency. The latter category would include step-parent adoptions and adoptions of the child by a foster carer. Whatever the type of adoption, the child will need to be placed with the prospective adopters before the adoption order can be made. The length of this placement will vary depending on who is adopting the child ( **Adoption and Children Act 2002 s 42)**. If the adoption is an agency adoption, students will need to be able to explain whether the child is placed with consent ( **Adoption and Children Act 2002 ss 19–20)**, or under a placement order ( **Adoption and Children Act 2002 ss 21–24)**. If the adoption is a non-agency adoption, prospective adopters will need to inform the local authority of their intention to adopt ( **Adoption and Children Act 2002 s 44)**.

In deciding whether to make the adoption order, the court is bound by the principle that the child's welfare is paramount and they will use the welfare checklist in **s 1(4)**to decide whether the child's welfare supports adoption. In addition, the consent of everyone with parental responsibility (PR) is needed before an adoption order can be made, although this can be dispensed with if the child's welfare demands it ( **Adoption and Children Act 2002 s 52(1)**.

As well as reforming adoption law, the **Adoption and Children Act 2002**also introduced special guardianship. Unlike adoption, special guardianship does not completely remove parental responsibility from the birth parents, but most aspects of parental responsibility can be exercised solely by the special guardian ( **Children Act 1989 s 14C)**. Students should be aware of the special guardianship order (SGO) and should be able to consider it as an alternative to adoption or a residence order where appropriate.

# QUESTION 43

Anna and Bertie were married five years ago, and had a daughter, Carrie, who is now two. Bertie was a famous footballer, but the marriage encountered difficulties when he began to experiment with drugs. One night, whilst under the influence of drugs, Bertie became violent and assaulted Anna, breaking her nose. Bertie was horrified by what he had done and voluntarily entered a rehabilitation centre, but Anna divorced him on the basis of his behaviour. Anna subsequently married David, and Carrie lives with them. David adores Carrie and would like to adopt her. Bertie has tried to maintain contact with Carrie.

▶ Advise Anna and David whether they will be able to adopt Carrie.

## How to Answer this Question

❖ Define adoption.
❖ Examine who can be adopted and who can adopt.
❖ Explain problem of step-parent adoption.
❖ Look at issue of parental consent and dispensing with it.
❖ See if s 1 would permit the making of the order.
❖ Consider alternatives to adoption.

## Applying the Law

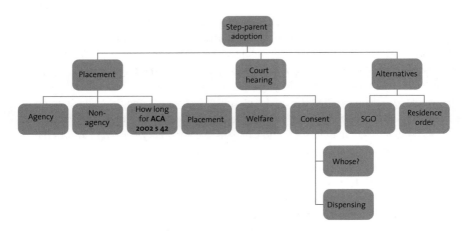

*The position of the David as a step-parent is illustrated here.*

# ANSWER

Anna and David want David to adopt Anna's daughter, Carrie. If the adoption is allowed this would mean that Carrie's birth father, Bertie, would be legally classed as a stranger to Carrie (**Adoption and Children Act 2002 s 46(2)(a)**). There are other ways of recognising and formalising David's relationship with Carrie and these should also be explored as the court may decide that they would be more appropriate.[1]

The first stage of the adoption procedure is the placement of the child with the prospective adopters. Under an agency adoption, the child is placed by the adoption agency. Under a non-agency adoption, the child is already living with the prospective adopters. As Carrie is already living with Anna and David, this is a non-agency adoption. The **Adoption and Children Act 2002** has reformed the law so that a step-parent who wishes to adopt his step-child no longer needs to adopt with that child's birth parent. As a result, in this case, it will just be David who is the adopter. David will need to inform the local authority that he intends to adopt Carrie (**Adoption and Children Act 2002 s 144**). The reason for this is so that the local authority can visit the placement and prepare welfare reports to help the court decide whether the adoption is in Carrie's welfare. Under the **Adoption and Children Act 2002 s 42**, Carrie has to be placed with David for six months before he can apply to adopt her.

The court will only make an adoption order in favour of David if it is in Carrie's welfare to do so. The welfare of the child is now the court's paramount consideration – **s 1(1)** and the court will use the welfare checklist in **s 1(4)** to determine what is in Carrie's welfare. From the facts, it seems that David has a good relationship with Carrie and would be able to care for her and meet her needs. The main problem for the court is the fact that an adoption order would terminate the parental responsibility of Bertie and make him a legal stranger to his daughter. Although the facts state that Bertie has been violent in the past, he has tried to maintain contact with his daughter and the court might well feel that it would not be in Carrie's interest to erase Bertie from her history. Furthermore, Bertie has tried to obtain help for his problem and it is far from clear that he would be violent again. One advantage that adoption might have over alternatives is that it is permanent and because it removes Bertie's parental responsibility there would be no danger of Bertie interfering in how Anna and David were raising Carrie. It is submitted, however, that this reasoning is less pertinent on these facts as Bertie does not seem to have undermined David and Anna's raising of Carrie.[2]

Furthermore, it should be noted that under the **Adoption and Children Act 2002 s 1(6)** the court does have to consider whether any alternatives to adoption could better promote

1   Adoption is the only way in which a mother or father with parental responsibility can lose that parental responsibility. Once the adoption order is made, the birth parent loses his or her parental responsibility and is legally a stranger in respect of the child.
2   Under the **Adoption Act 1976**, which was the previous adoption law, the child's welfare was the first consideration. The **Adoption and Children Act 2002 s 1(1)** changed this so that adoption was the paramount consideration. This means that not only does the child's welfare outweigh all other considerations, it outweighs all other considerations put together.

the welfare of the child. It is unclear why David wishes to adopt Carrie but if it is because he wishes to strengthen his rights in relation to Carrie, this could also be done through a residence order which would give David parental responsibility whilst not removing that of Bertie. Alternatively, under the **Children Act 1989 s 4A** it is now possible for a court to make a parental responsibility order in favour of the step-parent, meaning that in this case the court could award David parental responsibility without removing the parental responsibility of Bertie.

On the facts given, it is unlikely that the court would consider an adoption order to be in Carrie's welfare; however, if they were to do so, Bertie's consent to the adoption would be required. Under the **Adoption and Children Act 2002 s 52(1)** a birth parent's consent can be dispensed with if the welfare of the child demands it. The problem with this section is that once the court has decided that adoption is in the child's welfare, it is arguably very difficult for a parent to then argue that it is not also in the child's welfare for their consent to be dispensed with. As a result, if (and on the facts this is unlikely) the court decides that adoption is in Carrie's interest, it is very likely that they will dispense with Bertie's consent and the adoption order will be made.

# QUESTION 44

Tamsin is five. Tamsin's mother, Sarah, is an alcoholic and Tamsin is usually cared for by her maternal grandparents, Ruth and Peter. Although Tamsin usually lives with Ruth and Peter, occasionally Sarah demands that Tamsin leave her grandparents and come and live with her. Ruth and Peter feel that this is very disruptive and upsetting for Tamsin and they also feel that Sarah's lifestyle means that she is not properly meeting Tamsin's needs. They would like to be able to keep Tamsin with them, but they do not feel that they can refuse Sarah's demands to return Tamsin to them. Ruth and Peter would like to become Tamsin's permanent legal carers and are considering adoption as a way of achieving this.

▶ **Advise Ruth and Peter.**

## How to Answer this Question

❖ Can they adopt Tamsin – procedure? Would court make an adoption order?

❖ Alternatives to adoption – residence order?

❖ Alternatives to adoption – special guardianship order?

## Applying the Law

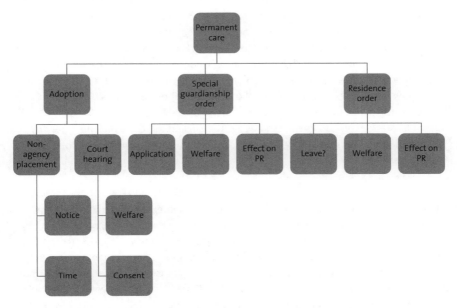

*Ruth and Peter's position and the key factors to consider are illustrated here.*

# ANSWER
Ruth and Peter want to become their granddaughter Tamsin's permanent carers.
They are considering adoption but it may be that other options, a residence order or a
special guardianship order, are more appropriate and more likely to be awarded by the
courts.

Under the **Adoption and Children Act 2002** there are two main types of adoption – an
agency adoption and a non-agency adoption. Under an agency adoption, the child is
placed with the adoptive parents by the adoption agency. Under a non-agency adoption,
the child does not need to be placed by the adoption agency because the child is already
living with the prospective adopters. In this case, Tamsin is already living with Ruth
and Peter so this is likely to be a non-agency adoption and they will have to give the
adoption agency notice of their intention to adopt Tamsin under the **Adoption and
Children Act 2002 s 144**. Although the facts do not state Ruth and Peter's ages, they will
be over 21 and therefore will meet the age requirements for adoption and, following the
introduction of the **Adoption and Children Act 2002 s 50**, they will no longer have to be
married in order to adopt as a couple. Under the **Adoption and Children Act 2002 s 42**,
Tamsin will have to be placed with Ruth and Peter for a minimum of three years before
they can apply to adopt her.

Under the **Adoption and Children Act 2002 s 1(1)**, the court will only make an adoption order in Ruth and Peter's favour if adoption is in Tamsin's welfare. In so doing, the court will consider the welfare checklist in the **Adoption and Children Act 2002 s 1(4)** and in particular, it will consider whether there are any other options for care which will better promote Tamsin's welfare. In favour of the adoption is the fact that Tamsin is already cared for by Ruth and Peter and therefore she will not be uprooted by the adoption; furthermore, the facts seem to suggest that they are better able to meet Tamsin's needs than her mother, who is an alcoholic. Moreover, at present Tamsin's mother, Sarah, is unsettling Tamsin by moving her from Ruth and Peter's home. If Tamsin is adopted, Sarah legally becomes a stranger to Tamsin and therefore no longer has any power to do this. This may strengthen Ruth and Peter's position and make Tamsin feel more secure.[3]

On the other hand, there are problems with adoption. If Ruth and Peter adopt Tamsin, it would mean that her grandparents would become her parents and her birth mother would be her sister. This would be difficult and confusing for Tamsin. Moreover, at present, Sarah is an alcoholic; if she were ever able to recover from this, she may be able to resume care of her daughter and therefore adoption, which permanently removes her parental responsibility, may not be the best option for Tamsin's welfare. When the court considers whether adoption is in a child's welfare, it also has to consider whether another option would better promote the child's welfare (**Adoption and Children Act 2002 s 1(2)**) and accordingly the court might want to consider whether a residence order or a special guardianship order would be more appropriate.[4]

A residence order determines whom the child lives with. Therefore if a residence order is made in Ruth and Peter's favour, Tamsin would live with them and Sarah would not legally be able to remove her. Furthermore, a residence order would give Ruth and Peter parental responsibility (**Children Act 1989 s 12**) and therefore enable Ruth and Peter to make decisions regarding their granddaughter (**Children Act 1989 s 3(1)**). Special guardianship (SG) would also give Ruth and Peter parental responsibility for Tamsin; however, whereas with a residence order they would share parental responsibility with Sarah, with special guardianship they would be in a privileged position and would be solely responsible for all but the most significant decisions. The advantage that both these orders have is that they do not distort the family tree – Ruth and Peter would still be Tamsin's grandparents although they would be the people raising her. On the other hand, neither residence

3   Under the **Adoption and Children Act 2002**, the child's welfare is the court's paramount consideration. This was a change from the **Adoption Act 1976**, where it was only the first consideration.

4   Adoption offers more permanence and security than alternatives such as a residence order or a special guardianship order. This is partly because it is not limited to the child's minority, but also because the birth parent(s) loses parental responsibility. They would need the leave of the court to apply for **s 8** orders which might be used to control the use of the carers' parental responsibility and this leave would only exceptionally be given.

orders nor special guardianship offers the same degree of permanency and stability that adoption provides. With both these orders, Sarah would still be Tamsin's mother and would still be able to apply for s 8 orders relating to her, and this potential upheaval and interference may be a strong argument against them and in favour of adoption.

On the scant facts, it is difficult to determine what order would be preferred by the courts. Nevertheless, it is possible that the fact that adoption would distort Tamsin's family set-up and potentially confuse her and cause further hostility between her grandparents and her birth mother is a strong argument against it and in favour of an alternative order. Another option for Ruth and Peter is to apply for a residence order rather than applying for adoption. Although Ruth and Peter do not have an automatic right to apply for a residence order (**Children Act 1989 s 10(4), s 10(5)**), their close connection with Tamsin means that they would almost certainly be given leave to apply (**Children Act 1989 s 10(11)**). Their application for a residence order would be decided on the basis of Tamsin's welfare (**Children Act 1989 s 1(1)**) and it is likely that it would be successful. It seems that Ruth and Peter are providing Tamsin with a good stable home and formalising this by giving them a residence order will not disrupt her.

## Common Pitfalls

This question is about permanent care and therefore adoption needs to be considered along with alternatives. Answers need to be clear on how adoption, special guardianship and residence orders differ, and need to be decided on the facts in the most appropriate order. As for adoption, it is important to understand when agency and non-agency procedure should be used and to be able to explain clearly what that procedure involves.

## Aim Higher

Good answers will show a sensitive and critical understanding of the issues involved as well as up to date knowledge of relevant case law.

# QUESTION 45

To what extent does the special guardianship order offer a useful alternative to the adoption order?

## How to Answer this Question

- ❖ What is the effect of the adoption order?
- ❖ What is the effect of the special guardianship order?
- ❖ The special guardianship order and kinship adoptions.
- ❖ The special guardianship order and permanence.

## Applying the Law

*The differences between special guardianship and adoption are shown here.*

# ANSWER

When an adoption order is made, parental responsibility belongs exclusively to the adoptive parents. The parental responsibility of the birth parents comes to an end and legally they become strangers to the child (**Adoption and Children Act 2002 s 46**). As well as reforming adoption law, the **Adoption and Children Act 2002** introduced special guardianship orders. Like adoption orders these are intended to offer a stable way of caring for and having responsibility for a child, but unlike adoption orders, the special guardianship order does not completely remove the parental responsibility of the birth parents. Under a special guardianship order, the special guardian will have exclusive parental responsibility for most decisions (**Children Act 1989 s 14C(1)(b)**); however, there is a core of especially significant decisions where the agreement of the birth parents, who have parental responsibility, is also required. This includes changing the child's surname (**Children Act 1989 s 14C(3)(a)**), removing the child from the jurisdiction for more than three months (**Children Act 1989 ss 14C(3)(b), 14C(4)**), and agreeing to the adoption of the child (**Children Act 1989 s 14C(20(b)**).

The idea behind special guardianship is that it offers a stable alternative to adoption in situations where adoption might not be appropriate. These situations are ones where, whilst the child may need a person to take on the responsibility of coming for them, they may not need or want a new parent and therefore adoption may not be suitable. The three situations that are most often thought to fulfil this are firstly the situation where a member of the child's family wants to adopt them (kinship adoption), secondly adoption of an older child, and thirdly adoption within a particular racial context. With an older child, he or she will often have formed a close bond with a birth parent that may make adoption and the legal extinguishing of that bond inappropriate. Special guardianship may be an appropriate way of responding to the child's need for care whilst recognising the reality of the relationship between the child and his birth family. On the other hand, it is important to note that the nature and reality of adoption has also developed and it is possible for an adoption order to be made that does allow for continued contact, indirect or direct, to be allowed after the order. As for the racial dimension, some groups do not adopt for religious or cultural reasons. Special guardianship orders allow these individuals to undertake the long-term care of children. This may well be a particular advantage to children who also come from those racial groups.

One situation where special guardianship might be more appropriate than adoption is where a member of the child's family, for example a grandparent, wants to adopt the child (*Re S (Adoption Order or Special Guardianship Order)* (2007)). One difficulty with adoption in this situation is that it distorts family relationships. The child's grandparent becomes their parent, their parent is now a sibling, and so on. Nevertheless, when a court has to determine whether to make an adoption order or a special guardianship order, it has to do so on the basis of the child's welfare (**Adoption and Children Act 2002 s 1(1)**) and although the potential distorting of family relationships may be an important factor in this it will not be the only consideration and there may be situations where adoption is preferred even in the kinship adoption context.

One advantage which adoption has over special guardianship is that is arguably more secure. When an adoption order is made, the birth parent becomes a legal stranger. One effect of this is that they no longer have a right to apply for any **s 8** orders in respect of the child and therefore the child's new family life cannot be disrupted by spurious **s 8** applications. In contrast, with a special guardianship order, the birth parent remains the child's parent and therefore the order always risks being disrupted by applications for contact or residence or the special guardian's exercise of parental responsibility being curtailed under **s 8** of the **Children Act**.

Along with adoption and residence order, the special guardianship order offers another means by which a person can have parental responsibility for a child and be responsible for their care. As it offers something between those two orders there will be situations where it will be the most appropriate way of promoting the child's welfare.

# QUESTION 46

Dawn is 25. She suffers from borderline personality disorder which is exacerbated by alcohol or drugs. Two years ago Dawn gave birth to a daughter, Evie. Evie was the result of a one night stand and neither she, nor Dawn, has seen Evie's father since. When Evie was about seven months old, a neighbour called the police after Evie was left alone whilst Dawn went out one night. This led to a police protection order and then to Evie being voluntarily accommodated under the **Children Act 1989 s 20**. Attempts were made to rehabilitate Evie with her mother, but sadly these always broke down, either as a result of Dawn's mental health, or because of her drinking and drug use. The local authority now believe that the best option for Evie is for her to be adopted and they have identified a couple they believe to be suitable, Fiona and Gary. Dawn has said that she is very unhappy at the proposed adoption and that she will not let Evie stay with Fiona and Gary. Dawn also has evidence that her own mental condition will worsen if the adoption is successful.

▶ Advise F and G on the procedure to adopt E and discuss whether the adoption would be successful.

## How to Answer this Question
### Placement of E for adoption:

❖ Is it an agency or a non-agency adoption? Because E is placed by the local authority it will be an agency adoption.
❖ How can the agency place E for adoption? With parental consent – whose? Or under placement order?
❖ Are the grounds for a placement order satisfied on the facts?
❖ How long is placement for and what will happen during placement?
❖ Can D remove E during the placement with F and G?

### Court Decision:

❖ What are the legal requirements for adopters and do F and G satisfy them?
❖ Adoption order would only be made if adoption is in E's welfare (**Adoption and Children Act 2002 s 1(1)**). Is it?
❖ What about the impact on D's health if the adoption order is made?
❖ Is D's consent needed? What if she refuses?

## Applying the Law

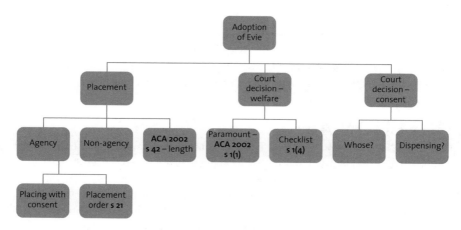

The key factors to consider in relation to the adoption of Evie are outlined above in relation to the relevant legislation.

# ANSWER

Having tried to rehabilitate Evie with her mother, Dawn, the local authority have now decided that Evie's needs will best be served by being adopted and have identified a suitable couple. As this is a case where the local authority would be placing the child for adoption, it would be an agency adoption. Agencies can place children either with parental consent – meaning with the consent of parents with parental responsibility, or through a placement order. In this case, Dawn will have parental responsibility as she is Evie's birth mother (**Children Act 1989 s 2(2)**); however, as Evie was the result of a one night stand, and the father has not been seen since, she is likely to be the only parent with parental responsibility for Evie. On the facts, Dawn is opposed to the adoption and therefore the local authority will only be able to place Evie for adoption if they are able to obtain a placement order.[5]

The grounds for obtaining a placement order are set out in the **Adoption and Children Act 2002 s 21(2)**. **Subsection 21(2)(a)** does not apply here, because although there has been local authority involvement, it does not seem, on the facts, that Evie has actually been made subject to a care order. Similarly, **s 21(2)(c)** is not relevant as Evie does have a parent, namely Dawn. Consequently, whether a placement order would be available depends on whether **s 21(2)(b)** is applicable. **Subsection (b)** refers to cases where the criteria in **s 31(2)** of the **Children Act 1989** are satisfied, in other words, it refers to children who are currently suffering, or who are at risk of suffering, significant harm. On the facts, Dawn has a drink and drug use problem which has made her incapable of meeting her daughter's needs; therefore a case could be made that were Evie to be returned to Dawn's care she would be at risk of significant harm through neglect. On this basis **subs 21(2)(b)** of the **Adoption and Children Act 2002** is satisfied, a placement order can be obtained and Evie can be placed for adoption with Fiona and Gary.

The purpose of the placement is to enable the adopters and the child to know each other and for social workers to check whether the adoptive placement does support the needs of the child. According to **s 42(2)** of the **Adoption and Children Act 2002**, Evie has to be placed with Fiona and Gary for a minimum of ten weeks. When the placement order is made, the local authority will obtain parental responsibility for Evie (**Adoption and Children Act 2002 s 25(2)**) and once Evie has been placed with Fiona and Gary, they will obtain parental responsibility for her (**Adoption and Children Act 2002 s 25(3)**). This is important because one of the attributes of parental responsibility is deciding where a child lives, and as Dawn is opposed to Evie staying with Fiona and Gary, their having parental responsibility strengthens their ability to have Evie with them during the placement without Dawn removing her. Furthermore **s 30(2)** of the

---

5   The first stage in the adoption process is the placement of the child with the prospective adoptive parents.

**Adoption and Children Act 2002 s 30(2)** makes it clear that Dawn does not have a legal right to remove Evie from Fiona and Gary's care during the placement order. Dawn could apply for the placement order to be revoked. To be successful in doing this, she would have to show that there has been a change in circumstances since the placement order was made, and on the facts, this does not appear to be the case.[6]

After placement, the next stage is for Fiona and Gary to apply to the court to adopt Evie. The court will have to check that the legal requirements for adoption are satisfied. Both Fiona and Gary must be over 21, which although the facts are not explicit, will be assumed that they are. The court will also need to check that Evie has been placed with them for long enough. Even if these legal requirements are satisfied, the court will only make an adoption order if it is in Evie's welfare so to do (**Adoption and Children Act 2002 s 1(1)**). Furthermore, because adoption does not only determine where a child lives and who raises that child, but also the child's family status, it would not be enough for Fiona and Gary to show that they are suitable carers for Evie; they would also have to show that adoption is the best way of meeting her needs.

Although there is not much information in the facts, it is arguable that Fiona and Gary would be able to convince the court that adoption would be in Evie's welfare. It does seem that Dawn is not able to provide a stable environment for Evie, and adoption does offer the child long-term stability. One issue is Dawn's health. She claims that were Evie to be adopted, her health would deteriorate. Sadly for Dawn, this is irrelevant for the court. It is Evie's welfare that is paramount: **Adoption and Children Act 2002**, which means that it outweighs all other considerations.

Even if the court decides that the legal requirements for adoption are satisfied and adoption does promote Evie's welfare, it still needs to check whether Dawn is consenting. The consent of every parent with parental responsibility is needed before an adoption order can be made. As has already been explained, Dawn would have parental responsibility for Evie so therefore her consent would be needed. Nevertheless, **s 52** of the **Adoption and Children Act 2002** makes it clear that parental consent can be dispensed with and under **subs 52(1)(b)** this can be done if the welfare of the child requires it. As the court will have already decided that adoption is in Evie's welfare, it is most likely that it would also decide that her welfare would require Dawn's consent to be dispensed with.[7]

---

6   Under the previous adoption law (**Adoption Act 1976**) the adoptive parents did not gain parental responsibility until the adoption order was made. This left the adoptive parents in a vulnerable position during the placement as they would not have parental responsibility but the birth parents still would.

7   Given that an adoption order will only be made if it is in the welfare of the child to do so, it is hard to see a situation where the court will decide that an adoption order ought to be made, but cannot because of the birth parent's refusal to consent.

## INTRODUCTION

It is common to find examination questions, whether problem or essay questions, that span a number of issues. Consider very carefully exactly what is being asked of you and ensure that you cover all issues carefully. The following questions attempt to bring together the various topics from earlier chapters.

## QUESTION 47

Nancy and Bill are lovers and are cohabiting in Bill's small flat. Bill has a drink problem and frequently returns home drunk, when he subjects Nancy to violent attacks. Nancy has just discovered that she is pregnant and is concerned about her well-being and that of her child if she stays with Bill. However, she has nowhere else to go, and is finding it difficult to obtain a job.

▶ Advise Nancy:

(a) whether, and on what basis, Bill may be excluded from the flat;
(b) what measures she can take to ensure that Bill is not violent to her in the future; and
(c) if she remains with Bill, whom she still loves, what steps the local authority could take in relation to her child.

### How to Answer this Question

(a) Look at provisions for occupation orders under the **Family Law Act 1996 (FLA)**; Nancy is a non-entitled applicant.
(b) Look at non-molestation orders under the **Family Law Act 1996 s 42**
(c) Local authority powers:
   ❖ mention duty to investigate (**s 47**);
   ❖ duty to assist voluntarily (**ss 17–20**);
   ❖ consider care order (**s 31**) and the criteria for the making of such an order;
   ❖ emergency protection order (**s 44**).

## Applying the Law

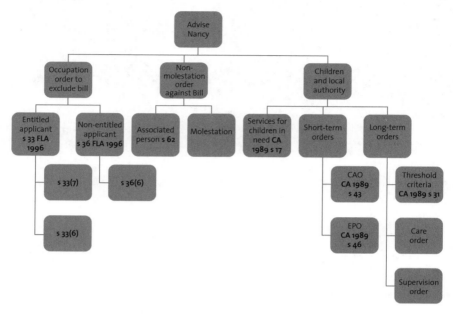

*Nancy's legal options are shown in the flowchart above.*

## ANSWER

(a) In advising Nancy on whether, and on what basis, Bill may be excluded from the flat, it is necessary to realise that the flat is owned or rented by Bill, and he would seem to be an entitled respondent within the **Family Law Act 1996**. Nancy, however, appears to have no right to occupy the flat by virtue of a beneficial interest or contractual entitlement or by virtue of any enactment. Since she is Bill's lover, she has no matrimonial home right to occupy either and so she would be a non-entitled applicant within the **Family Law Act 1996**.

The court nonetheless has jurisdiction to entertain her application for an occupation order if she and Bill have lived together as husband and wife and are accordingly cohabitants within **s 62**. Nancy is a non-entitled applicant and Bill seems to be an entitled respondent and so **s 36** will apply. This would require the court to first consider the making of an occupation rights order, giving Nancy the right to occupy the home, which she would not otherwise have, and then to make a regulatory order excluding Bill.

In making an occupation rights order the court will take all the circumstances of the case into account, including the housing needs and resources of the parties and any relevant child; the financial resources of the parties; the likely effect on the health, safety and well-being of the parties and relevant child of any order or no order being made; the conduct of the parties in relation to each other and otherwise; the length of time they have lived together as husband and wife; whether there are any children; the time that has passed since they lived together; and the existence of any proceedings between the parties under the **Children Act 1989** or in relation to ownership of property (**s 36(6)**).

In the present case Nancy has nowhere to live and has no job or financial resources. Since she is pregnant she is physically more vulnerable and clearly needs somewhere to stay. However, the flat is Bill's and he also needs somewhere to stay. His drink problem means that he is also vulnerable, but his behaviour towards Nancy has been blameworthy, and his violence could clearly put her and the unborn child at risk. Even though the couple are cohabitants, the facts would seem to suggest that Nancy should be allowed to occupy the flat for a short period of time. This might, then, see her through her pregnancy and, once she has a baby, she will be a greater priority housing need for local authority accommodation.[1]

If an occupation order is made, then the court can make a regulatory order excluding Bill from the home or restricting his occupation. The factors influencing the court in determining whether to make such an order are the housing needs and resources of the parties; their financial resources; the effect of any order or failure to make an order on the health, safety or well-being of the parties or relevant child; the conduct of the parties in relation to each other and otherwise; the likelihood of significant harm to the applicant or child if no order is made; and the likelihood of significant harm to the respondent if an order is made. With non-entitled cohabitants, unlike the position with entitled applicants, there is no compulsion to make an order on the basis of a risk of significant harm. This puts cohabitants at a disadvantage over spouses, who will usually be entitled applicants by virtue of their matrimonial home rights.

In this case, however, there have been significant violent episodes, which would clearly continue if Bill were allowed to remain in the flat. He is a single male whose behaviour has been blameworthy and violent. The court is likely to be prepared to exclude him from the home. Such orders are of limited duration, however, and are for an initial six-month period, with the possibility of one further six-month extension. This would, nevertheless, be sufficient to see Nancy through the difficult period of her pregnancy.

Since there has been violence in the past, it seems likely that Nancy would be allowed to occupy the flat and exclude Bill for a limited period of time.

(b) The measures that Nancy could take to protect herself from Bill's violence in the future would be to seek a non-molestation order under the **Family Law Act 1996 s 42**

----

1    Nancy is a non-entitled applicant and therefore applies for an occupation order under **s 36**. There is no provision in **s 36** which corresponds to the presumption in favour of an order in **s 33(7)**.

Nancy would need to show that she and Bill are associated persons within s 62. This could be satisfied by showing that they were living together as husband and wife, and were cohabitants, or that they lived together in the same household. Once the baby is born, they will also be associated since they are the parents of the same child.

It is then possible for Nancy to apply for a non-molestation order on its own or as an adjunct to other family proceedings, such as an occupation order. The court has a discretion whether or not to make the order and will look at all the circumstances of the case, including the need to secure the health, safety and well-being of the applicant and the relevant children. There is no requirement that the respondent has to have been violent, and the order can be widely drafted to afford protection, not just from violence, but from pestering and harassment. In the present case there have been several violent episodes which look likely to continue, posing a grave risk to Nancy's health and that of the unborn child. The court will almost inevitably grant a non-molestation order.

The order can be for a limited time or until further order (s 42(7)), and here it is likely to be a continuing order.

(c) Nancy is concerned that if she remains with Bill, whom she still loves, the local authority may take steps in relation to her child once it is born. The local authority have a duty to investigate cases where they have reasonable cause to suspect the child is suffering, or likely to suffer, harm: **Children Act 1989 s 47**. The local authority will, through their social workers, consult with the family and try to work in partnership to assess the needs of the child. If Nancy's child is deemed to be a child in need, then the local authority have an obligation to provide services for that child under s 17 and, in extreme circumstances, to provide accommodation for the child under s 20. These are exercised on a voluntary basis in co-operation with the parent, and so it is important for Nancy to realise that, even if she tries to patch up her relationship with Bill, the local authority will be there in the future to help her and her child should she turn to them. However, the real problem lies in that the local authority may decide that their cause for concern is sufficient to justify them applying to the court to exercise compulsory powers over Nancy's child.[2]

There is a power for the local authority to apply to the Family Proceedings Court for a care order under the **Children Act 1989 s 31**. In order to grant a care order, the court must be satisfied that the child is suffering, or is likely to suffer, significant harm. Harm is defined in the Act as including ill-treatment or impairment of health and development. The concept of ill-treatment includes sexual abuse and physical and mental ill-treatment. There is no evidence that Bill will necessarily ill-treat the child, but his violence and alcoholism raise serious concern about his ability to control himself whilst drunk. Although Nancy's child will not, at birth, be suffering significant harm, there is obviously

---

2   Wherever possible the local authority should try to work in partnership with the child's parents, and providing services to support a family in difficulty is preferred to coercive measures.

the argument that it is likely to do so. The local authority will be able to satisfy the threshold criteria if they can show there is a real significant likelihood of harm. Clearly, Bill's alcoholism, the extent to which he is able to control it, and his willingness to try to reform so as to assist with the upbringing of his child, will be crucial in determining the likelihood of harm. The time for assessing the likelihood of harm is the time at which the local authority intervene to assist the child. It is not necessarily the case that harm must be shown at the time of the hearing. This was the outcome of *Re M (A Minor)* (1994) in which the House of Lords held that the time when the child is actually suffering, or is likely to suffer, significant harm is the point at which the local authority first take protective steps.

This harm or likelihood of harm has to be attributable to the care being given to the child or likely to be given to it if the order is not made, not being what it would be reasonable to expect a parent to give it; or the child being beyond parental control. Obviously, it is the first of these that is applicable in the present case. There is nothing on the facts to indicate that Nancy will be an unsuitable parent. She is expressing concern over the welfare of her child and she does not have any previous history of bad parenting. However, the concern is expressed over Bill and his violent and unpredictable nature. Clearly, his violence, if it is directed against the child, is unacceptable and unreasonable. The court will not necessarily make an order just because the threshold criteria are satisfied. The non-interventionist policy of the Act (s 1(5)) means that the court will only make an order if this is better than leaving things as they are. The court recognises the need to act without delay (s 1(2)) and the paramount consideration is, as ever, the welfare of the child (s 1(1)).

The welfare, then, of Nancy's unborn child will, once it is born, be the paramount consideration and will determine whether or not a care order will be made. Clearly, the child's welfare is usually best served by its upbringing in a family environment but, whilst Nancy remains determined to live with Bill, serious concern will be expressed over the ability of herself and Bill to promote their child's welfare. Since the child is a newborn child there is no real status to maintain and it may be that the court will take the view that a care order does enable the local authority to have a wider discretion as to what to do to promote the child's welfare. Clearly, the philosophy of the Act is that compulsory measures are a last resort and that children are better off with their natural families. However, where there is serious concern over their natural ability to care for the child, it may be that a care order is the best option. This care order does not mean that the child will necessarily be taken away from Nancy and Bill, but it does give the local authority the opportunity to keep a close eye on the child's progress. Consequently, it seems likely that the local authority may seek to obtain a care order. Care orders are obtainable on notice being given to the parents in the case.

If the local authority decide that more speedy measures are needed, they can apply for an emergency protection order under the Act. An emergency protection order is available under s 44 if the local authority can show that there is reasonable cause to believe that the child is likely to suffer significant harm if he is not removed from the accommodation where he is, to accommodation provided by the local authority. It is also possible that the local authority may apply for an emergency protection order if they are making enquiries with regard to the child under s 47, and those enquiries are being frustrated by access to the child being unreasonably refused, and there is reasonable cause to believe that the access to the child is required as a matter of urgency. Therefore, if, after the child's birth, Bill appears to be violent or, for example, Nancy does not co-operate with the local authority's enquiry, then the local authority may seek an emergency protection order.

Such an order is a significant measure and it gives the local authority parental responsibility for the duration of the emergency protection order. The order only usually lasts for eight days (s 45(1)), although it can be extended for a further seven days. The emergency protection order will authorise the child's removal to local authority accommodation and the court will direct whether contact is to be permitted between the child and any other person. It is likely that Nancy would still be able to see her child because she is not abusing it but Bill may have contact restricted or refused. The emergency protection order can be challenged after 72 hours have passed by the parents or by the child unless they were present and were heard at the hearing. This emergency protection order is very speedily obtainable without notice and could help the local authority prepare their application for the care order.

The effect of the care order, if made, would be to vest the parental responsibility in the local authority who would need to exercise it in the child's best interests. Nancy would not lose her parental responsibility if the local authority acquire it under a care order and the local authority are under an obligation to work in partnership with the parents, consulting them where possible and taking their views and the views of the child into account (s 22 of the Act). Thus, it seems that the local authority could possibly obtain a care order and may need an emergency protection order should Bill remain violent.

The court can make an interim care order, under the **Children Act 1989 s 38**, if there are reasonable grounds for believing that the threshold criteria in s 31 will be met. Should it appear that if Bill is excluded from the home the child will cease to suffer or cease to be likely to suffer significant harm, and if Nancy is able and willing to care for the child and consents to Bill being excluded, then an exclusion requirement can be made requiring Bill to leave the home, or the area the home is in, and prohibiting him from entering the home. A power of arrest can also be attached to this. This exclusion requirement is also an option if the local authority apply for an emergency protection order, but it is only going to be possible if Nancy agrees to Bill's exclusion (**Children Act 1989, 44A**).

# QUESTION 48

Amy and Benedict went through a ceremony of marriage four years ago, when Amy was 16 and Benedict was 20. Amy's parents were unhappy with the marriage, and so refused their consent. Amy and Benedict eloped and were married in a country church one month later. The banns were read using Amy's middle name, Louise, instead of Amy, and Benedict shortened his name to Ben, as he was commonly called.

Twins were born subsequently, and are now aged two and a half. However, the marriage has broken down, and Amy wishes to end the marriage.

▶ Advise Amy:

(a) on what basis her marriage to Benedict may be ended;
(b) on the status of the two children of the marriage;
(c) whether Benedict is liable to pay maintenance for the children and, if so, on what basis.

## How to Answer this Question

(a) Look at possible ways of ending marriage:
  ❖ nullity on basis that void under s 11 (used false names; parental consent irrelevant);
  ❖ nullity on basis that voidable under s 12 (no real evidence).
(b) Status of children and their legitimacy:
  ❖ the Legitimacy Act 1976 s 1 (belief that marriage is valid renders children legitimate).
(c) Liability to pay maintenance under the Child Support Act 1991 (CSA):
  ❖ explain the statutory formula.

## Applying the Law

*Part a and Part b – factors to consider for nullity of marriage.*

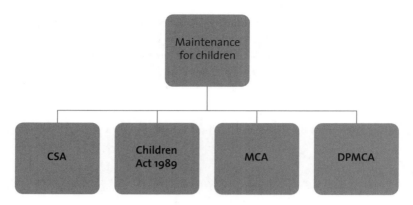

*Part c – maintenance for children in relation to the relevant legislation.*

# ANSWER

(a) The marriage between Amy and Benedict may be ended by an application for nullity if the marriage is void under the **Matrimonial Causes Act (MCA) 1973 s 11** or if the marriage is voidable under the **Matrimonial Causes Act 1973 s 12**. An application for divorce is also possible under the **Matrimonial Causes Act 1973 s 1**.

A void marriage is one that is a complete nullity: *De Renville v De Renville* (1948). Technically, there is no need to apply for a decree of nullity in the case of a void marriage; however, Amy would be advised to do so in order to achieve certainty, and in order to avail herself of the provisions for financial security in the **Matrimonial Causes Act 1973**.

Examining the criteria which make a marriage void in **s 11**, it can be seen that these defects occur if the parties have married within the prohibited degrees: if either party is under 16, which does not apply here; or if they have married in disregard of certain formalities under the Marriage Acts. In this case, the marriage took place according to the rites of the Church of England and there is serious concern as to whether the banns have been duly published. The purpose of calling banns is to ensure publicity and to enable those with objections to object to the marriage. It is possible to marry in an area in which the couple do not live, provided they have established residence for the qualifying period, as is the case for Amy and Ben. The banns have been read using somewhat different names from the couple's legal names. In the case of Benedict he is usually known as Ben and so there could be an argument that he did not intend to deceive anyone by the use of his abbreviated name, as in *Dancer v Dancer* (1948). However, Amy, by the use of her middle name, could arguably have been said to have deceived and to have removed the possibility of persons objecting to her marriage. Much might depend upon how frequently Amy was known by the name of Louise, but it does seem that there may be an intention to deceive here.

The couple have also married without parental consent. In the case of Amy, she is under 18 and parental consent is required. However, the lack of parental consent is not a defect that renders the marriage void: **Marriage Act 1949 s 48(1)(b)**. It does seem here that Amy and Ben have married in church without objections being made and therefore, subject to the fact that the banns may not have been duly published because of the concealment, the marriage may nevertheless be valid. The marriage will only be void if the banns were not duly published and both parties knowingly and wilfully married in disregard of this. It is somewhat contentious whether both Ben and Amy married in disregard of this: if they did, the marriage is void and a nullity decree should be sought under **s 11**.

If, however, the marriage is valid, then the only other options open to Amy are to apply for nullity on the basis of the marriage being voidable under the **Matrimonial Causes Act 1973 s 12** or to apply for a divorce under the **Matrimonial Causes Act 1973 s 1**. There is insufficient evidence on the facts of this case to indicate what has gone wrong with the relationship after the marriage. However, if it can be shown that either the basis for declaring the marriage to be voidable exists or the basis for a divorce exists, then the marriage between Amy and Benedict may be ended.

(b) Second, the status of the two children of the marriage depends upon the **Legitimacy Act 1976 s 1**, as amended. Historically, children of a void marriage would have been deemed illegitimate and this somewhat harsh consequence could flow after many years of the marriage and even after the death of both parties to the marriage. The **Legitimacy Act 1976 s 1** mitigates this rule by deeming a child to be legitimate if either or both parents believe that the marriage was valid at the time of conception or the time of the marriage, whichever is the later. **Section 1** only applies if the father is domiciled in England and Wales at the date of the birth, which appears to be the case here. The question then turns on whether either Amy or Ben or both of them reasonably believed that their marriage was valid. It is already established that the marriage is void if they realised that the banns had not been duly published. However, it is not clear under **s 1** whether any mistake of law that they may make can ever be reasonable. Thus, it could be argued that if Amy and Ben, whilst realising that they had used different names, reasonably believed that that did not affect the validity of their marriage, then their children will be legitimate. This is a somewhat unsatisfactory position. The status of the two children in the present case will depend, therefore, upon whether the marriage was void; if so, there is the additional uncertainty of the **Legitimacy Act s 1**.

The consequence of this may be that the children in this case are legitimate, in which case both Amy and Ben have parental responsibility under the **Children Act 1989 s 2(1)**. If, however, the children are illegitimate, then only Amy will have parental responsibility under the Act; whereas if the marriage was merely voidable or was ended on divorce, the children will be legitimate.

(c) Ben's liability to pay maintenance will lie under the **Child Support Act 1991**. This Act applies by imposing a maintenance requirement on the natural father of the children.

These two children have been born in wedlock and are presumed to be the natural children of Amy and Benedict. Benedict may dispute paternity, in which case paternity will need to be established before he can be held liable under the Child Support Act

The first step is to assess whether there are qualifying children, and both twins are qualifying children under the Act. Benedict would be termed a non-resident parent and he would pay 16 per cent of his gross income for the support of his two children. Amy's income would be ignored, and there are no allowances for Benedict's housing costs, etc. However, this figure may be adjusted downwards, if Benedict acquires a second family, or if the children spend time living with him.

# QUESTION 49

Felicity and Greg married in February 1997, and have a son, Edmund, who is now seven. When they married, Felicity agreed that Greg's widowed mother, Iris, could come and live with them if she ever became unable to look after herself, and Greg agreed that the same would apply to Felicity's mother.

Three months ago, Greg's mother, Iris, became ill and moved in with Felicity and Greg to convalesce. Iris has often been difficult, criticising the way Felicity and Greg bring up Edmund, and often taking sides in the increasingly frequent matrimonial rows. Felicity finally confronted Greg, telling him that either his mother should leave, or she, Felicity, would leave. Greg responded by saying that Felicity had overreacted, at which point Felicity stormed out.

▶  Advise Felicity:

(a)  whether she can divorce Greg;
(b)  whether she can exclude Greg's mother from the matrimonial home, in the event of there being no divorce;
(c)  whether she can prevent Iris seeing Edmund.

## How to Answer this Question

(a)  Basis for divorce:
  ❖  irretrievable breakdown and the five facts;
  ❖  only real possibility is behaviour;
  ❖  problem as to behaviour;
  ❖  could separate and wait two or five years.
(b)  Seek occupation order under the Family Law Act 1996 s 33 as entitled applicant.
(c)  Contact between grandmother and child:
  ❖  parental responsibility and ability to act independently;
  ❖  need to apply for s 8 order;
  ❖  welfare and the s 1(3) checklist.

## Applying the Law

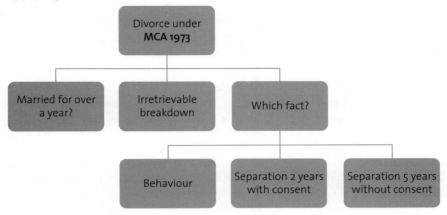

*Part a – how the law relates to divorce in this scenario.*

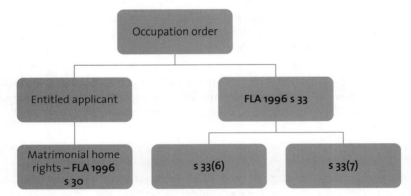

*Part b – factors to consider in relation to an occupation order.*

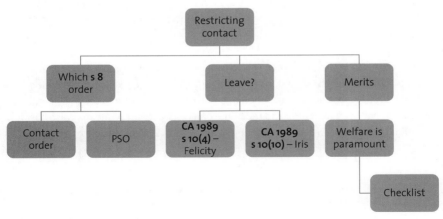

*Part c – factors to consider in relation to restricting contact.*

# ANSWER

(a) In order to divorce Greg, Felicity must establish that their marriage has broken down irretrievably: MCA 1973 s 1(1). This must be done by reference to one of the five facts in the MCA 1973 s 1(2): *Richards v Richards* (1972). In the present case, it may be argued that, even if one of the five facts were established, Felicity would have difficulty in establishing irretrievable breakdown, as in *Biggs v Biggs* (1977). The couple appear to have experienced temporary difficulty during the stay of Iris, rather than a permanent breakdown in their relationship. However, if Felicity established one of the facts, then the court will grant the decree (s 1(4)) unless it is satisfied that the marriage has not irretrievably broken down.

The only possible basis for an immediate divorce is to present a petition based on s 1(2)(b), that is, that the respondent, Greg, has behaved in such a way that she cannot reasonably be expected to live with him. There needs to be some behaviour or conduct on Greg's part that is referable to the marriage. Felicity's complaint appears to centre on Iris' behaviour, and this cannot form the basis of a petition based on Greg's behaviour. Instead, Felicity would have to argue that his uncaring response to her problem is symptomatic of his neglect and lack of concern. This does seem somewhat flimsy, and it would then be necessary to show that, given the individual characteristics of the spouses (*Ash v Ash* (1972)), it would be unreasonable to expect Felicity to continue to live with Greg (*Livingstone-Stallard v Livingstone-Stallard* (1974)). The mere fact that Greg is unconcerned or undemonstrative in the face of his wife's demands for attention may well not suffice: *Pheasant v Pheasant* (1972). However, given the special procedure for obtaining a divorce, it is possible that Felicity's petition would not face much scrutiny.[3]

She could, however, continue to live apart from Greg, that is, in two separate households: MCA 1973 s 2(6). Felicity must also recognise that the marriage is at an end (*Santos v Santos* (1972)), although this does not need to be communicated to Greg. If this continues for two years, and Greg consents to the granting of the petition, then a divorce may be obtained under the MCA 1973 s 1(2)(d). If Greg refused consent, then Felicity will not be able to argue constructive desertion as she did not have good reason to leave. Instead, she will need to wait until she and Greg have been separated for five years, and petition under the MCA 1973 s 1(2)(e).

(b) In order to exclude Greg's mother, Felicity will need to make an application for an occupation order under the provisions in the Family Law Act 1996. Felicity is an entitled applicant within s 33 as she has matrimonial home rights in relation to the dwelling house, which has been her home and the home of her spouse, Greg. She may also have some other entitlement to occupy, either by virtue of a legal or beneficial entitlement.

---

3    The behaviour fact is the most used of the facts in s 1(2). This may be because it is very flexible and in reality, thanks in part to special procedure, it is quite easy to establish.

Accordingly, Felicity can apply for an order under s 33 against a respondent who is an associated person within s 62. Greg's mother is an associated person since she is a relative by virtue of being Greg's mother, and she is also an associated person by virtue of living in the same household as Felicity.

The order can require the respondent to leave the home or otherwise regulate the occupation of the home by the parties. In determining whether and what regulatory order to make, the court will take into account the circumstances of the case, including the housing needs and resources of the parties; their financial resources; the likely effect of any order or failure to make an order on the health, safety or well-being of the parties or relevant child; and the conduct of the parties in relation to each other and otherwise. The court can then exercise its discretion over whether to make an order. Felicity will argue that she and her child need to remain in the house, and that, since Iris has not given up her own home, she could return there without difficulty. She will also argue that Iris' behaviour is having a detrimental effect on her health and the well-being of the family. However, the position is slightly complicated by the fact that Iris is in the home with the agreement of Greg, and, initially, of Felicity herself. In addition to this, Iris is sick, although it is not clear how severe her illness is.

If, however, under s 33(7) it appears that the applicant or relevant child is likely to suffer significant harm attributable to the conduct of the respondent if the order is not made, then the court must make an order, unless the respondent or relevant child is likely to suffer equal or greater significant harm if the order is made. This requires the court to first consider whether there is the likelihood of significant harm, and then balance the harm of making an order with the harm of not making an order.

Harm is defined in s 63 to mean ill-treatment or impairment of mental or physical health with the additional criteria of impairment of development for a child. Ill-treatment includes both physical and sexual abuse in relation to a child, and development is widely defined to include physical, emotional, intellectual, social or behavioural development. The concept of 'significant' is likely to mean considerable or important, if guidance in earlier cases on the meaning of such wording in other statutes is followed: *Humberside County Council v B* (1993).

It is difficult to see how, on the facts, Felicity would be able to sustain such an argument, so there would be no statutory presumption in favour of the order being made. It seems rather harsh to exclude Iris from the home, since she is only there temporarily until she recovers, but much would depend on the nature of her behaviour towards Felicity. This is a case where the court might be prepared to accept an undertaking from Iris that she will do her best not to interfere in Felicity and Greg's domestic arguments and to stop her criticism.

(c) The issue of Iris' contact with the child Edmund will be affected by whether Edmund has remained with his father and grandmother in the matrimonial home, or whether he has left and is staying with his mother. Since Felicity and Greg are married, they both have parental responsibility for Edmund: **Children Act (CA) 1989 s 2(1)**. This is defined as 'all the rights, duties, powers and responsibility that a parent has by law in relation to the child and its property': **CA 1989 s 3(1)**. However, both parents are entitled to act independently in the exercise of their parental responsibility, and this means that there is no automatic veto.

Consequently, if Edmund has remained with his father, Felicity will be unable to prevent her son seeing Iris, unless she seeks a residence order to enable Edmund to live with her, or a prohibited steps order to prevent Iris having contact with Edmund: s 8 CA 1989. If, however, Edmund is living with Felicity, she can prevent contact in the immediate future, but should be advised that Iris might apply for a contact order under s 8.

In any application for a s 8 order, the child's welfare will be the paramount consideration (s 1(1)), and must be determined by reference to the checklist in s 1(3). The court will be aware of the risk of prejudicing welfare by unnecessary delay (s 1(2)), and will only intervene if necessary (s 1(5)).

In this case, Felicity, as a parent, can apply for a s 8 order as of right, whereas Iris, as a grandparent, will require leave. However, given that Iris has a good relationship with her grandson, it is likely that the court would recognise her genuine concern and grant leave. There are two possible issues here: namely, where Edmund should live; and whether there should be contact with his grandmother. Advice has been sought on this latter issue only, and this advice would be given, first, on the basis that Edmund lives with Felicity, and, second, that he lives with his father.

If Edmund lives with Felicity, then she should be advised that the courts tend to view contact with other members of the family with whom the child has a good relationship as being in the child's welfare. The s 1(3) checklist would require the court to take into account the ascertainable wishes and feelings of the child in the light of his age and understanding. Edmund is seven, and will almost definitely have a view as to whether he wishes to continue to see his grandmother. Although this view would not be conclusive, since he is only seven, it will be taken into account. Edmund's needs can be met by his grandmother, and since he has an existing relationship, he may be disturbed at any enforced change. There is no evidence that Edmund is at any risk of harm from Iris, and it may be that she has love and guidance to give that would be of benefit to Edmund. It seems likely that contact would be allowed, unless it was genuinely upsetting and distressing for Felicity, so as to be detrimental to Edmund's welfare.

Likewise, it is extremely unlikely that the court would regard it as in Edmund's welfare to prohibit contact with Iris should Felicity seek a prohibited steps order. This seems to be a vindictive action on Felicity's part, and she should be wary of making such an application, since it does not give the impression that she has her son's welfare at heart.

# QUESTION 50

In matters of the family, the child should come first, last and always. Discuss to what extent English family law provides for children's welfare.

## How to Answer this Question

Requires an examination of various areas of family law in which the welfare of a child could be affected:

- ❖ Children Act 1989, disputes over upbringing and local authority powers;
- ❖ adoption – Adoption and Children Act 2002 changed the law so welfare is now paramount;
- ❖ divorce – granting – no consideration of welfare;
- ❖ ancillary relief – welfare first consideration;
- ❖ Child Support Act 1991 and possible conflict with welfare;
- ❖ property disputes – no consideration of welfare;
- ❖ occupation of home – just one of a number of considerations.

## Answer Structure

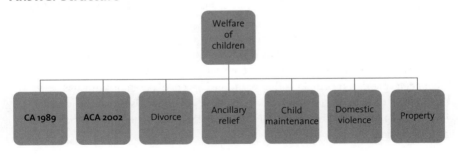

# ANSWER

Where a family contains children and problems are encountered, the children are inevitably affected by what their parents do. It is not just the obvious cases where the dispute concerns the upbringing of the child; many disputes which appear to be solely between the adults have effects that impinge on their children's welfare. It is necessary, therefore, to examine to what extent English family law takes into account the child's welfare, and whether it does so in an adequate manner.

The **Children Act 1989** is a crucial piece of legislation which does a great deal to make family law child-centred and responsive to the child's needs. The Act covers both the child and their relationship with the parents, as well as the role of the State and local authority powers. As its cornerstone, it provides that in matters of the child's upbringing and welfare, the child's welfare is the court's paramount consideration: s 1(1). This removes any doubt that existed by the old phrase 'first and paramount', and it is clear that ultimately the court must rule in favour of the option that best promotes the child's well-being and interests. The s 8 orders will only be made on the basis that they promote welfare, and local authority powers will only be exercisable under the Act if in the child's best interests. To assist the court in determining what is in the child's welfare, s 1(3) provides a checklist of factors. Importantly, this checklist begins with the need to consider the child's ascertainable wishes in the light of its age and understanding. This reinforces the *Gillick* concept that, as children become more mature, they should have a greater say in their own lives, provided they have sufficient maturity and understanding.

There are two other general principles in the Act which highlight the importance of considering the child's welfare. The first, in s 1(2), provides that the court must be mindful of the fact that delay is often prejudicial to the child's welfare, and imposes a positive duty on the court to set a timetable for the conduct of the proceedings. The second is the non-interventionist policy in s 1(5), whereby the court should only intervene and make an order if doing so is better than not making an order. This discourages routine orders and tries to encourage the parties to reach a consensus on the upbringing of the children when possible.

There is a substantial body of case law which has shown how welfare may be promoted, and the **Children Act 1989** has done much to bury the notion that parents 'own' their children and can do as they wish. The concept of parental rights has been replaced by the notion of parental responsibility, which emphasises that the parents have an obligation to nurture their child and promote its well-being, rather than treat it as a possession.

As welcome as the provisions of the **Children Act 1989** are, they do not extend to all disputes which affect children. Adoption is one of the most significant decisions that can be made about a child and it is dealt with in the **Adoption and Children Act 2002** rather than the **Children Act 1989**. The **Adoption and Children Act 2002** s 1(1) makes it clear that the child's welfare is paramount in decisions relating to adoption. This is a change from previous legislation where adoption was only the court's first consideration (**Adoption Act 1976 s 6**). Moreover, both the adoption agency and the court must have the child's welfare as their paramount consideration. The **Adoption and Children Act 2002** has set out a checklist that details how a child's welfare should be assessed. Whilst this is similar to the checklist in the **Children Act 1989 s 3**, it does have specific criteria that reflect the fact that adoption is a lifelong decision and that adoption severs the link between the child and its birth family.

When a couple divorce, the basis of divorce is irretrievable breakdown, as evidenced by one of the five facts: **MCA 1973 s 1(2)**. There is no consideration of the effect on the children if their parents divorce. Critics have argued that the adults involved should have to face up to the effect their divorce is having on their children, and there are those who argue that divorce is detrimental to children's welfare. The majority argue that it is the breakdown of the relationship that is detrimental to the children and there is no legislation that can force couples to get along amicably. To complicate divorce and the breakdown of a relationship by introducing a consideration of the children's welfare could lead to a party, who is denied a divorce on these grounds, resenting his or her children.

When ancillary relief and property matters are determined on divorce, the child's welfare is merely the first consideration, and even then only whilst it is a minor. The financial implications of divorce and the re-housing of the parties can have important repercussions on a child, but its welfare is of first, not overriding, importance. The factors in **s 25** must be considered, and a solution reached by taking into account those factors will not always be one that is in the child's best interests. Indeed, the consideration of conduct, where it would be inequitable to disregard it, to reduce a spouse's financial entitlement, may have repercussions on the children if that spouse is the parent with care of the children.

In considering financial obligations for children's maintenance, the provisions of the **MCA** apply to financial support for children of the family who are not the natural children of the payer. Again, their welfare is a first consideration, and although the court is directed to consider their needs, the manner of their education, any physical or mental disability, the court also considers the parties' needs and resources, and the extent and basis of their assumption of responsibility for the child. It is not possible to aggressively promote a child's welfare by awarding high levels of financial support if this would have the effect of economically ruining the payer.

Financial responsibility for natural children is governed by the **Child Support Act 1991**, and one of the criticisms of the Act is that it often disregards the welfare of the children involved. The obligation on the mother to name the father if she receives State benefits could be detrimental to the child's welfare if it puts the mother under pressure and causes her distress. It can also re-involve the father in the children's lives, which is not always to their advantage, especially if he has been abusive or a bad influence in the past. Contact disputes may well increase, as many payers feel they are entitled to see the child they are being forced to support, and this is not in line with the consensus approach of the **Children Act 1989**. Where a mother is in receipt of benefits, the child support payments do not actually benefit her or her child; instead, there is a reduction in her benefit to match any child support received. There is often little financial benefit to the children, and the assessment has often had dire financial consequences for the payer. The children suffer if their father is impoverished by the payments with no corresponding benefit to the mother. In addition, the extra costs may make it difficult for some payers to afford to maintain contact with their children as such contact can involve travel expenses, etc which are not routinely taken into account under the Act but require a departure direction.

Where there are property disputes between couples that have to be resolved by reference to the normal rules of property law, the welfare of the children is not a consideration. If there is no divorce, there may be a situation where a parent and child have no interest in the home and cannot remain there. Cases like *Burns v Burns* (1984) illustrate that even where there has been a lengthy relationship with children, no account can be taken of the children's needs in determining equitable interests. This depends on a common intention to share, contributions and detrimental acts, for which caring for children does not suffice. However, the **Children Act 1989 Sched 1** does contain a provision whereby the court can allow occupation of a house and transfer of interests if that is for the welfare of the children. This is a relatively new area and it remains to be seen how frequently it will be used to promote welfare of the child.

In matters concerning the occupation of the home under the **Matrimonial Homes Act 1983**, the welfare of the children was just one consideration, and does not override the others: *Richards v Richards* (1984). The **Family Law Act 1996** contains important reforms in the area of domestic violence and the exclusion of persons from the home. These powers have strengthened the protection available for children, and it seems that the Act may have elevated the level of a child's interests beyond that in the previous law. Thus, it can be seen that whilst the welfare of the child is frequently considered in family law matters, it is not always an overriding consideration. Delicate balance has to be maintained between the welfare of the child and the rights of its parents, but English law has gone a long way towards ensuring that the child's welfare is always borne in mind.

# Index